Induction
An essay on the justification
of inductive reasoning

NICHOLAS RESCHER

Induction

*An essay on the justification
of inductive reasoning*

BASIL BLACKWELL
OXFORD

© Nicholas Rescher 1980

First published 1980 by
Basil Blackwell Publisher
5 Alfred Street
Oxford OX1 4HB
England

British Library Cataloguing in Publication Data
Rescher, Nicholas
  Induction.
  1. Knowledge, Theory of
  2. System theory
  I. Title
  121   BD161

ISBN 0–631–10341–4

TYPESET IN 11/12 pt MONOPHOTO TIMES
PRINTED BY
BILLING AND SONS LTD.
GUILDFORD, LONDON, OXFORD, WORCESTER.

The author dedicates this book
to four inductive theorists
from whose work he has profited greatly

Max Black
Risto Hilpinen
Henry E. Kyburg, Jr
Wesley Salmon

Table of Contents

Preface

The much-controverted problem of the justification of induction provides the agenda of this book. Proceeding in the belief that induction *is* a rational cognitive process, it explores by means of a new, methodologically-oriented approach the issue of just *why* this process qualifies as such.

The book is the final installment of my "Systems Epistemology" trilogy. Its first member, *Cognitive Systematization* (Oxford: Basil Blackwell, 1979) analyzes the central role of systematization for the constituting of our knowledge. The second, *Scepticism* (Oxford: Basil Blackwell, 1980) shows how our potentially fallible processes of systematizing inquiry can indeed yield something deserving of the proud title of *knowledge*. The present book examines the legitimacy of orthodox inductive reasoning within this systems-oriented framework.

The ruling line of thought of the book was initially set out with telegraphic concision in Chapter II ("A Pragmatic Justification of Induction") of my book on *The Primacy of Practice* (Oxford, 1973). On discussing that book with some readers, and, especially, on reading some reviews, it came home to me that the position set out there stood in need of a fuller and more telling exposition. The present disquisition accordingly offers a response to the motley mixture of misunderstanding and incomprehension encountered by that earlier discussion.

The book was drafted in Oxford during the summer of 1978. It formed the basis of a series of lectures on induction delivered at the University of Pittsburgh during the Winter Term of 1979 and also given concurrently at the University of Rochester. A somewhat condensed version of these lectures was then given in the Faculty of Literae Humaniores of the University of

Oxford during the Trinity Term of 1979. I am grateful to the Sub-faculty of Philosophy for inviting these lectures and to Corpus Christi College for affording me an academic home in Oxford on this as on many previous occasions.

I am grateful to those whose participation in the discussion of these materials contributed materially to their development. I want to thank Jean Roberts for reading an early version of the manuscript and offering various suggestions for its improvement. I am also indebted to Mrs Virginia Chestek and Ms Catherine Miller for seeing the typescript through a series of revisions, and to John Horty for help with the proofreading.

PITTSBURGH
October 1979

Introduction

This book will grapple with a fundamentally Kantian question: How can limited experience of nature provide a suitable basis for the claims to generalized knowledge needed to render empirical science possible? From one perspective of consideration, this is simply once more a key problem of Kant's successors – the central theme of Fichte's *Wissenschaftslehre* regarding the theoretical foundations of our knowledge, of Hegel's *Science of Logic*, and of the theory of science of William Whewell and Charles Sanders Peirce. It is a major issue of traditional epistemology, perhaps even the main one. Peirce wrote in 1878:

> Late in the last century, Immanuel Kant asked the question: "How are synthetical judgments *a priori* possible?". . . . But before asking *that* question he ought to have asked the more general one, "How are any synthetical judgments at all possible?" How is it that a man can observe one fact and straightaway pronounce judgment concerning another different fact not involved in the first. Such reasoning, as we have seen, has, at least in the usual sense of the phrase, no definite probability; how then can it add to our knowledge? This is a strange paradox . . .[1]

This issue of the legitimation of inductive reasoning represents the focal topic of this book.

Throughout the present discussion, induction will be understood in the broadest appropriate sense. Rather than construing it narrowly, as a method for reasoning to a universal

[1] Charles Sanders Peirce, *Collected Papers*, ed. by C. Hartshorne and P. Weiss, vol. II (Cambridge, Mass, 1933), sect. 2.690.

generalization from its supportive instances,[2] induction is understood to include all of our rational devices for reasoning from evidence in hand to objective facts about the world. Induction, thus understood, will encompass the whole of "the scientific method" of reasoning, and in treating of the justification of induction we take in hand the validation of the processes of reasoning in the sciences.

The concerns of the theory of inductive reasoning fall into two main groups which are set apart by rather distinctive problems:

(1) *The mechanics of induction:* How induction works – the setting out of the actual working details of the various forms of inductive reasoning to exhibit the structure of inductive inference as properly practiced. A study of the tactics and strategy of induction: its *modus operandi.*

(2) *The legitimation of induction:* Why induction works – what justifies induction. A detailing of the rational credentials of induction by showing that – and how – a rationale can be provided for the inductive reasonings of (1) that shows them to be rationally appropriate.

The present discussion is addressed primarily at item (2), and so does not provide a manual of inductive inference.[3] To be sure, the issue of why induction works cannot be altogether separated from that of *how* it works. But it will be presupposed that the reader already has some general idea of its *modus operandi* and is familiar with the rudiments of the "how it's done" techniques of scientific method, statistical theory, the

[2] Cf. J. S. Mill's characterization of induction as "the operation of discovering and proving general propositions." Induction is generally viewed as the latter-day equivalent of Aristotle's *epagōgē*, which he construes as the process of establishing universal propositions of the form "All *X*'s are *Y*'s" on the basis of particular cases falling under them.

[3] For a survey of various types of inductive inferences see John P. Day, *Inductive Probability* (London, 1961), pp. 15–25; Arthur Pap, *An Introduction to the Philosophy of Science* (New York, 1962), pp. 141–147; Rudolf Carnap, *The Logical Foundations of Probability*, 2nd ed. (Chicago, 1962), pp. 205–208; Henry E. Kyburg, Jr., *Probability and Inductive Logic* (London, 1970); Richard Swinburne, *An Introduction to Confirmation Theory* (London, 1973). A critical survey of recent literature is given in Henry E. Kyburg, Jr., "Recent Work in Inductive Logic," *American Philosophical Quarterly*, vol. 1 (1964), pp. 249–287.

design of experiments, and cognate matters relating to the working details of inductive argumentation. Thus, the central question is: what sorts of considerations *validate* our reliance on induction as a method for reasoning in building up our knowledge of the ways of the world? The aim of this explicative endeavor is to clarify how and why the standard inductive reasoning yield results that qualify as rationally acceptable. The pivotal issue is that of the norms and criteria of rational preferability that militate on behalf of orthodox inductive arguments *vis-à-vis* their actual or hypothetical rivals.

To be sure, someone might argue as follows:

A demand to justify induction must arise from some supposed deficiency or imperfection. Only if there were some visible deficiency to induction would it make sense to ask for its justification. But there is no such defect. Only if we could take a stance outside the range of inductive praxis could we ask for an argument to lead us within. But we do not and ought not to take such a stance. And so induction simply needs no justification.

This objection is untenable. Even when all is well with a position and even when one stands firmly committed to it, one can still ask for "the reason why." It is not only possible but sensible to seek out the grounding basis of those matters we feel confident of, even as we inquire into the standing of those we view as problematic. The philosopher has the task of probing the rational basis of our certainties no less than those of our more hesitant commitments. (He thus wants a justification of our *deductive* praxis no less than one of our *inductive* praxis.) A philosophical request for a justification of induction nowise impugns inadequacy to it.

In line with this governing objective, it is the aim of the book to expound a new and promising line of approach to the justification of induction, namely the methodological-pragmatic approach. Viewing induction as a characteristic sort of cognitive *method* – a method, that is, for answering our information-in-hand transcending questions about the world (rather than as a characteristic process for drawing conclusions – a variant style of argumentation or inference) – it becomes possible to assimilate the justification of induction to those *pragmatic* devices that are natural to the justification of methods in general. It will be argued that such an approach has the merit of making it possible to avoid all of the well-known difficulties to which the more familiar and established approaches to the justification of induction are subject.

The ensuing discussion falls into four parts. Chapters I–III lay out the general structure of the methodological approach to inductive reasoning. The central chapters, IV–VI, develop the specifically pragmatic justification whose elaboration is the *raison d'être* of the book. Chapters VII–VIII endeavor to remove some tempting but untenable objections to this approach. Finally, Chapters IX–XII indicate the strengths of this approach and examine its advantages over other strategies for the justification of induction. In all, the present book endeavors to present a rounded argument for a characteristically methodological-pragmatic line of approach to one of the key classical problems of the philosophical theory of knowledge.[4]

---

[4] It may be useful to offer some brief guideposts to this literature of the justification for induction. A helpful survey of the field is Max Black's article on "Induction" in vol. 4 of *The Encyclopedia of Philosophy*, ed. by Paul Edwards (New York, 1967), where bibliographic references are given. More extensive bibliographies are given in Rudolf Carnap, *Logical Foundations of Probability*, 2nd ed. (Chicago, 1962), and in Marshall Swain (ed.), *Induction, Acceptance and Rational Belief* (Dordrecht, 1970), There are several useful anthologies covering the recent literature: M. H. Forbes and M. L. Martin (eds.), *Probability, Confirmation, and Simplicity: Readings in the Philosophy of Inductive Logic* (New York, 1966); Sidney A. Luckenbach, *Probabilities, Problems, and Paradoxes: Readings in Inductive Logic* (Encino and Belmont, 1972); and Richard Swinburne (ed.), *The Justification of Induction* (Oxford, 1974).

I

Induction as Truth-Estimation

SYNOPSIS

(1) Induction is an ampliative methodology of inquiry – one designed to provide answers to our information-in-hand transcending questions regarding factual matters. (2) Induction is not something idealized; it is a matter of doing the best we can in the epistemic circumstances in which we find ourselves. (3) An inductive inference can always be viewed as an aspiring but failed deductive inference – an enthymeme in which some crucial premiss is lacking. In a cogent inductive argument, this missing premiss represents the most promising available way of filling in the information-gap at issue: the inductively appropriate answer to a factual question is that in which the information-in-hand is supplemented in a plausibilistically optimal manner. Induction is thus not a method of "inference to the best *explanation*," but to the best *systematization*. (4) Induction is an instrument of inquiry; it affords a mechanism for arriving at our "best available estimate" of the correct answer to our factual questions. (5) This view of induction as a process of plausibilistically guided truth-estimation establishes the conditions and circumstances in whose light various otherwise puzzling features of induction are readily accounted for. (6) Inductive appropriateness does not hinge on considerations of probability, but on considerations of systematic best fit in which more than maxi-probability is involved.

1. THE TELEOLOGY OF INDUCTION: THE SEARCH FOR BEST AVAILABLE ANSWERS TO QUESTIONS

At the basis of the cognitive enterprise lies the fact of human curiosity rooted in the need-to-know of a weak and vulnerable creature emplaced in a difficult and often hostile environment in which it must make its evolutionary way by its wits. For we must act – our very survival depends upon it – and a rational animal must align its actions with its beliefs. We have a very real and material stake in securing viable answers to our questions as to how things stand in the world we live in. Our *questions* stand at the very center of the cognitive stage, providing the impetus from which our knowledge – or putative knowledge – of the world is arrived at.

Questions arise most pressingly where the information-in-hand does not suffice – when they are not answerable in terms of what has already been established. Exactly here arises the requirement for an *ampliative* methodology of inquiry – ampliative in C. S. Peirce's sense of going beyond the evidence in hand.[1] We need to do the very best we can to resolve questions that transcend accreted experience and outrun the reach of the information already at our disposal. And so it becomes necessary to have a device for obtaining the best available, the "rationally optimal" answers to our information-in-hand transcending questions about how things stand in the world.

Its relationship to question-answering, to *inquiry*, provides the characterizing mandate of our inductive methodology.[2] The definitive task of induction is to provide an ampliative methodology for acquiring information in the domain of "matters of fact and existence," extending our informational horizons by basing larger contentions upon lesser data. Induction is at bottom a mechanism for enlarging the stock of (purported) truths that we accept about the world – a resource

---

[1] For Peirce, "ampliative" reasoning is synthetic in that its conclusion goes beyond ("transcends") the information stipulated in the given premisses (i.e., cannot be derived from them by logical processes of deduction alone), so that it "follows" from them only inconclusively. Cf. *Collected Papers*, vol. II, 2.680 *et passim*.

[2] Most philosophical writers on induction lose sight of its crucial correlativity with the question-answering process. However the mathematician Georgy Polya has not done so. See his *Induction and Analogy in Mathematics* (Princeton, 1954).

comparable in this regard to observation and memory. This *erotetic* (i.e., question/answer oriented) perspective offers a natural account for the fact that predictive success is so important an aspect of the teleology of induction and so pivotal a factor in the assessment of its adequacy. For questions about the future are among our most prominent and important factual concerns.

Dictionaries sometimes define induction as "inference to a general conclusion from particular cases." But such inferences – e.g., from "spaniels eat meat," "schnauzers eat meat," "corgis eat meat," etc., to "all dogs eat meat" – illustrate only one particular kind of inductive reasoning. Nor will it do to add merely those inferences to a particular conclusion that move from effects to causes – from the smoke to the fire; or from the bark to the dog. For this does not go far enough. Inference from sample to population and its inverse, from part to whole (from the jaws to the entire alligator), from style to authorship, from clue to culprit, from symptom to disease, etc., are all also modes of inductive inference. The crucial thing about induction is its movement beyond the evidence in hand – from informatively lesser data to relatively larger conclusions.

2. INDUCTION A MATTER OF DOING THE BEST WE CAN

Induction is an instrument for question-resolution in the face of imperfect information. It is a tool for use by finite intelligences, capable of yielding not the best *possible* answer (in some rarified sense of this term), but the best *available* answer, the best we can manage to secure in the existing conditions in which we do and must conduct our epistemic labors. Of necessity, its reach is restricted to what lies within our cognitive range: it obviously cannot deal with issues that might lie outside our conceptual horizons (as quantum electrodynamics lay beyond those of the physicists of Newton's day). The "available" answers at issue have to be found within some limited family of alternative possibilities within our intellectual reach. Induction is not an occult matter of an intellectual alchemy that transmutes ignorance into knowledge; it is a mundane and realistic human resource for doing the best we can in the epistemic circumstances in which we do – or with reasonable further exertion can – actually find ourselves.

Consider a question of the form: "Are the F's also G's?" The situation here is akin to that of a multiple-choice examination, where one can respond:

(1) Yes, all of them are.
(2) Never – none of them are.
(3) No, some are and some aren't.
(4) Don't know; can't say.

This pretty well exhausts the range of alternatives. Now when in fact *all* of the observed F's (over a fairly wide range) are indeed G's, our path seems relatively clear. Alternative 4 is not an answer – it is a mere evasion of the question, a response of last resort, to be given only when all else has failed us. Alternative 2 is *ex hypothesi* ruled out in the circumstances. The choice between 1 and 3. And we naturally opt for the former. The governing consideration here is the matter of plausibility – specifically that of uniformity. For 1 alone extends the data in the most natural way, seeing that this response alone aligns the tenor of our general answer with the specific information we actually have in hand. It is, accordingly, this resolution that affords the "inductively appropriate" answer in the postulated circumstances.

To be sure, in saying that induction represents the search for plausibilistically optimal answers, we are not saying that it does not (like all question-answering devices) enjoy the privilege of maintaining silence, and responding "can't say" as the proper reply in certain circumstances. Quite the reverse. If we ask, "Which side of this (fair) die will come up?" this is exactly what induction would reply: we just cannot effect a rationally defensible resolution here. No inductively appropriate answer is available. (And this situation would still obtain even if the die were loaded in favor of one side.) Yet this sort of negativity is something the inductive enterprise seeks to minimize.

But why not always opt for safety in answering our questions, systematically selecting the noncommittal pseudoalternative "none of the above"? Why not decline all risk of error and simply follow the path of scepticism? The answer is simple:

Nothing ventured, nothing gained. The object of the cognitive enterprise is clearly to secure truth (and not simply to avert error!). This, after all, is a definitive task of inquiry, the venture of cognitive gapfilling – of securing information insofar as possible.[3]

Nevertheless, the "best available answer" at issue here is intended in a rather strong sense. Its acceptability-claims must not only be stronger than those of the alternatives, but this difference in comparative strength must be substantial – and, in particular, more substantial than is reflected in any mere difference in probability, since the most probable cannot *eo ipso* be reasonably claimed as true. The quest for information hinges on the distinction between good and bad answers, between answers that have little or nothing to be said for them and answers for whose acceptance there is adequate systematic warrant, everything taken into account. An inductively appropriate answer must qualify as our *best* estimate of the true answer in a noncomparative sense that encompasses being a *good* answer pure and simple. We want not just an "answer" of some sort, but a *viable* answer – an answer to whose tenability we are willing to commit ourselves. Induction is not to be a matter of "*mere guesswork*" but of "*responsible estimation*" in a serious sense of the term: it is not *just* an estimate of the true answer that we want, but an estimate that is sensible and defensible: *tenable*, in short. The provision of reasonable warrant for rational assurance is the object of the enterprise.

[3] Stephen Barker has formulated the point at issue clearly and cogently:

Of course it is true that further observations would be bound to eliminate many of these competing hypotheses; but to say that we ought to suspend judgment and wait for more data is to miss the point, for our problem here is to use the data that we have got and in the light of them make a reasonable judgment about which hypothesis we should accept. It is inappropriate to appeal to data that are not yet obtained, for our decision always has to be based upon the evidence that we have got, not upon evidence that we have not got. We never obtain more than a finite quantity of data, and no matter how excellent these data may be there will remain always innumerable different hypotheses consistent with them. We cannot forever defer our choice among the competing hypotheses, forever waiting for more data to be collected; we must be able to come to some reasonable decision in the light of a finite collection of evidence. ("Formal Simplicity as Weight in the Acceptability of Scientific Themes," *Philosophy of Science*, vol. 28 [1961], pp. 162–171 [see p. 164].)

3. INDUCTION AS ENTHYMEMATIC DEDUCTION: THE PROLIFERATION/REDUCTION MODEL OF INDUCTION AS PLAUSIBLE REASONING

The term "induction" is derived from the Latin rendering of Aristotle's *epagōgē* – the process for moving to a generalization from its specific instances.[4] Gradually extended over a wider and wider range, it has ultimately come to embrace all nondemonstrative argumentation in which the premisses do (or are purported to) build up a case of good supportive reasons for the conclusion while yet falling short of yielding it with the *demonstrative* force of logical deduction (seeing that it always remains *logically* possible with inductive arguments to admit the premisses and deny the conclusion).[5]

This informational shortfall reflects a crucial facet of the matter. It means that an inductive inference can always be looked upon as *an aspiring but failed deductive inference*, an enthymeme, an argument in whose formulation some crucially necessary premiss is lacking, so that a larger conclusion is based on lesser premisses. This is exemplified by such cases as the following:

Spaniels eat meat
Schnauzers eat meat
Corgis eat meat
⟨The remaining species of dogs (terriers, dobermans, etc.) all eat meat⟩

∴ All dogs eat meat

There is smoke yonder
⟨Where(ever) there's smoke, there's fire⟩

∴ There is fire yonder

[4] See W. D. Ross, *Aristotle's Prior and Posterior Analytics* (Oxford, 1949), pp. 47–51.

[5] See the excellent article on "Induction" by Max Black in *The Encyclopedia of Philosophy* ed. by P. Edwards, vol. 4 (1967).

Two thirds of the items in the sample are defective
⟨The sample is representative of the whole⟩

∴ Two thirds of the items in the whole population are
defective

(Here the enthymematically tacit premises needed to make
the argument deductively cogent have been bracketed.)

This enthymematic approach takes the step of transforming
an inductive argument into a deductive one, by dwelling on the
conception of a missing premiss that is required to make the
argument *fully* – i.e., *deductively* – cogent, but suppressed in its
actual formulation. We must accept the burden of Hume's
critique of induction to this extent at any rate, that we take
inductive arguments as normally presented to be incomplete
and thus – in requiring the addition of further premises – to
fail as they stand to present a deductively cogent process of
reasoning.[6]

What is at issue on this enthymematic perspective is a complex maneuver which takes the following form. We begin with
a certain question Q (What do dogs eat? What does yonder
smoke portend?) Within the setting afforded by the body K of
the Q-relevant information that is already in hand,[7] we then
engage in a conjectural process of alternative-proliferation to
determine the alternative answers $A_1, A_2, \ldots A_n$ which (in the
context of the relevant information) are "worth bothering
about" in that they exhaust or span the whole spectrum of the
feasible alternatives. In each case, we then identify the contextually most plausible enthymematic (because information-
extending) premiss E_i – that is, the (maximally plausible) supplemental supposition which can underwrite a deductively
valid argument leading from K to A_i. We thus arrive at a series

---

[6] It might be objected that in physics and other branches of empirical science one
standardly solves one's problems by wholly deductive reasoning. But while this is
indeed true of textbook exercises, it is clear that, in applying such calculations to
underwrite contentions about the real world, information-in-hand transcending
issues inevitably arise to endow the overall situation with an enthymematic structure.
(Humean worries regarding the continued operation of existing laws are only one
instance of this.)

[7] In general, this body K of Q-relevant information consists of two components, the
body D of data specific to the inductive problem at hand, and a more diffuse body B of
"background knowledge," so that $K = D \& B$.

of arguments leading to the various conclusions A_i that afford diverse answers to our inductive question Q:

$$
\begin{array}{ccc}
K & K & K \\
\langle E_1 \rangle & \langle E_2 \rangle & \langle E_n \rangle \\
\hline
\therefore A_1 & \therefore A_2 & \therefore A_n
\end{array}
$$

In each case, E_i is the K-relatively most plausible supplementation to K that is capable of underwriting the deductive move from K to the particular A_i at issue.

Thus in our example we might have (among others):

(a)	(b)	(c)
There is smoke there (and suitable background considerations)	There is smoke there (and suitable background considerations)	There is smoke there (and suitable background considerations)
$\langle$This smoke is being caused by a fire$\rangle$	$\langle$This smoke is being caused by a smoke-flare$\rangle$	$\langle$This smoke is being released from a storage container$\rangle$
There is fire there.	There is a smoke-flare there.	There is a smoke-discharging storage container there

The inductive task is to determine which one of these alternative answers to the question "What does yonder smoke portend?" is to qualify as the "most promising" in the sense of identifying the particular addendum E_i that is, relative to the given data of K, the *plausibilistically optimal* alternative at our disposal – where the "plausibility" at issue turns on the matter of "best fit" with respect to the cognitive commitments of K. The inductively appropriate answer to the question at issue corresponds to the outcome of this search for the enthymematic premiss that is plausibilistically optimal (in the context of K) – namely that premiss E_i which (relative to the information in hand) represents the smoothest enthymematic supplementation of the background information. (In the case of the previous example, this will, of course, be the enthymematic premiss of (a).)

The enthymematic-plausibilistic analysis of induction is thus predicated on the stance that wherever there is an "inductively appropriate inference" from the information K to the conclusion C, there *ipso facto* is an inductive question Q with a correlative range of possible answers $A_1, A_2, \ldots,$ $A_i = C, \ldots, A_n$, and, corresponding to each A_j, an enthymematically supplemental thesis E_j of such a sort that, first of all, the argument

$$
\begin{array}{l}
K \\
E_i \\
\hline
\therefore A_i (= C)
\end{array}
$$

is *deductively* valid, and (moreover) for any $j \neq i$, if

$$
\begin{array}{l}
K \\
E_j \\
\hline
\therefore A_j
\end{array}
$$

is deductively valid, then E_j is *less plausible* (relative to K) than E_i is.[8] On this enthymematic analysis, inductive argumentation involves a characteristic two-step process:

(1) *possibility-elaboration*, that is, the conjectural proliferation of the spectrum of alternative possible answers,

---

[8] It deserves note that the "missing" enthymematic premiss of an inductive argument need not be *minimal* in the sense of adding nothing over and above what is needed to move from premisses to conclusion. We can, for example, make the inductive move of sampling-generalization from "These (randomly selected) apples from the barrel are all sour" to "All apples in the barrel are sour" *via* the perfectly workable enthymeme:

These apples from the barrel are sour (& the indications are that all the apples in the barrel are of the same kind)

⟨All the apples in the barrel are like these in taste-relevant respects⟩

∴ All the apples in the barrel are sour.

The enthymematic premiss here is clearly stronger than what is *minimally* required from the move from premiss to conclusion. But since it is no less plausible than its more restricted cousins, it serves just as well for present purposes. (Cf. the author's *Plausible Reasoning* [Assen, 1976].) In general, it should be said that contextual *plausibility* – and neither content-paucity nor *probability* as such – determines the inductive appropriateness of enthymematic premisses. (To say this is not, of course, to deny that these other factors can play a role in the assessment of plausibility.)

accompanied by a process of finding the appropriate
enthymemes for each such answer by determining the
best ways of closing the "epistemic gap" that separates
those answers from the given "data of the problem."
(This survey need not include *all* theoretically available
alternatives, but can merely span them by some suitable covering process.)

(2) *possibility-reduction*, that is, the reduction of these alternatives through elimination of some of them. This is
to be done by assessing the relative plausibility of the
materials needed to close the enthymematic gap encountered en route to the solution in question. That is,
we use an analysis of comparative plausibilities as a
reductive device for seeking out the plausibilistically
optimal alternative(s) within this manifold of
possibilities.[9]

A natural transition thus leads from the question-answering
view of inductive reasoning to an enthymematic approach.
The information at hand (K) only takes us part of the way
towards obtaining an appropriate answer (A) to a factual
question (Q). We must also traverse the remaining "epistemic
gap" separating K from A, and must somehow secure the
information that enables us to cover the residual distance. This
gapfilling is done not so much by an "inference" as by a leap –
an "inductive leap."

Induction is accordingly not so much a process of inference
as one of estimation – its conclusion is not so much *extracted*
from data as *suggested* by them. And, clearly, we want to accomplish this gapfilling step in the least risky, the minimally
problematic way, as determined by plausibilistic best-fit
considerations.

Induction *leaps* to its conclusion instead of literally *deriving*
it from the given premisses by *drawing* the conclusion from
them through some extractive process. Whewell put the point

---

[9] This perspective indicates that it is desirable to distinguish between an *inductive
argument* (which is simply an enthymematic argument) whose factual conclusion
outruns the information provided by its premisses), and *inductive argumentation*
considered as the general procedure of inductive reasoning, a complex process in the
course of which very different sorts of reasonings – including not only deductive
inference but also conjectural and plausibilistic argumentation – will enter in.

nicely. "Deduction," he wrote, "descends steadily and methodically, step by step: Induction mounts by a leap which is out of the reach of method [or, at any rate, mechanical routine]. She bounds to the top of the stairs at once. . . ."[10] We cannot pass by any sort of inference or cognitive calculation from the "premises" of an inductive "argument" to its "conclusion" because (*ex hypothesi*) this would be a deductive *non sequitur* – the conclusion (in the very nature of the case) asserts something regarding which its premises are altogether silent.[11] Clearly the paradigm mode of *inference* – of actually deriving a conclusion from the premises – is actual deduction,[12] and this paradigm does not fit induction smoothly. As one recent writer has felicitously put it, our inductive "conclusions" are "not *derived* from the observed facts, but *invented* in order to account for them."[13]

For the sake of a concrete illustration of this abstract formulation, consider the following situation. Several observers have seen a three-letter scrawl inscribed almost illegibly (in an English-language setting). They agree that they could make out all of the letters *except for the first one*, thus yielding the result that the word in question is of the pattern (?)*AN*. Only three of the observers thought they could make out the first letter. One interpreted it to be a *G*, another made it out as a *Q*, and third as an *O*. What conclusion can be drawn from these data as to the identity of the uncertain letter?

Note first of all that the data authorize no decisive answer to the question of the problematic letter. No definite conclusion can be drawn from them by deductive means. We must proceed inductively, since the body of explicitly given information does not suffice to determine (deductively entail) any one of

---

[10] William Whewell, *Novum Organon Renovatum* (London, 1858), p. 114.

[11] The force of Dickinson Miller's principle must be acknowledged: "There are no intermediate degrees between following from premises and not following from them. There is no such thing as half-following or quarter-following." (Dickinson S. Miller, "Professor Donald Williams vs. Hume," *The Journal of Philosophy*, vol. 44 [1947], pp. 673–684 [see p. 684].)

[12] This perspective supports F. H. Bradley in his critique of J. S. Mill's view of induction on the basis of the consideration that *inference* as such is impotent to accomplish the move from particulars to universals: that it is only legitimate to argue from some to all if it is premissed that the particulars at issue share some universal character.

[13] Carl G. Hempel, *Philosophy of Natural Science* (Englewood Cliffs, 1966), p. 15.

the possible answers to our question as correct.

As we begin with our conjectural canvassing of feasible alternatives for the missing letter, a plurality of (incompatible) possibilities confront us. Given that an English-language context is at issue, this letter could be anything from *A* to *Z*. Accordingly, the process of alternative elimination must be gotten under way. Here we may treat the thesis that "An ordinary English word is at issue" as a fixed constraint (i.e., a maximally plausible thesis which we would only abandon *in extremis*). And so – supposing that names can be ruled out – it emerges that the more limited list *BAN, CAN, FAN, MAN, PAN, RAN,* etc., encompasses the possibilities (i.e., all are proper English words). The specified consideration of plausibility thus still leaves before us a sizable (but nevertheless limited) spectrum of alternative feasible answers to our question. But note further that all of the usable reports agree on one point: the letter in question has a C-shaped left-hand side. Thus just four of the theoretically possible alternatives – the letters from *A* to *Z* – namely *C, G, O,* and *Q,* have a higher plausibility than the rest. (Note that we have not at this stage inferred or concluded that the missing letter does actually have a C-shaped left-hand side, we simply accord a higher plausibility value to the prospects that realize this circumstance.) Since only one of these alternatives, viz. *C,* also meets the preceding condition of yielding an ordinary English word, we accept it as yielding the appropriate solution. On this basis, our reductive analysis will issue in *CAN* as the plausibilistically "proper" result that affords our best estimate of the word at issue.

Other possibilities for information gapfilling are available – lots of them – but they are just not as epistemically advantageous because each requires the sacrifice of some thesis of relatively higher plausibility. The operation of plausibility gradings here is clear. The theses to which the analysis gives relatively high plausibility rankings are:

(1) "An ordinary English word is at issue" as highly plausible relative to its alternatives.

(2) "The missing letter has a C-shaped left-hand side" as highly plausible relative to its alternatives.

The first of these derives its plausibilistic advantage on grounds of consonance and regularity: it provides for greater uniformity in the context of "background knowledge." And the second case too rests on similar considerations. Here again a greater analogy and uniformity within "data-in-hand" is preserved by this particular enthymematic premiss than by its rival alternatives. Our "inductively appropriate conclusion" accordingly emerges on the enthymematic analysis by supplementing the background information of the case in hand with premisses whose high plausibility *vis-à-vis* their alternatives is assured through the operation of the parameters of inductive systematicity.

To be sure, the reasoning which moves from the given data to this conclusion (viz., that the word at issue is *can*) is quintessentially inductive in that the conclusion at which we ultimately arrive moves well beyond the information-content of the initially given premisses. And it does so subject to the guidance of considerations of plausibility as determined with reference to the circumstances of the problem in hand. (Note also that the situation is also such that no definite probabilistic conclusion can be drawn from it, seeing that information about observer reliabilities, word-frequencies in contexts of the sort at issue, etc., do not form part of the conditions of the problem.) This cycle of conjectural possibility-elaboration followed by a phase of possibility-reduction on the basis of plausibilistic best-fit considerations characterizes the structure of the enthymematic analysis of inductive reasoning.

Seen in this light, induction is a gapfilling device that is not a matter of characteristic rules of *inference* but a characteristic process of *premiss introduction* – one that paves over deficiencies in our information by an optimal exploitation of such information as is available. Induction emerges as a method of truth-estimation in erotetic situations that must be resolved enthymematically, by means of plausibilistic considerations.

On such an approach, inductive reasoning is not a matter of using a characteristic sort of "inductive logic," but is a matter of leaping to conclusions by gapfilling, by supplementing the resources of ordinary (deductive) logic with *substantive* materials. Such a substantively committal process can never be validated *a priori* by reasoning from general principles alone.

(As will be seen below, this fact means that induction itself will eventually have to play a prominent part in the justification of induction.)

*   *   *

This "best available answer" approach to induction bears some points of kinship to the "inference-to-the-best-explanation" approach (seeing that in many cases the route to the best answer is bound to proceed via the best explanation).[14] However, the two approaches are by no means identical, and the advantages lie with the former. Thus suppose, for example, that we want to know "Is *p* the case or not?" in a circumstance where Smith, a generally reliable source, reports that *p* (and where no other significant information regarding the truth status of *p* is otherwise available). Our present, enthymematic-plausibilistic approach would lead us to maintain that *p* is true – which is clearly the inductively appropriate answer to the question at hand. Its reasoning would run roughly along the lines of the enthymeme:

Smith generally speaks the truth [*ex hypothesi*]
⟨This case conforms to the general run⟩
───────────────────────────────────────
∴ Smith speaks the truth in this case
(In this case) Smith says that *p* [*ex hypothesi*]
───────────────────────────────────────
∴ *p* is the case

The enthymematic premiss at issue ("This case conforms to the general run") is clearly more plausible than the available alternatives in the circumstances assumed to be operative –

[14] As far as I know, this approach was first formulated by Max Black as a (mis-?-) interpretation of Popperianism: "Those who agree [with Popper] would rewrite putatively inductive inferences to make them appear explicitly as [optimal] hypothetical explanations of given facts." (Art. "Induction" in *The Encyclopedia of Philosophy*, ed. by P. Edwards, vol. 8 [New York, 1967], p. 173.) Its rationale is given fuller articulation by Gilbert Harman in "The Inference to the Best Explanation," *Philosophical Review*, vol. 63 (1966), pp. 241–247; and also in "Knowledge, Inference, and Explanation," *American Philosophical Quarterly*, vol. 5 (1968), pp. 164–173.

including the absence of counter-indications of any sort. And so, given the conditions of the problem, the argument runs a smooth course to the desired conclusion. By contrast, however, an "inference to the best explanation approach" would not enable us to get past "Smith believes that p" – which is, after all, a vastly better explanation of Smith's saying that p than p's being the case would be.[15]

Again, suppose it to be known that someone won a prize for good work in language-study at an American school early in the present century. The question is: What sort of prize was he awarded? Given the circumstances, the inductively indicated answer is clearly *a book*, considering their predominant popularity for this sort of purpose. But there is no "inference to the best explanation" operative here. For what is being explained? That he was given a book? But this is the very item in question and not a given fact in need of explanation. That he won a prize? Surely the best explanation of this is that he did superior work. While the model of inference to the best explanation works splendidly in some inductive contexts (the move from the smoke to the fire, for example), it simply does not work in general. Accordingly, induction is on our approach rather a matter of "inference to the best *systematization*" than one of "inference to the best *explanation*."[16]

4. INDUCTION AS TRUTH-ESTIMATION

Induction represents a cognitively serious effort at closing an information-gap in such a way that – everything considered – we can regard it as epistemically well-advised to accept the indicated results. This quest for a cognitively optimal answer makes induction a matter of systematization geared to considerations of best fit within the framework of our cognitive commitments.

The widespread, indeed virtually universal tendency is to think of induction as a process of *inference* – a matter of characteristic modes of ampliative inference for drawing larger

[15] To be sure, p's being the case may well in its turn form part (but only part) of the best explanation of Smith's believing that p. But that's another matter.

[16] For a more detailed account of what is at issue throughout the plausibilistic deliberations of this chapter, see the author's *Plausible Reasoning* (Assen, 1976).

conclusions from informatively lesser premises. The present approach is very different in its orientation. It sees induction not as a characteristic mode of drawing conclusions, but *as an estimation technique*, a methodology for obtaining answers to our factual questions through optimal exploitation of the information at our disposal. Thus regarded, induction is at bottom an *erotetic* (question-answering) rather than an *inferential* (conclusion-deriving) procedure. Instead of *inferring* "All X's are Y's" from premises of the form "X_i is Y", we take the line that the former is the best available answer to the question "What is the Y-status of the X's?" given the epistemic situation created by the premises. Induction thus conceived is the methodology of ampliative reasoning for securing the "best available answer" to our questions – for rational optimization in our quest for information that transcends the "materials in hand." It accordingly represents a method of *estimation* – specifically a method for estimating the correct answer to a question as well as this can be done through cognitive systematization on the basis of the (inherently insufficient) information in hand.

The need for such an estimative approach is easy to see. Pilate's question is still relevant. How are we humans – imperfect mortals dwelling in this imperfect sublunary sphere – to determine where "the real truth" lies in matters of scientific fact? The consideration that, at the level of matters of generality, we have no *direct* access to the truth regarding the world, that, indeed, it is doubtful if one can make any sense at all of the notion of "direct access" here – is perhaps the most fundamental fact of epistemology. The demand for necessitarian certainty is pointless here – hyperbolic assurance, precision, accuracy, etc., are simply unavailable in matters of scientific inquiry. We have no lines of communication with the Recording Angel. We live in a world not of our making where we have to do the best we can with the means at our disposal. We must recognize that there is no prospect of assessing the truth – or presumptive truth – of claims in this domain independently of the use of our imperfect mechanisms of inquiry and systematization. And here it is *estimation* that affords the best means for doing the job. We are not – and presumably will never be – in a position to stake a totally secure and unblinkingly final claim to the truth in matters of scientific interest. But we certainly can indeed make our best estimate of the truth of the matter.

We can and do *aim* at the truth even in circumstances where we cannot make failproof pretentions to its attainment, and where we have no alternative but to settle for the *best available estimate* of the truth of the matter – that estimate for which the best case can be made out accordingly to the appropriate standards of rational cogency. And systematization in the context of the available background information is nothing other than the process for making out this rationally best case. In the enthymematic circumstances of the case we have and can have no logically airtight guarantee that the "inductively appropriate" answer is true. The inductively appropriate answer is the correct one, not categorically, but "as best we can determine it" – true according to the best available judgment of the matter.[17] Induction is and remains an estimation procedure. The fact that we have an inductively warranted answer in hand must never be taken as a basis for shutting the door to further inquiry.

Induction, on the present approach, is seen as a method (or family of methods) for arriving at our best *estimate* of the correct answer to questions whose resolution transcends the reach of the facts in hand. In view of the unescapable equation of "correct" with "true" we may characterize induction as a process of truth-estimation. Given the information-transcendence at issue in such truth-estimation, we *know* that induction does not *guarantee* the truth of its product. Indeed, if the history of science has taught us any one thing, it is that the best estimate of the truth that we can make at any stage of the cognitive game is generally to be seen, with the wisdom of hindsight, as being far off the mark. Nevertheless, the fact remains that the inductively indicated answer does in fact afford our best available *estimate* of the true answer – in the

---

[17] Of all writers on induction, it is Hans Reichenbach who has come closest to taking this line. He writes:

The inductive inference is a procedure which is to furnish us the best assumption concerning the future. If we do not know the truth about the future, there may be nonetheless a best assumption about it, i.e., a best assumption relative to what we know. (Hans Reichenbach, *Experience and Prediction* [Chicago, 1937], pp. 348–349.)

sense of that one for whose acceptance as true the optimal overall case be constructed with the instruments at hand.

It is in just precisely this sense of affording the best-attainable assurance of rational cogency that we propose to "justify" induction in this discussion. It is certainly not a failproof, sure-fire instrument for generating certified correct answers, something which would in the very nature of the case be infeasible in these information-transcending cases. Rather, it is a method for doing the job at issue – that of truth-estimation – as well as it is possible to do in the epistemic circumstances of the case.

Since a process of truth-estimation is at issue, inductive cogency as such is not purported to provide a theoretically failproof basis for answering our questions about how things stand in the world. Indeed, the history of our cognitive endeavors shows the fallibility of induction only too clearly. There is no justification – and no need – for maintaining that induction is an inherently idyllic mode of truth-estimation – all that need be argued is that it's the best one we've got. The accuracy or "validity" (as it is generally called) of an estimation process – its capacity in general to yield estimates that are close to the true value – cannot in the present case be assessed directly but will reflect itself in our confidence in the estimates it yields, a confidence which, in the context of a "best fit" process, will turn on the issue of the tightness of fit.

Such a view of induction as a procedure for truth-estimation contrasts importantly with certain alternative approaches. For one thing, it rejects the notion that induction is a *theory about the constitution of nature*. (How, save inductively, could such a theory ever be substantiated?) And, as we have said, it denies that induction is a *rule of inference* that moves ampliatively from lesser premises to larger conclusions. For the legitimation of such a rule would call for a rule-warranting thesis whose status would be vitiatingly problematic. As will be seen, its avoidance of such difficulties yields important advantages for the estimative approach to induction from the standpoint of justificatory argumentation.

5. ASPECTS OF ESTIMATION

To set the stage for the present approach to induction as an estimation procedure, consider the following passage from Rudolph Carnap:

> Both in everyday life and in the practice of science, estimates are made of the unknown values of magnitudes. The treasury makes an estimate of the income to be expected from a new tax, a hostess makes a guess as to the number of guests who will come, a general estimates the strength of the forces the enemy has now or will have tomorrow at a certain place, a physicist tries to find the best value for the velocity of light on the basis of several measurements which have yielded slightly different values. An estimate we make cannot be asserted with certainty. Strictly speaking, it is a guess. That does not mean that it is necessarily an arbitrary guess, that "any guess is as good as any other." Sometimes it is a "good guess," that is to say, the estimate is made by a careful procedure; but even for the most careful estimation there is no guarantee of success. To make a careful estimate means to utilize all relevant knowledge available and to reason well in deriving the estimate from this knowledge. Since the procedure of estimation cannot lead to a certainty, it is not a deductive but an inductive procedure.[18]

The only alteration needed here issues from the fact that whereas Carnap construes estimation as a form of induction, the present approach takes the inverse perspective. It looks on induction as a form of estimation, viewing induction as a device, nay the preeminent device, for truth-estimation in the factual domain – an estimation process based on our commitment to the idea that truth is systematic. Its task is to provide an answer that is qualified to serve (at any rate *pro tem* – until epistemic circumstances change) as our truth-surrogate in factual contexts.

[18] Rudolph Carnap, *Logical Foundations of Probability* (Chicago, 1962), pp. 512–513.

This, of course, means that induction must conform to the usual rules and requirements for estimates in general. The following principles are especially important here:

(1) *Character requirement*

We intend our estimate $X^{\#}$ of an item X to serve as surrogate for X. Estimates must thus have exactly the same character as their estimanda; they must have the same logical structure and obey the same laws. An estimate of a length must be a length, and not a temperature; an estimate of an integral value must be an integral value (etc.). Any necessary or essential feature of X must likewise pertain to $X^{\#}$ as well.

(2) *Uniformity requirement* ("Reliability")

A process of estimation must be consistent in the sense of uniformity. It must yield similar results in informationally similar circumstances.[19] A principle of sufficient reason holds for estimates: they should only vary where (and insofar as) differences in the conditions of estimation constrain such differences in the resultant estimates. The standard methodological principle of similar operation in similar cases must hold to assure the reproducibility of results. This sort of uniformity is usually indicated by speaking of the "reliability" of estimates.

(3) *Coordination requirement* ("Data-Sensitivity")

Our estimates must correlate positively with the structure of their data-base. Specifically, the more proximate the conditions of our estimation, the more proximate must our estimates be (if all else is equal). And conversely, substantial divergencies in the nature of our data-base of estimation must be reflected in appropriate differences in the estimates we base on them. In sum, our estimates should be sensitive to the relevant data: if added data reinforce (or counterindicate) a

---

[19] This rule thus encorporates (*inter alia*) what Wesley Salmon has called "the criterion of linguistic invariance" which requires that: Given two logically equivalent (i.e., informationally indiscernbile) formulations of a body of evidence, no rule of estimation may yield distinct (i.e., mutually inconsistent) results on the basis of these statements of evidence. (Cf. Salmon's "The Pragmatic Justification of Induction" in R. Swinburne [ed.], *The Justification of Induction* [Oxford, 1974], pp. 85–97 [see p. 92].)

result, our estimation procedure should reflect this in appropriate changes in an appropriate manner and degree.

(4) *Correctness-in-the-limit requirement* ("Consistency")
An estimation process should be such that, as the data on which we base our estimate grow increasingly complete – as we have DATA-IN-HAND → COMPLETE INFORMATION (for example, as SAMPLE → POPULATION) – the estimate-as-based-on-the-data should eventually approximate the true answer being estimated. And thus with a *complete* information base, the estimation process should (demonstrably) yield the correct result. This requisite is often characterized as *consistency*. The statistician R. A. Fischer has characterized this as the "fundamental criterion of estimation."[20] Given that K is the data-in-hand, it requires that *in the limit* our K-based estimate of a parameter should converge on the true value θ of this parameter: that as $K \to$ (total information), $\theta^{*(K)} \to \theta$, where $\theta^{*(K)}$ is our chosen estimate of θ relative to the data-base K.[21]

(5) *Accuracy requirement* ("Validity")
An estimation process should in general yield estimates that are close to the true value, insofar as this is verifiable. It should, insofar as we can determine, achieve accuracy. Its "track record" should be good. This requisite is generally characterized as validity.

Such characteristic conditions governing the process of estimation in general are also to be taken to apply to the particular mode of estimation that is at issue in induction. Moreover,

[20] R. A. Fischer, *Statistical Methods and Scientific Inference*, 2nd ed. (Edinburgh, 1959), p. 141. See also his "On the Mathematical Foundations of Theoretical Statistics," *Philosophical Transactions of the Royal Society of London*, Series A, vol. 222 (1922), pp. 309–368 (see p. 316).

[21] It is of interest to consider in the light of this principle the rule of so-called "counterinductivism," based on the precept: "If $X\%$ of the sample exhibit a feature F, then estimate that $(100-X)\%$ of the whole population will do so." Let f be the actual frequency in the whole population. Then, as *sample → population*, the observed frequency will $\to f$. And then, according to the specific rule, the predicted frequency for the whole population will be $1-f$. Accordingly, this rule stands in violation of Fischer's principle. (For a further discussion of counterinductivism, see sect. 3 of Chapter VII, below.)

since an instrumentality – a means to an end – is at issue with respect to our estimation methods, the normal cost/benefit principles of procedural economy and efficiency will apply. And so, other things equal, our estimation procedures ought to be as effective, efficient, versatile, simple, etc. as possible. (This final condition might be characterized as the *Effectiveness Requirement*.)

The operation of these requirements in relation to induction, duly construed as a truth-estimation method, will, as we shall see, come to play an important role in its justification.

6. INDUCTION AND PROBABILITY

The substantive *content* of our estimate is one thing and our *confidence* in this outcome is something else again. These two factors do not coincide – separate considerations are at issue here. Specifically, the fact that induction specifies a particular answer as appropriate does not of itself yield any information about the proportion of like outcomes in like cases. As C. S. Peirce ultimately came to see (unlike the legion of probabilistic inductivists of his day and since), probability as such has little direct bearing on induction.[22] (In particular, the fact that a claim is highly probable does not of itself underwrite the inductive appropriateness of this contention.)

With a factual question Q, there are, generally, *infinitely many* theoretical available ways of adding material to the body K of Q-relevant information-in-hand so as to obtain a given answer A to this question. And specifically, given any general theory T and any limited body of evidence E (duly consonant with T in the best hypothetico-deductive manner), there will always be many, and generally *infinitely* many, rival theories – each contrary to T, but consonant with E – so that no body of evidence can render T probable in the context of such an infinitistic spectrum of alternatives. Given such infinite ranges of ineliminable alternatives, probabilistic considerations will prove of little avail.

---

[22] *Collected Papers*, vol. II, sect. 2.780. It is important to note in this connection that in the absence of inductive considerations we would not even be in a position to make use of probabilities!

Think again of Hume's examples. We reason that this sort of bread, which has nourished us to date, will also nourish us tomorrow, or that fire, which has burned flesh in the past, will also do so in the future. But the information that confirms us in these conclusions does not yield any specific probability value for the contentions at issue.

To be sure, an answer cannot be inductively appropriate in circumstances where some comparably detailed alternative answer is more probable: probabilistic inferiority would *preclude* inductive appropriateness. (This follows from the simple consideration that if the answer *A* at issue were less likely than some comparable alternative, then the very considerations that establish the greater likelihood of the other alternatives would of themselves block realization of that "best fit" needed to establish the inductive appropriateness of *A*.) But the fact that such probabilistic inferiority blocks inductive acceptability certainly does not mean that probabilistic superiority of itself entails inductive acceptability. Think of a die loaded heavily in favor of six. In these circumstances we might be well advised to bet on (the truth of) "The next toss will yield a six." But this contention is not something we are entitled to propound as an inductively validated conclusion.

Induction is a matter of obtaining the optimum truth-estimate in terms of the systematic best fit secured through plausibilistic cogency. Its aim is to provide an answer that we can responsibly maintain to be true, and this is not a matter of simply identifying whatever answer is most probable in the sense of the mathematical calculus of probabilities. Thus, if we draw at random an integer from the range 1 to 1,000, it is very likely that 555 will *not* result. But it is not an inductively acceptable answer to the question "What number will be obtained" to respond, "Well, at any rate it won't be 555." An inductive "conclusion" must be offered with full assertive interest: it will not do to say something like "Well, I can't (or won't) really commit myself, but such-and-such would be the safest bet." The truth-estimative mission characteristic of the inductive enterprise goes beyond any mere probabilism.

Consider the case of prediction. It is one thing to deem a certain eventuation likely and quite another to predict that it will actually happen. Prediction calls for assertoric commitment: to predict that something will occur is to take the stance that "*p* will occur" is *true* and not just that this is something that is likely. If something does not happen, the man who predicted its eventuation has spoken falsely, while the man who merely called it highly probable need make no retractions. It is one thing to deem an eventuation likely and another actually to predict it. Prediction is a mode of truth-estimation and is as such a quintessentially inductive process. (This is why its predictive success is a crucial facet of adequacy with any inductive procedure.)

The considerations that establish a certain answer to a factual question as inductively appropriate will not themselves be wholly articulable in strictly probabilistic terms. This leads back to the interesting issues of inductive theory posed by the "Lottery Paradox" which results from a decision-policy for propositional acceptance that is based upon a probabilistic threshold value.[24] Thus suppose an acceptance threshold of 0·80, and consider the six statements resulting from the schema "*This (fair and normal) die will not come up i when tossed*" when *i* ranges from 1 to 6. According to the specified standard, each and every one of the resulting six statements must be accepted as true. Yet their conjunction results in a patent absurdity.[23] Moreover, the fact that the threshold was set as low as 0·80 instead of 0·90 or 0·9999 is wholly immaterial. To recreate the same problem with respect to a higher threshold we need simply assume a lottery wheel having enough (equal) divisions to exhaust the spectrum of possibilities with individual alternatives of sufficiently small probability. Then the probability that each specific result will *not* obtain is less than 1 minus the threshold value, and so can be brought as close to 1 as we please. Accordingly we should, by accepting each of these claims, be driven to the impossible conclusion that there is no

[23] The derivation of the paradox presupposes that "acceptance" is acceptance *as true*, and that truths obey the standard conditions of mutual consistency, conjunction (i.e. that a conjunction of truths be a truth), and of closure (i.e. that the logical consequences of truths be true).

[24] The lottery paradox was originally formulated by H. K. Kyburg, Jr., *Probability and the Logic of Rational Belief* (Middletown, Conn., 1961). Regarding its wider implications for inductive logic see R. Hilpinen, *Rules of Acceptances and Inductive Logic* (Amsterdam, 1968; *Acta Philosophica Fennica*, fasc. 22), pp. 39–49. Cf. also I. Levi, *Gambling With Truth* (New York, 1967), chs. II and VI.

result whatsoever. This Lottery Paradox effectively manages to rule out a propositional acceptance rule that is based upon a probabilistic threshold.

Such considerations indicate that there is reason to think that probabilistic considerations are not in themselves sufficient for our inductive concerns.[25] Inductive appropriateness turns on systematic best-fit as articulated through considerations of plausibilistic cogency, and not merely on considerations of probability. And the quantitative question of *how probable* the inductively appropriate conclusion is (in the epistemic circumstances at hand) is generally something additional to and supervenient upon the qualitative question of exactly *what* this conclusion should be.

[25] A recent book in which this thesis has been argued in an interesting and cogent way is L. J. Cohen, *The Probable and the Provable* (Oxford, 1977).

II

Inductive Argumentation as Cognitive Systematization

SYNOPSIS

(1) The conception of "plausibility" operative in induction is such that *the parameters of cognitive systematization* themselves afford the criteria of inductive plausibility. (2) Induction thus emerges as *plausibilistically* guided truth-estimation, with systematicity itself providing the operative standard of plausibilistic cogency. Such a perspective leads back to an "Hegelian Inversion" of the truth/system relationship. (3) Induction is a process of truth-estimation through systematization with experience that effects the optimally plausible blending of conjecture with information-in-hand. (4) This approach to induction as systematicity-geared truth-estimation can accommodate in natural and straightforward fashion all of the various standard forms of inductive argumentation, including: induction by simple generalization, (5) statistical reasoning, (6) "demonstration by signs," (7) curve fitting, and (8) philological reasoning. (9) The various standard modes of inductive inference can all be fitted into the present (erotetic-enthymematic) model of induction as "systematization with experience" subject to the plausibilistic guidance of the parameters of cognitive systematization. While this redescription of induction leaves the question of its justification unresolved, it puts the matter on a more tractable footing.

1. PLAUSIBILITY AND SYSTEMATICITY

Considerations of plausibility play a central role in the truth-estimation model of inductive reasoning, providing the eliminative process through which we arrive at the "best estimates" of correct answers to our information-transcending questions. This approach leads straightaway to the problem of where these plausibilities come from.

The reply is straightforward. Throughout inductive contexts, plausibility is a matter of cognitive systematicity: *the standards of inductive plausibility inhere in the parameters of cognitive systematization.* We must accordingly undertake a brief examination of the ideas at issue in the traditional concept of a system as an "organic unity" of mutually collaborative units. The principal factors at issue here – the *parameters of systematicity*, as we may dub them – include preeminently the following items:

(1) *completeness:* comprehensiveness, avoidance of gaps or missing components, inclusiveness, unity and integrity as a genuine whole that embraces and integrates all its needed parts

(2) *cohesiveness:* connectedness, interrelationship, interlinkage, coherence (in one of its senses), a conjoining of the component parts, rules, laws, linking principles; if some components are changed or modified, then others will react to this alteration

(3) *consonance:* consistency and compatibility, coherence (in another of its senses), absence of internal discord or dissonance; harmonious mutual collaboration or coordination of components, "having all the pieces fall into proper place"

(4) *functional regularity:* lawfulness, orderliness of operation, uniformity, pattern conformity, normality (conformity to the "usual course of things")

(5) *functional simplicity and economy:* elegance, structural economy, tidiness in the collaboration or coordination of components, harmony and balance, symmetry[1]

[1] On the range of considerations at issue here cf. Elliot Sober, *Simplicity* (Oxford, 1975).

(6) *functional efficacy:* efficiency, effectiveness, adequacy
to the common task, versatility and range and power
of operating principles.

These are some of the characterizing parameters of systematization. After all, systematization is not just a matter of constructing a system, however jerry-built it may prove to be, but of
constructing it under the aegis of certain standard criteria. A
system, properly speaking, must exhibit all of these various
parameters. (Think, for example, of the control system for a
manufacturing process or the life-support system of a space
capsule.) But a system need not exhibit all these facets of
systematicity to an equal degree – let alone perfectly.
They reflect matters of degree, and systems can certainly
vary in the *extent* to which they embody these characteristics,
and in the *manner* of their embodiment as well, since the
rather schematic nature of these "parameters" leaves a good
deal of context-specific detail to be filled in. But no system can
be found or constructed that lacks a substantial combination of
these desiderata. For they afford the guiding standards which
govern the process of systematization and determine the
claims of its products to be characterized as a "system." If a
system (an economic or social system, for example) were to
lose one of these characteristics in substantial measure – if its
coherence or harmony of functioning, or end-realizing effectiveness were substantially diminished – then its very existence
as a system would be threatened.[2]

To be sure, our present concern is not with systematicity *per
se,* but specifically with *cognitive* systematicity as based on the
conception that our information about the world is to constitute part of a system of knowledge. Accordingly, the parameters of systematicity must, in this present context, be construed in a specifically cognitive sense. And the key fact for our
purposes is that, thus construed, they afford our criteria of
inductive plausibility – of the acceptability-qualifications of
our answers to information-transcending questions.

This reliance upon the parameters of systematicity as inductive norms – as standards of plausibility and presumption
in the inductive domain – means that systematicity becomes

[2] For a further development of these issues, and a fuller exposition of the parameters of systematicity, see the author's *Cognitive Systematization* (Oxford, 1979).

the *arbiter* of acceptability-as-true, to use the well-chosen word of F. H. Bradley.[3] After all, we seek to articulate our knowledge by shaping its structure in the most systematic way, the way that endows the resulting manifold of cognitive commitments with the greatest attainable degree of systematic order. But systematicity is not merely ornamental; it is not just a matter of endowing the exposition of our knowledge with certain aesthetic features. Instead of merely representing a facet of the organization of our (otherwise preexistent) knowledge, systematicity is to provide an operative force in the very *constituting* of this knowledge. For while inquiry is a process of enlarging the information at our disposal, of yielding new items to be added to the stock of our acceptances, such question-answering is not just a matter of getting an answer, but a *tenable* answer – one that *merits* acceptance within that body of "already established" information that provides the materials for our further systematizations. And systematicity itself furnishes us with the operative norms here, so that inductive acceptability becomes a matter of systematic fit – and indeed a matter of the tightness of that fit. In sum, we use system not just as organizer of what we accept, but as a Bradleian *arbiter* of acceptability – a standard of what we are to accept, or at any rate endorse *pro tem* until such time as discordant counter-indications come to view.

The connection between induction and systematicity is thus mediated through two governing ideas: *optimality* and *plausibility*. This emerges from the following chain of considerations: (1) Induction seeks to present the best available (i.e., contextually *optimal*) answers to our questions – specifically, our information-in-hand transcending questions about the world. (2) The idea of "best available" in relation to possible answers is to be understood with reference to plausibility considerations, with the best available solution as that which involves a minimum of implausibilities. (3) Systematicity is the arbiter of plausibility in factual contexts. The parameters of systematicity serve as guidelines for the assessment of acceptability.

The definitive features of the present analysis of induction are

---

[3] See F. H. Bradley, "On Truth and Coherence," *Essays on Truth and Reality* (Oxford, 1919), pp. 202–218 (esp. p. 210), where Bradley endorses "the claim of system as an arbiter of fact."

two. First, *inductive reasoning is seen as part and parcel of the enterprise of cognitive systematization* – the systematic structuring and rounding out of our knowledge or presumptive knowledge of matters of fact. Second, in this process of systematic attunement, *the parameters of systematicity (uniformity, simplicity, and the rest) are themselves taken to provide the requisite yardsticks of the plausibility-assessment* that guides deliberations of acceptability.[4] And the second point is bound up with the first: it is because induction is part of the enterprise of cognitive systematization that the parameters of systematicity are to be taken as standards of plausibility in inductive contexts.

Let us consider one, admittedly crude, example of this process. Suppose we have the question "What are the values of the (empirical) quantities x and y?" in a situation where our database contains only the two items of information: $x + y = 2$ and $x^2 + 2xy + y^2 = 4$; items which, so we shall suppose, are obtained independently, their contentual redundancy notwithstanding. Yet because of this redundancy of these items, the situation is mathematically underdetermined: we cannot provide any demonstrably cogent answer to our question on the basis of the information in hand. But since (so let it be supposed) the whole body of our relevant background knowledge indicates nothing to upset the situation of seeming parity between x and y, we could project the enthymeme:

B [= our relevant "background knowledge"]
$$\left. \begin{array}{l} x + y = 2 \\ x^2 + 2xy + y^2 = 4 \end{array} \right\} \quad [= D, \text{ the "data of the problem"}]$$

[4] In an oft-cited passage, John Stuart Mill wrote:

Why is a single instance, in some cases, sufficient for a complete induction, while in others, myriads of concurring instances, without a single exception known or presumed, go such a little way towards establishing a universal proposition: Whoever answers this question knows more of the philosophy of logic than the wisest of the ancients and has solved the problem of induction. (*A System of Logic* [8th ed.; London, 1895], Bk. III, chap. iii, sect. 2.)

But the matter is not all that arcane. It is precisely the matter of *systematic best-fit* that distinguishes between some instance-indicated generalizations and others in inductive argumentation – the mere *number* of instances is in itself secondary and insignificant. The decisive factors are fit, enmeshment, and that Whewellian "consilience" to which Mill never gave due credit.

⟨what holds of *x* holds of *y*: $x \approx y$⟩ [an enthymematic supposition that is, *ex hypothesi*, supported by *B*]

∴ $x = y = 1$

To be sure, the enthymematic thesis of parity $x \approx y$ is not more *probable* than other alternatives relative to the information afforded by the body of our knowledge-in-hand, $K = D \& B$. Rather, it is, on this basis, just more *systematic* (uniform, simple, regular, etc.) – and thus more data-consonantly *plausible* than the other alternatives (assuming *B* to be suitably benign). In these circumstances we would reach a definite resolution to our question on inductive grounds, setting both *x* and *y* at 1. This example illustrates the inductive recourse to system – the use of *K*-based plausibilities to arrive at an inductively appropriate answer through system-geared blending of question-resolving conjecture with the data afforded by our information-in-hand.[5]

2. TRUTH ESTIMATION AND THE HEGELIAN INVERSION

To obtain a clear view of the underlying rationale for the present conception of induction, let us glance back once more to the epistemological role of systematicity in its historical aspect. The point of departure was the traditional Greek view (present in Plato and Aristotle and clearly still operative with rationalists as late as Spinoza) which – secure in a fundamental commitment to the systematicity of the real – took *cognitive* systematicity (i.e., systematicity as present in the framework of "our knowledge") as a measure of the extent to which man's purported understanding of the world can be regarded as adequate. On this classical view, the principle of *adaequatio ad rem* is so applied as to yield the result that since reality is systematic an adequate account of it must also be so.

A long line of philosophers, then, has seen system as a crucial aspect of truth. The tradition they represent has

---

[5] The defect of this conveniently oversimple example lies in the fact that – short of making extreme demands on the background knowledge *B* – the tightness of fit is not sufficient for an inductive conclusion to be drawn with sufficient confidence.

stressed the overall systematicity of "the truth," holding that the totality of true theses must constitute a cohesive system. This classical approach saw systematization as a two-step process: first determine the truths, and then systematize them. (Think of the analogy of building: first assemble the bricks, then build the wall.) With the tradition from Leibniz through Kant to Hegel, however, we come to an inversion that leads to a single-step process: the determination of the right components through the very process of their assembling (the choosing of just those bricks which will fit together to make up a sturdy wall). We shift from *true→systematic* to the reverse transition *systematic → true*. Fit itself affords the criterion of rightness. From a *desideratum of the organization* of our "body of factual knowledge," systematicity accordingly came to be metamorphosed into *a qualifying test of membership* – a standard of facticity.[6]

We thus arrive at the "Hegelian Inversion" of the traditional relationship of systematicity to truth. Beginning with the implication-thesis that what belongs to science can be systematized ("If properly belonging to science, then systematizable"), we then transpose it into the converse: If a proposition is smoothly systematizable with the whole of our (purported) knowledge, then it should be accepted as a part thereof. This Hegelian inversion brings down to earth the old metaphysicians' equation

the truth = the perfect system of judgments

by replacing it with the equation

our best estimate of the truth =
                the optimal systematization we can devise

From being a characteristic of science (as per the regulative idea that a body of knowledge-claims cannot qualify as a science if it lacks a systematic articulation), systematicity is transmuted into a testing standard of (presumptive) truth – an acceptability criterion for the claims that purport to belong to science. The key idea at issue is simply an extension of the old

<hr>

Compare F. H. Bradley, "On Truth and Coherence," *op. cit.*

idea that simplicity – or now, rather, systematicity in all its various dimensions – is the identifying hallmark of truth (*simplex sigillum veri*). Accordingly, the Hegelian Inversion sees the transformation of systematicity from a framework for *organizing* knowledge into a mechanism for *determining* adequate knowledge-claims. Fit, attunement, and systematic connection thus become the determinative criteria for assessing the acceptability of claims, the monitors of cognitive adequacy.

On this approach, then – to which the present view of induction fully conforms – the assurance of inductively authorized contentions turns exactly on this issue of tightness of fit: of consilience, mutual interconnection, and systemic enmeshment. Systematicity becomes our test of truth, the guiding standard of truth-estimation. Our "picture of the real" is thus taken to emerge as an intellectual product achieved under the control of the idea that systematicity is a regulative principle for our theorizing. The linkage between truth and systematicity does not, then, take the form: "*systematic because true (since the truth is a system)*." Rather, it takes the reverse form: "*true because systematic (since systematicity is the test of truth)*."

To be sure, we have here weakened this second linkage somewhat. For our epistemological position moves from systematicity not to correctness itself, but rather to *the rational warrant of claims to correctness*. The operative transition is not from "systematic" to "correct," but rather from "systematic" to "rationally claimed to be correct." The role of systematicity is, in the first instance, epistemic (and only derivatively on · tological). The "best available answer" at issue is so only in the sense of affording us the best available *estimate* of the truth.[7]

3. INDUCTION AS SYSTEMATIZATION "WITH EXPERIENCE"

Induction emerges as a tool of system-building – a device for the plausibilistically optimal meshing of question-resolving conjecture with the data of the relevant information-in-hand where the parameters of cognitive systematization themselves

---

[7] It must, to be sure, be noted that while the remarks of this section simply *explain* the operation of a truth-criteriology based on systematicity, they do not *justify* it. This remains as a task to which the ensuing chapters will be devoted.

provide the requisite standards of plausibility. Induction, thus regarded, is a mechanism of question-resolution through the systematic rounding off of the background information that is at our disposal with enthymematic conjecture – the optimally systematic blending of conjecture with available information-in-hand. It is a process of dovetailing our experientially guided plausible conjectures into their wider experiential context on the basis of plausibilistic best-fit considerations. Here, support and systematicity are inextricably correlative.

The line of thought of these deliberations depicts induction as a particular sort of cognitive systematization with "the data." For systematic "best fit" is always a matter of fitting *with something* and this is where the matter of the *data* – of information already in hand to provide a "background" – plays its indispensable part.[8] (Note, however, that our "data" are invariably fallible – that our sources of information afford misinformation as well; the process of fitting things with the data also makes for a smoothing out of the data themselves.)[9] But just what are these *data*? They may stem from many sources: observations, records, or even (in such contexts as hypothetical exercises) mere assumptions. At bottom, however, the data-base of our inductive theorizing is afforded by the body of our *funded experience* (as William James called it).

One very important point must be stressed in this connection. To someone accustomed to thinking in terms of a sharp contrast between organizing the information already in hand and an active inquiry aimed at extending it, the idea of a *systematization of conjecture with experience* may sound like a very conservative process. This impression would be quite incorrect. Our approach must not be construed to slight the dynamical aspect. The present analysis sees systematization itself as an instrument of inquiry – a tool for aligning question-resolving conjecture with the (of itself inadequate) data at hand. The factors of completeness, comprehensiveness, inclusiveness, unity, etc. are all crucial aspects of system, and the ampler the information-base, the ampler is the prospect for

---

[8] Note here the crucial role of this background knowledge K as part of the information-base relative to which the plausibilities of the case are determined.

[9] Compare the author's treatment of data in *The Coherence Theory of Truth* (Oxford, 1973).

our systematization to attain them. The drive to system embodies an imperative to broaden the range of our experience, to extend and expand the data-base from which our theoretical triangulations proceed. In the course of this process, it may well eventuate that our existing systematizations – however adequate they may seem at the time – are untenable and must be overthrown in the interest of constructing ampler and tighter systems. Cognitive systematization is emphatically not an indelibly conservative process which only looks to what fits smoothly into heretofore established patterns, but one where the established patterns are themselves ever vulnerable and liable to be upset in the interests of devising a more comprehensive systematic framework.

4. INDUCTION BY SIMPLE GENERALIZATION

The preceding discussion has given an abstract characterization of inductive reasoning as a process of truth-estimation proceeding by way of a systematization of question-answering conjecture relative to experience. Specifically, inductive argumentation was depicted as a matter of enthymematic reasoning requiring supplementary information to be provided on the basis of plausibility considerations determined by the standard parameters of cognitive systematicity (comprehensiveness, unity, regularity, simplicity, etc.). Let us now examine the detailed workings of this erotetic-enthymematic model of inductive inference more closely and, in particular, let us see how this general approach can actually be put to work to accommodate various standard forms of inductive argumentation.

A most rudimentary but also common form of inductive argumentation is *induction by simple generalization,* the process of inductive reasoning which moves from an observed uniformity across the examined cases of a certain sort to the conclusion that *all* cases of this sort have the feature in question. The instances at issue – all drawn from a family Z of cases – share a property ϕ. The argumentation then moves from the fact that all of the *observed* Z-instances have ϕ to the conclusion that *all* Z-instances do so. Its structure is one of reasoning from $(\forall x)(x \in Z_s \supset \phi x)$ to $(\forall x)(x \in Z \supset \phi x)$, where Z_s is the set of all the observed or sampled instances of Z (so that clearly $Z_s \subseteq Z$). We now face the problem: just what is it that makes this conclusion "inductively appropriate"?

Consider the matter from our present perspective. We begin by confronting the question "What is the ϕ-status of the Z's?" The answers include:

(1) "All Z's are ϕ"
(2) "No Z's are ϕ"
(3) "Some Z's are ϕ and some aren't"
(4) "Can't say"

Here (4) is a non-answer, while (2) is untenable in the circumstances under hypothesis. Only (1) and (3) afford workable answers. And (1) is clearly the "inductively appropriate" answer to our question. But how do we arrive at it? How, given our enthymematic approach, do we close the enthymematic gap schematized by the premiss E of the argument:

$B[=$ our relevant "background knowledge" regarding Z, Z_s, and ϕ]
$(\forall x)(x \in Z_s \supset \phi x)[= D$, the "data of the problem"]
$\langle E \rangle$

$\therefore (\forall x)(x \in Z \supset \phi x)$

The characteristic inductive situation of a conclusion that moves beyond the available information is clearly present here. In the face of the given information $K (= D \,\&\, B)$, various rather different answers are available with respect to our focal question of the ϕ-status of the membership of Z as a whole. For given the premiss that all Z-members have ϕ, there will be many different conjecturally available ways to fill the information-gap with respect to the ϕ-condition of the *residual* Z-population outside of Z_s. The given premiss $(\forall x)(x \in Z_s \supset \phi x)$ is clearly compatible with $(\exists x)(x \in Z \,\&\, \sim \phi x)$, or even with $(\forall x)(x \in (Z - Z_s) \supset \sim \phi x)$. When we canvass the range of possibilities for moving beyond the premiss $(\forall x)$

$(x \in Z_s \supset \phi x)$, by way of enthymematic supplementation, we thus obtain not only the "appropriate" E, namely

(i) $(\forall x) (x \in (Z - Z_s) \supset \phi x)$ ["All the remaining Z-members have ϕ"],

but also such alternatives as

(ii) $(\forall x) (x \in (Z - Z_s) \supset \sim \phi x)$ ["None of the remaining Z-members have ϕ"]

(iii) $(\exists x) (x \in (Z - Z_s) \& \phi x) \& (\exists x) (x \in (Z - Z_s) \& \sim \phi x)$ ["Some of the remaining Z-members have ϕ and some don't"]

(iv) $Z_s = Z$ ["There are no further Z-members"].

All these contentions afford diverse routes towards filling in the gap in our information regarding the ϕ-status of the remaining, Z_s-external elements of Z. (In fact, these alternatives span the whole spectrum; insofar as other answers to the question of the ϕ-status of the remaining Z-population outside Z_s are possible, they would simply be special cases of (iii).) Here (i) points us towards (1), while (ii) and (iii) point towards (3) as answers to our basic question. (Case (iv) can in general be dismissed in its claim of finitude for what is in general a potentially infinite range.) Now how is (i) to be validated here? Given that induction is "systematization with experience," and that experience has *ex hypothesi* furnished us with $(\forall x) (x \in Z_s \supset \phi x)$, how can we resolve the choice between these various supplementation-moves and establish (i) as the inductively appropriate member of this family of alternatives?

To resolve this issue, it becomes necessary, as we have seen, to seek the plausibilistic guidance needed for possibility-elimination. This needed guidance is conveniently accessible in terms of considerations of systematicity, and particularly – in the present case – through the following:

Uniformity Principle

In the absence of explicit counter-indications, a thesis about unscrutinized cases that *conforms to a uniformity present throughout the data at our disposal* is more plausible than any of its regularity-discordant contraries – and the more extensive this pattern-conformity, the more highly plausible the thesis.

This principle articulates the precept that when the initially given evidence exhibits a marked logical pattern, then pattern-concordant claims relative to this evidence are, *ceteris paribus*, to be evaluated as more plausible than pattern-discordant ones, and the more comprehensively pattern-concordant, the more highly plausible. (For example, in text-reconstruction, if the missing letter follows a Q it is presumably a U or if the missing word follows an article, it is plausible to suppose it to be a noun.)

Let us apply this line of consideration to the preceding example. Here we begin with the premissed fact that $(\forall x) (x \in Z_s \supset \phi x)$. Barring ominous indications within our background knowledge B, it is at once clear on this basis that thesis (1) is the maximally plausible alternative because *it and it alone places the Z_s-included and the Z_s-excluded members of Z on precisely the same footing.* Thesis (i) alone reflects the plausibilistic priorities of the Uniformity Principle, envisaging an uniform, homogenous situation as between Z_s and $Z - Z_s$. It thus emerges as winner in the competition among alternatives in point of data-relative plausibility. And now, once this thesis $(\forall x) (x \in (Z - Z_s) \supset \phi x)$ is conjoined as the enthymematic premiss to the initially given $(\forall x) (x \in Z_s \supset \phi x)$, we have it that $(\forall x)(x \in Z \supset \phi x)$. This example shows how the erotetic-enthymematic approach furnishes a plausibilistic basis for inductive validation in the specific case of the standard process of induction by simple generalization.

5. STATISTICAL REASONING

Statistical reasoning of the most familiar sorts is also readily accommodated within the operation of an erotetic-enthymematic model of inductive reasoning. Take, for example, the move from sample to population in the type of statistical reasoning often characterized as "proportional induction." Here we resolve the basic question "What proportion of the F's are G's?" by arguing from the given data that "the proportion of F's that are G's (within our sample population Z_s) is r" to the conclusion that the same situation obtains in the population as a whole. The inductively indicated transition from the sample frequency of r to the population frequency of just this same value can once again be rationalized straightforwardly through the mechanisms of the enthymematic approach.

Reliance on the Uniformity Principle to align the situation within the unobserved $Z - Z_s$ with that of the observed population Z_s is patently clear here. A proportion r of F's that are G's within the sample Z_s means that *the selfsame proportion* in the residual group $Z - Z_s$ will be necessary and sufficient to yield an identical overall proportion for the whole population X. (Compare Figure II.1.)

Figure II.1

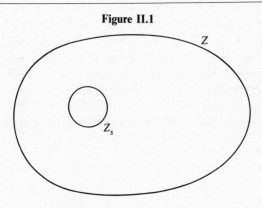

Note: If the proportion of the trait in view is r within Z_s then the identical proportion of r in $Z - Z_s$ is sufficient (and necessary) to yield this same overall proportion for Z as a whole.

In the absence of counter-indications, the most systematic (simple, uniform, etc.) course is to assilimate the question of the situation in $Z - Z_s$ to that of Z_s. Uniformity considerations again provide the plausibilistic guidance required to engender straightforwardly the standard inductive result.[10]

Here too, then, we have the conjectural projection of various possibilities followed by a reductive elimination – subject to plausibilistic considerations – of all those case that conflict with the "inductively appropriate" conclusion. And the guidance

[10] Note that when $r = 100\%$, the present case is effectively identical with the situation of induction by simple generalization. This sort of systemic uniformity is clearly an indispensable requisite for any adequate analysis.

of plausibility-assessments by uniformitarian considerations again yields a basis for validating this "inductively appropriate" answer.

6. "DEMONSTRATION BY SIGNS"

One very common type of inductive reasoning occurs when we make an inference to the usual cause of an observed effect (or conversely) – for instance, when we answer the question "What is it that has produced the effect *R*?" by simply indicating the cause which, in the ordinary and usual cause of events, leads to the realization of *R*. In such cases, it is supposed that a general relationship of the form "Normally *R* only when *S*" obtains and then the presence of *R* is taken to betoken *S*. Aristotle characterizes this as a "demonstration by signs" (*kata to sēmeion apodeixis*),[11] and he gives a neat example of this sort of reasoning: "Normally the ground is wet (= *R*) only after a rainfall (= *S*); the ground is wet; so it has been raining."

This mode of argumentation is readily assimilated to the present erotetic-enthymematic model of inductive reasoning via an enthymematic inference that proceeds along the following lines:

> *B* [= the background information]
> Normally (relative to *B*) we have it that *R* only
>   when *S* [by hypothesis]
> *R* in this case [given datum]
> ⟨This is a normal case⟩
> _____
> ∴ *S* in this case

In the absence of counter-indications within *B*, it is the simplest and most straightforward course – and thus the data-relatively most plausible one – to take the present case of *S* to be one that falls within the "normal" range. And so, in the circumstances of the case, *S* is the most smoothly systematic answer to the question "What is it that has produced *R*?" (To be sure, its reliance on an inherently defeasible enthymematic

[11] *Soph. Elen.*, 167b10–20; but cf. the more detailed discussion in *Anal. Pr.*, 70a6ff.

presupposition that makes patent the fragility of this reasoning.)

7. CURVE FITTING

The problem of generalizing from particular data is often compared to that of tracing the smoothest curve through a given family of points. As A. A. Cournot wrote well over a century ago:

> En général, une théorie scientifique quelconque ... peut être assimilée à la courbe qu'on trace d'après une défi-nition mathématique, en s'imposant la condition de la faire passer par un certain nombre de points données d'avance.[12]

Given that there is a curve which passes through the points at issue the question of how we are to estimate the form of this curve is to be resolved on inductive principles in the most systematic (uniform, simple, smoothly continuous) way.[13] The fitting process at issue is, of course, readily accommodated to the plausibilistic process of the present "best fit" model, with the standard parameters of systematicity – uniformity, simplicity, and the rest – playing their usual determinative role.[14]

8 PHILOLOGICAL REASONING

Philological reasoning affords yet another straightforward in-stance of the capacity of our enthymematic model to accom-modate the standard varieties of inductive argumentation.

Suppose the occurrence of the following inscription on an ancient, weather-eroded tombstone in an old New England graveyard:

Tl ᴄs. Taⳕlɔˉ

1ˉʔᴄ-17ʂʔ

---

[12] *Essai sur les fondements de nos connaisances*, vol. I (Paris, 1851), p. 82.

[13] Cf. John S. Kemeny, "The Use of Simplicity in Induction," *The Philosophical Review*, vol. 62 (1953), pp. 391–408.

[14] This is elaborated in greater detail at pp. 174–178 below.

It is not difficult to figure out that this must be presumed to be

Thos. Taylor
1736–1782

To be sure, conjectural proliferation will generate a sizable spectrum of possible alternatives. But plausibility considerations can be evolved around issues such as

(1) the usual style and phraseology of inscriptions of the sort at issue;
(2) physical fit of missing or incomplete symbols;
(3) making unproblematic sense within the general context;

and the like, to facilitate the reduction of these possibilities to manageable proportions. The standard parameters of cognitive systematization – uniformity, simplicity, economy, normalcy, etc. – take hold once again to supply the considerations needed for the assessment of the data-relative plausibility that guides the process of informational gapfilling.

9. SUMMARY

As this survey illustrates, the various standard modes of inductive reasoning can readily be fitted into the erotetic-enthymematic model of induction as a process of truth-estimation that proceeds by "systematization with experience" – invoking the usual parameters of cognitive systematization (and, above all, the factors of uniformity, simplicity, and normality) to furnish the plausibilistic guidance needed to implement this approach.[15]

Admittedly – and this is a point that requires emphasis – the preceding deliberations have been largely a matter of *description*, of characterizing (from a suitable point of view) the way in which inductive reasoning proceeds. The question of *justifi-*

[15] The mechanisms of the theory of plausible reasoning that underlie the deliberations of this chapter are set out in greater detail in the author's *Plausible Reasoning* (Assen, 1975). The use of the parameters of systematicity as indices of plausibility is considered in *Cognitive Systematization* (Oxford, 1979).

cation still remains untouched. But this "mere re-description" does enable us to see the problem in a different focus. The issue is now clearly seen not as a matter of legitimating a peculiar form of inferential reasoning, but one of validating or justifying our recourse to the plausibilistic guidance of the standard parameters of epistemic systematicity as a basis for resolving our information-in-hand transcending questions. The issue of justifying induction is now itself recast into one of validating our reliance on system-indicated plausibilities as a basis for truth-estimation in the factual domain. There is, as we shall see, good reason to regard this reformulation of the problem as substantially facilitating its resolution.

III

The Pragmatic Approach to Justifying Induction

SYNOPSIS

(1) The two basic questions regarding the appropriateness of the present approach to induction are: Why *systematization*?, and why systematization *with experience*? (2) Why *systematization*? Because the object of the enterprise is the attainment of the best available answers to our questions, and systematization is the appropriate means towards this end of the realization of cognitive rationality. (3) Why systematization *with experience*? Because the aim is to secure information *about the world* – and experience is our only route to this destination. A this-or-nothing principle is at work. (4) A conspectus of the task that lies before us in justifying induction when the issue is approached along these lines.

---

1. WHY SYSTEMATIZATION WITH EXPERIENCE?

Any ampliative mode of argumentation, induction preeminently included, substantiates a conclusion on an evidential basis that is deductively insufficient, so that divergent resolutions always remain theoretically possible. How then are we to justify a specific resolution, given that alternative possibilities exist? The answer in the case of induction is that we do so by fixing upon that alternative which best and most smoothly fits our overall data-basis, so that the rationale for our inductive imputations of truth is provided in terms of the general process of cognitive systematization. The tactics characteristic of inductive reasoning all emerge from one and the same fundamental strategy – the drive towards cognitive systematicity. It is a matter of resolving our questions by filling gaps in an informational framework – a process of truth-estimation that is carried through on the basis of best-fit considerations. The invocation of *uniformity* and *simplicity*, to take only two examples, are just so many applications of the parameters of systematicity in their regulative, methodological guise as means of enhancing the systematic structure of our cognitive commitments. From this standpoint, induction comes to be seen as part and parcel of a drive to place our claims to knowledge on a footing of systematic best fit on the basis of experience.

But what considerations validate such a process of reasoning? This problem divides into two components: Why *systematization*?, and why systematization *with experience*? Let us begin with the first.

2. WHY SYSTEMATIZATION? THE SEARCH FOR OPTIMAL ANSWERS

A truth-estimate must, of course, be justified – or at any rate be capable of justification. Now in the cognitive setting, "to justify" is itself nothing other than to systematize. It lies in the very nature of the thing that *validation* must proceed in cognitive contexts by way of systematization, fitting the answers to our questions as smoothly as ever we can into the context of the background information provided by "the evidence at hand" or "the body of available data."[1] Systematization, in sum, affords the standard methodology of cognitive validation. And this circumstance is particularly clear in inductive situations. In giving an answer to a question whose resolution transcends the information in hand, we rationally make (to just exactly this extent) a "leap in the dark." In doing this we

[1] The root idea here goes back to Leibniz, who held the acceptability of an hypothesis to hinge upon its *power* and its *simplicity* – that is, on the number of the phenomena it would explain and the fewness of the assumptions it involves. The factors of systematization and experiential enmeshment are simply extensions of Leibnizian ideas. Cf. the discussion of Leibniz' position in the author's *Studies in Modality* (Oxford, 1974), pp. 57–70.

want to minimize the extent to which we create further problems and difficulties for ourselves. Securing a systematic best
fit of our answer within the overall framework of our cognitive
commitments is precisely the way to assure this desideratum.

The aim of inquiry is, after all, twofold: (1) to obtain answers to our questions, and (2) to do so (if possible) in such a
way as to move the whole corpus of our cognitive commitments nearer to completeness. That is, in inquiry with respect
to a question Q we want to obtain an answer to Q in a way that
will shift our existing "body of knowledge" to a successor state
in which Q is answered, and moreover the overall range of
unanswered questions is reduced or at any rate rendered as
small as is possible in the circumstances. It is thus built into the
very goal-structure of inquiry that the answers we seek should
minimize difficulties – that they should not only resolve the
particular question from which we set out, but that they
should fit smoothly within the overall body of our cognitive
commitments to the greatest feasible extent.

The answer to the question "Why systematize?" can thus be
given in straightforwardly purposive terms. The object of the
enterprise of inquiry is to obtain the "best available" answers
to our questions, in the sense of securing those answers for
whose adoption the strongest case of rational justification can
be developed. And, given what is at issue in rationale-
development, systematization is the natural and appropriate
means to this end. The search for optimal answers requires
systematization because the conditions of the "optimality" at
issue with answers are determined on this very basis.[2]

These considerations clearly have a direct and immediate
bearing on the rational legitimation of induction. For induction represents a process of reasoning that can be seen to
conform to the general canons of rationality through its assimilation to the strategy of coherent systematization. Once
cognitive rationality is construed (as it should be) in terms of
the introduction of systematic order into our understanding of
things, and induction seen as simply a natural instrument for
the realization of systematicity (as is indeed the case), then the
rational warranting of inductive reasoning becomes relatively
straightforward.

[2] Cf. the author's *Cognitive Systematization* (Oxford, 1979).

3. WHY EXPERIENCE?

Why should induction be a matter of the systematization of question-resolving conjecture *with experience*? The answer lies in the consideration that system-building is not an end in itself – it is a process subject to objectives and desiderata of extra-systematic provenience. A crucial control is exercised over our systematizing by the very objects of the enterprise, the root issue of the aims and purposes of inquiry.

The starting point here is set by our factual questions – questions about the world to which we want and need to have the best available answers. Now at this juncture a "this-or-nothing" argument comes into operation. Our only access to information about nature is through *interaction* with it. And such interaction is what experience is all about. (Here, of course, "experience" must be broadly construed to encompass the whole gamut of interaction-with-nature-generated cues and clues that serve as grist to the mill of inquiry.) Our cognitive machinery must have inputs to provide knowledge of nature, and experience is the only source of inputs we have. The empiricist insight holds good: we have no alternative but to fall back on experience as the *fons et origio* of our factual information about the world.

To be sure, experience itself cannot do the whole job for us. For one thing, it only relates to particular cases. Our questions about the world standardly involve some element of generality, and empiricists have always had to confront the vexing problem of rationalizing the cognitively crucial step from particular experiences to the reasoned acceptance of empirical generalizations. Still, while our questions generally call for answers that *transcend* experience, we must nevertheless give them answers that *align* with it insofar as possible. There is simply no alternative to relying on experience for the reference points of the theoretical triangulation through which our knowledge of the world is generated. If information about matters of objective fact is to be obtainable at all, then this *must* be so on the basis of *experience* (supplemented by whatever principles and rules of inductive systematization are needed to make its rational exploitation possible). Observation is our only avenue of contact with what happens in the world. (The all-knowing Recording Angel does not whisper it into our ears, and if he did, it is doubtful that we would understand him!) If *anything* can validate claims to generalized factual knowledge, then experience – limited and, no doubt, imperfect experience – can validate such claims.

Thus when Russell, in his *Problems of Philosophy*, asks whether "*any* number of cases of a law being fulfilled afford evidence that it will be fulfilled in the future,"[3] we must answer the question with yet another: What *would* you be prepared to count as evidence here? What do you think it appropriate to ask for? If you are not prepared to let our experience of observed cases count as evidence *vis-à-vis* the future, then just what sort of evidence is it that you demand? Experience is the only route to the destination in these matters of generality; it is the only game in town. There is just no chance of winning if we do not play the game at all. It is appropriate in this context to invoke William James' principle that: "a rule of thinking which would absolutely prevent one from acknowledging certain kinds of truth if those kinds of truth were really there, would be an irrational rule."[4] It is thus irrational – being altogether self-defeating from the standpoint of the cognitive enterprise – to assume *a priori* a sceptical stance on the view that claims to factual knowledge can be validated experientially. If we want information about the world – to be in a position to make correct cognitive claims about it – then we *must* use experience as a basis for making such claims, and we *must* treat such experientially based claims (at any rate provisionally) as being correct, as affording genuine knowledge.

Here we encounter a characteristic instance of the generic process of "*this-or-nothing argumentation*" in philosophical inquiry. Bosanquet explained the principle at issue in the following terms:

[A] general consideration . . . [of cognitive justification] might be rendered by some such formula as "This or nothing," which, empirically speaking, we do often make use of in representing the ground of a conviction. The

[3] Bertrand Russell, *Problems of Philosophy* (Oxford, 1912), p. 96.
[4] "The Will to Believe," sect. X.

essence of ... [this sort of justification] would be in showing of any suggested assertion that unless we accepted it, our province of truth would as a whole be taken from us.[5]

The structure of the situation is such that if one is not prepared to rely on experience, then there is no choice but to abandon the whole project of inquiry aimed at securing answers to our questions regarding matters of objective fact. Given that we want to ask about the course of nature as we *can* experience it, we have no choice but to base our answers in some way or other in the course of nature as we *do* experience it. As John Henry Newman wrote: "We are in a world of facts, and we use them; for there is nothing else to use."[6] If we do not call on experience to validate our cognitive claims in the factual sphere, then *nothing* can do so: if *anything* can, then *experience* can. A "nothing to lose" perspective lies in the background here. If we wish to realize a certain goal and only one route to this destination lies open, we have little choice but to try it, however unpromising it may seem.

A rational animal facing the uncertain future must triangulate from past experience: it must make its way in a difficult world by its cognitive wits. Its reliance on experience is natural and inevitable, and thereby also legitimate, seeing that no rationally superior alternative lies to hand. What other warrant could – or need – there be? There is no room for any feelings of dissatisfaction here. For we must face the fact that, in the circumstances, this sort of argumentation is the strongest that can reasonably be asked for, because it is the strongest that can possibly be had. And it must always be remembered in this context that the epistemic obligations of rational credence cannot and do not outstrip the limits of the possible. (The old Roman legal maxim applies: *Ultra posse nemo obligatur.*)

To be sure, nothing said here should be construed to assert that experience is a gift horse into whose mouth we are not entitled to look. Just what status is to be accorded to the "data

[5] Bernard Bosanquet, *Implication and Linear Inference* (London, 1929), pp. 3, 19 and *passim*. Cf. also A. C. Ewing, *Idealism* (London, 1934, 3rd ed. 1961), p. 237.
[6] J. H. Newman, *A Grammar of Assent* (London, 1870), chap. IX, sect. 1.

of experience" within the framework of inductive inquiry? Clearly they are not "fixed points," not absolute and incorrigible axioms. As the ancient sceptics stridently – and rightly – insisted, there is nothing irrefragably trustworthy about our senses. The "data of experience" are certainly not incontestable absolutes. Sight tells us the stick held at an angle under water is bent, while touch tells us it is straight. The "data of experience" – of sight, memory, and the rest – are certainly givens, but they are NOT *given truths*. They are simply raw materials that serve as *inputs* into the process through which our best available answers to our questions are arrived at. Their status is not *definitive* but *presumptive*. In the course of systematization, they may themselves come unstuck. The epistemic bearing of these data is nothing final and absolute – they are themselves part and parcel of the systematizing process, and are themselves not only *materials* but also *objects* of inductive inquiry.

Inductive reasoning is thus a matter not only of systematization *with* experience but of the systematization *of* experience as well. (It is not sensation but inductive theorizing that enables us to make sense of the bent-stick-under-water phenomenon.) Experience itself is not something wholly selfsufficient and altogether indifferent to the formative pressures of systematization. Our "sources of knowledge" need not be regarded as something sacred and sacrosanct. Dreams, intimations, hunches, omens, and the like, once held equally undisputed sway alongside the five senses and memory. As these examples show, even the claims to merely presumptive truth that can be made out for certain sources can eventually come to be undone.

It deserves stress, moreover, that such a demolition of some sector of our experiential data can only come about in situations of conflict where the stronger prevails over the weaker. And in such a conflict as is at issue here it is not possible for *all* of the rival competitors to kill each other off; that which prevails as the stronger will thereby survive the competition. The idea that *all* of our cognitive sources can become unstuck in this way can thus be dismissed out of hand. One cannot argue from the potential unviability of *any* source to the prospect that all of our sources may prove unviable *en bloc*.

Accordingly, the sceptical imposition of a standard which, on the basis of theoretical general principles, would preclude all prospects of an experiential validation of factual claims is *eo ipso* improper and illegitimate. Being the only route, experience must be allowed to serve as a possible route – its inherent problems and difficulties notwithstanding. Whatever *factual* information we can attain regarding the arrangements of the world must be *empirical* and ultimately based on our experiential encounter of it. There is no real alternative for the *modus operandi* of our truth-estimation than the systematic exploitation of experience.

4. THE PROBLEM OF JUSTIFICATION

The problem, however, still remains of just what it is that establishes the results of an optimal systematizing of experience as actually affording "the best available answers" to our factual questions about the world. The *aim* of the cognitive enterprise is to attain the truth (no doubt of that!). What then leads us to regard the systematization of experience by the usual inductive standards is the appropriate route to this ultimately decisive destination – how can we effect the transition from "optimally systematic" to "presumably true"? What qualifies the conclusions to which experience leads us in inductive systematization to be taken as actually representing *knowledge*?

Induction is certainly not a sure-fire device for getting correct answers. (As Hume has shown, this is an impossibility in the very nature of the case.) Instead, the best we can hope to show is that induction is a means for doing the job of truth-estimation as well as it is possible to do in the epistemic circumstances in which we live and work. Such an approach casts induction as an optimal method of goal attainment – a means for countering our questions with those answers for whose acceptability the most rationally cogent case can be made out. To be sure, this contention that induction (i.e., systematization with experience) represents an *optimal* method of inquiry rests at the present stage of the discussion as a mere claim – something that still needs to be established.

Given an approach that views induction as a matter of

truth-estimation through "systematization with the data," it becomes clear that what a justification of induction must accomplish is a validation of the governing role of our standard criteria of cognitive systematization (simplicity, uniformity, economy, and the rest). After all, very different parameters could in theory be employed in cognitive systematization, and corresponding functional equivalents of systematicity – we might call them tystematicity and wystematicity, etc. – can certainly be envisaged. What needs to be accomplished by a "justification" of induction is to show that induction as we practice it – subject to our familiar recourse to the standard parameters of scientific systematization – is indeed legitimate relative to purposes for which the whole venture of rational inquiry is ultimately instituted. This is the task to which the subsequent discussion will have to be addressed.

IV

The Methodological Turn
A: Initial Justification

SYNOPSIS

(1) Induction is a methodological device for *doing* something, namely a truth-estimation method for making the "inductive leap" needed to realize answers to our information-in-hand transcending questions. (2) The natural criterion for assessing the appropriateness of any method is the instrumentalist standard of its promise for working out – its potential for purpose-realization. (3) And here, *faute de mieux* considerations can serve our justificating purposes by establishing the "practical necessity" created by absence of any more promising alternative. (4) Such frail considerations can bear substantial weight because the standards of proof are weaker in the methodological domain whose norms are ultimately governed by practical (pragmatic) rather than theoretical (cognitive) considerations. Above all, this means that a justification can be provided in the absence of any initial preguarantee of effectiveness. (5) Argumentation along these *faute de mieux* lines can also be marshalled to provide an adequately supportive initial justification for our specifically *cognitive* methods, including our inductive practices. (6) This methodological course of (initial) justification for induction is itself free from any inductive involvements. (7) But while such *faute de mieux* argumentation gets the justificatory argument off to a good start, it does not in itself bring the matter to a satisfactory conclusion.

1. THE INDUCTIVE LEAP AND THE METHODOLOGICAL-
PRAGMATIC ASPECT OF INDUCTION

The epistemic predicament of man is such that his only access to information about "the real world" is through the epistemological resources and instrumentalities at his disposal in sensing and reasoning – that we are so constituted as to have no *direct* access to such information, unmediated by the epistemic processes of controlled inquiry. This circumstance that our only route to information about the world is through theoretical triangulation from interaction with nature is a fundamental reality that must be faced up to and reckoned with. Being inevitable, it is in no way a focus of appropriate regret; here, as elsewhere, there is little point in lamenting what cannot in the very nature of things be helped. We must do the best we can by the means at our disposal, and our epistemological mechanisms are just that: means to an end. One cannot understand induction aright without viewing it in this perspective, as a cognitive tool for obtaining optimally plausible and thereby *presumptively* true answers to our questions about the world.

The enthymematic model of induction as a question-answering process of truth-estimation casts induction in the role of a gapfilling technique – a method for securing answers to our questions in situations of imperfect information. Its work is genuinely ampliative rather than merely inferential: it does not lie in unravelling the inner ramifications of a preexisting state of informational affairs, but in bringing about a new state through augmenting or supplementing the information at our disposal. Such gapfilling requires committing ourselves to something that is merely suggested, rather than already covertly present and extractible by derivation; it calls for the accomplishment of a task that goes beyond any mere *inference* as such.

Induction thus emerges as a methodological device for *doing* something, namely for making the "inductive leap" needed to fill gaps in our available information. It involves an enthymematic supplementation of given data that is not an inferential step capable of validation by any logical or quasi-logical means, but rather is the product of a *decision* – a decision to bridge over an epistemic gap by a certain data-transcending "act of acceptance."

This aspect of *accepting* something not already assured by the informative data actually at our disposal makes induction a matter of practical reasoning (in Aristotle's sense): the attainment of the "conclusion" involves implementation of a decision and accordingly represents an act, albeit an intellectual one. This tacit element of decision – present throughout all our so-called inductive "inferences" – renders inductive argumentation a matter of action, namely the action of undertaking an assertoric commitment in line with a certain cognitive policy of procedure. The present approach to the justification of induction is thus predicated on the recognition that induction is neither a substantive *theory* about the nature of things, nor a quasi-logical *inference-process*, but a *technique of truth-estimation* – an instrumentality of inquiry. Accordingly, induction is the operative method of a goal-oriented activity: it is at bottom a matter of *praxis*, a process ultimately of practical rather than strictly theoretical character. This fact is critically important from the standpoint of justification or validation, since it means that the justification needed here will thus properly proceed along methodological or instrumental lines.

2. INSTRUMENTAL JUSTIFICATION

Instrumental justification is justification in terms of end-conduciveness. To be justified *instrumentally* is to be justified in the way inherently appropriate to an instrumentality, tool, method, procedure, *modus operandi,* technique, or the like. The fundamental idea in this area is that of *agency,* for by their very nature, all such instrumentalities are means for doing things of a certain sort in the endeavor to realize a particular objective. Accordingly, an instrumental justification is one that is naturally "fitting and proper" with regard to a *means* as such – methods included. A *method*, after all, is something intrinsically purpose-relative, and its capacity for goal-realization is an essential aspect of its very *raison d'être*. And, as a "means for doing things of a certain sort," a method will have to be legitimated in a *teleological* or purpose-relative manner. A method is, of course, never a method pure and simple, but always a method-for-the-realization-of-some-end, so that the inevitably teleological question of its *efficacy and effectiveness* in the realization of its purposes comes to play the central, controlling role.

With specific regard to methodology, at any rate, the pragmatists were surely right: there can be no better or more natural way of justifying a *method* than by establishing its capabilities with respect to the objectives at issue. The proper test for the correctness or appropriateness of anything instrumental is plainly and obviously posed by that paradigmatically pragmatic question: Does it *work*? Does it attain its intended purposes? Does it – to put it crassly – deliver the goods? The rational legitimation of a method is not a question of *theoretical* considerations that turn on matters of abstract general principle, but is essentially *practical* in its orientation.

The pragmatic justification of induction to be developed here proposes to apply these abstract strictures regarding methodology-in-general to the specific case of induction as a method of inquiry. Viewing induction as a cognitive method, it sets out to approach the question of the justification of induction from the angle of the justification of methods in general.

3. METHODOLOGICAL JUSTIFICATION: STAGE I – *FAUTE DE MIEUX* REASONING

While there is no question that the proper justification of a method must ultimately hinge on the pragmatic standard of purposive efficacy, this ultimate destination is, however, far removed from the point at which we must begin. For methods govern actions, and actions take place within the course of time. It is expedient to distinguish between *initial* justification (correlative with the question "Why should I adopt this method and 'give it a try'?") and eventual or *ultimate* justification (correlative with the question "Why should I *continue* to use the method?"). Moreover, it is important to realize that the question of the utility of a method is always a *comparative* matter to be considered relative to the alternatives at hand. The crucial question in this sphere is: What are our *other* options regarding methods for realizing the goals at issue.

In the first instance, the justification of a method calls for developing a line of considerations to show that use of the method in the apposite circumstances is reasonable (rational, etc.). And it is clear that, at this *initial* stage, the use of a method need not be rationalized through a preassurance of success. The *faute de mieux* validation of method-adoption is perfectly proper at the outset. If we need to achieve an end, we are perfectly entitled – *rationally* entitled – to use a method that offers better promise of success than any alternative that lies to hand. Given that we are to attain a certain destination, we are (*ex hypothesi*) justified in adopting what appears as the best way to it that we can find. Hans Reichenbach has offered an instructive example:

> [Consider the situation] of a man who wants to fish in an unexplored part of the sea. There is no one to tell him whether or not there are fish in this place. Shall he cast his net? Well, if he wants to fish in that place I should advise him to cast the net, to take the chance at least. It is preferable to try even in uncertainty than not to try and be certain of getting nothing.[1]

There is no guarantee that the method at issue will succeed. There is no assurance that some other method (perhaps praying to the fish-god to rain fish from the heavens?) will not succeed better. Nevertheless, to the best of our knowledge and belief, no alternative seems more promising. *Faute de mieux. . . .* This situation illustrates the tenor of a practicalist approach to justification – at any rate in its basic or initial stage. For at this initial stage the justification of doing the best one can – insofar as one can tell this in the circumstances in which one finds oneself – is always a perfectly appropriate practical justification in the practical domain. Its being the best available alternative – its comparative promise – can provide all the justification of which a method initially stands in need.

[1] *Experience and Prediction* (Chicago, 1938), pp. 362–363.

It is pivotally important to note that the "optimality" at issue in the present argumentation does not rest on the strong, existentially oriented premiss that *there is* no other more efficient method for accomplishing the ends at issue, but merely on the weaker, epistemically oriented premiss that no such method is *recognized*, that none lies within the horizons of our knowledge or beliefs in the matter. We need not claim that *there cannot be* some other, superior method, but merely that none such lies within the range of alternatives that we have contemplated. To substantiate the theoretical point that the chosen method is inherently superior, one would indeed need to establish its claims *vis-à-vis* all other *possible* alternatives. But this theoretical point (and the often practically unmanageable task it poses) is quite dispensable for present purposes. For in the practical domain – where we must act here and now, under the prevailing circumstances and conditions as we find them – we are perfectly warranted in confining our attention to the methods that are actually available – those that lie within the range of our cognitive horizons. The issue that there may be a superior method – that someday somebody might find a better way to attain these ends than any we have thought of – is simply irrelevant from the standpoint of the practical realities of the case. It is for us perfectly sufficient, and rationally sufficient, to do the best we can with the means at hand – with the instruments actually and realistically at our disposal. In this practical context, the "best alternative" at issue in rational justification is not "the best there is," in some theoretical sense, but simply the best that is realistically available – the best that we can think of. More than this – the attainment of some theoretically extant but effectively unavailable optimum – cannot legitimately be asked for. (*Ultra posse nemo obligatur.*)

This argumentation hinges on the issue of justification on the fact of *ostensible optimality* ("this method is as promising as any in sight") or, equivalently, on the circumstance of *practical necessity* ("this or nothing better"). If we adopt the abbreviative conventions:

M = the method under consideration is being used (in this case)

$S =$ optimum prospects of success are being attained (in this case)

then practical necessity comes to:

$$\sim M \to \sim S, \text{ or equivalently } S \to M.$$

That is, the optimal prospect of success (i.e., *realistically optimal,* given the visible alternatives) requires the method under consideration. But note that this is something very different from, and something that by no means implies, the converse claim that the use of the method under consideration assures optimal prospects of success:

$$M \to S.$$

That is, the *actual efficacy* of the method, its capacity to "deliver the goods" remains very much of an open issue. The *necessity* of the method *vis-à-vis* the objective, then, does not afford any assurances for its *sufficiency*. Nevertheless it does afford a substantial incentive for use of the method in such practical situations – even if it is one that is provisional and still in need of the reassurance of effectiveness.

Three considerations are thus paramount at this initial stage of method-justification: (1) *Potential efficacy:* There is *some* reason (however small) to think the method does – *or indeed only may or can work;*[2] for example, success has occasionally attended use of the method. (2) *Ostensible optimality:* There is no good reason to think that any other particular *available* alternative holds better promise of working, and there is no equally promising alternative that is more convenient. (3) *Safety:* There is no good reason to think that use of the method offers any foreseeable threat to realization of our larger aims: there is no threat of a potential loss of such a magnitude as to outweigh the benefit that attends our use of the method if all goes well. These three considerations link method-use to the promise of success, if only weakly. They set the standards by

---

[2] It is clear that the possibility at issue in this "*may or can* work" is not just a *logical* possibility, but a possibility of real potentiality.

which the initial justification of a method through *faute de mieux* argumentation can proceed.

This *faute de mieux* approach to methodological justification is closely related to that of Sect. 3 of the preceding chapter, where we argued by means of "this or nothing" considerations that our factual knowledge of the world must be based upon interactive *experience* of it. *Faute de mieux* reasoning is in fact a slight variant of this – a matter of "this or *nothing better*" rather than strict "this or *nothing*" argumentation. The two are clearly both forms of a common pattern, linked by the obvious principle that the only alternative is automatically the best one. There is, however, an important difference here. In the present context, "this or nothing" means this or nothing at all, while "this or nothing better" means "this or nothing better *that we know of.*" Argumentation of the strict "this or nothing" sort must be implemented *a priori*. But "this or nothing better" argumentation will in general involve experience. For while experience does not tell us that there *is* no other road to success, it does reveal that we *have found* no better, and that's quite good enough here. Thus "this or nothing better" argumentation can – in practical contexts – be implemented *a posteriori* (experimentally), as a principle of justificatory reasoning, when experience indicates that among the methods we have actually come upon and tried none affords a better promise of success.[3] And "this or nothing better" justification can quite appropriately be developed *ab ignorantia* by way of the consideration that the course of experience has brought to light no indication of the superiority of any alternative method that has come to view.

4. THE APPROPRIATENESS OF *FAUTE DE MIEUX* ARGUMENTATION AND THE ROLE OF INSUFFICIENT REASON

The validity of such a relatively weak form of reasoning as

[3] Note that the argumentation does *not* proceed inductively *à la* sample-to-population reasoning from "no method already found in the past has been superior" to "no method to be found in the future will be superior."

faute de mieux argumentation turns crucially on considerations characteristic of the *practical* realm. In the *theoretical* sphere, we certainly cannot reason that adoption of the best alternative at hand is automatically warranted, that we are justified without much further ado in accepting the best alternative we can think of.

To base a conclusion upon the absence of any good visible reasons to the contrary is clearly not an acceptable practice in the cognitive domain. A thesis – a theoretical commitment – can be rationally preferable only when there is *good reason not to adopt* any of its competing alternatives. But a method – a practical resource – can be rationally preferable when there is *no good reason* to adopt any of its alternatives. While the former circumstance calls for something positive and information-requiring, we can get by in the latter with something negative and ignorance-tolerating.

The justificatory situation is thus different in the practical domain because its probative groundrules are far weaker. Where actions rather than beliefs are at issue, the matter of "adequate justificatory support" stands quite differently. For in the strictly theoretical or purely cognitive case we can always postpone a decision until "all the returns are in," whereas in the context of praxis, inaction is itself a mode of action. We can defer decisions in purely theoretico-cognitive settings, but doing so in practical situations exacts the penalty of foregoing goal-attainment. We can always suspend belief but over action is an inescapable imperative: in *this* regard, there is a decisive difference between purely intellectual and "real" actions. With the latter, inaction is a mode of action, but not with the former, where nonacceptance is wholly noncommittal. This difference in urgency is the basic reason why lesser evidence can carry greater weight in this practical domain.

Very different situations thus obtain as regards presumption and burden-of-proof in the theoretical and practical spheres. In the practical domain, we are standardly constrained as to a resolution; but in the theoretical domain, we can in principle always defer decisions. A different pressure of urgency thus operates with action as opposed to belief. Accordingly, the justification of the adoption of a procedure or method has a mien very different from that of the justification of the adoption of a thesis.[4] We are in a position to impose far weaker probative demands in practical matters. In the sphere of human praxis we have it as a principle of practical reason that whenever there is no visible reason for changing the way of doing something, a change need not be made.

It is tempting to suppose that the only route to the justification of a method lies in establishing *in advance* the crucial pragmatic claim that it actually works, but this view is very much mistaken. The rational validation of a method – the establishment of the appropriateness of its use – demands no prior assurance of success. After all, the justification of a method can simply be a *comparative* matter – a matter of its *relative* potential or possibility *vis-à-vis* the alternatives in hand. In practical situations, the adoption of a method, however modest its demonstrated promise, is perfectly rational and justified whenever there is no better alternative in sight as a potential means to accomplishing the task in hand.

An *ontological* principle of argumentation from ignorance (*argumentum ab ignorantia*) to the effect that "If there is no reason to think that *p*, then *p* will not hold of reality" is patently problematic. And one certainly cannot claim an *epistemological* principle to the effect that "If there is no *known* reason for maintaining *p*, then we may safely conclude that not-*p*." But with methods and practical instrumentalities the situation is very different. For one may safely conclude that a method for realizing a goal is acceptable if no sufficient impediments to its acceptance are visible.

---

[4] This line of thought was inaugurated by the ancient academic sceptics, revived by Hume, and exploited by Kant:

> ... reason has, in respect of its *practical employment*, the right to postulate what in the field of mere speculation it can have no kind of right to assume without sufficient proof. For while all such assumptions do violence to [the principle of] completeness of speculation, that is a principle with which the practical interest is not at all concerned. In the practical sphere reason has rights of possession, of which it does not require to offer proof, and of which, in fact, it could not supply proof. The burden of proof accordingly rests upon the opponent. (CPuR, A776–7 = B 804–5.)

Our present theory of induction in effect uses this Humean line of thought in defence against Humean conclusions. For we have no inclination to say that a "merely practicalistic" defense of induction will leave the matter on a basis that must be viewed as deficient from the angle of "rigorously theoretical considerations."

But argumentation from ignorance (in its currently operative guise) is, of course, a merely *methodological* principle. Such a principle is inherent in the theory of practical reasoning and the methodology of action-justification, governed by the idea that when there is no jolly good reason to change one's ways, then one need not do so.[5] What is basically at issue here is a principle of rational economy, a principle of least effort: any change in one's own manner of doing things involves an effort, and so there must be some compensatory visible gain for its exertion. This sort of argumentation is perfectly acceptable in the practical realm, even though its use in the theoretical sphere is very dubious indeed. (It must thus be recognized, and indeed *stressed*, that it is not our inductive "conclusions" that we are justifying by this-or-nothing-better reasoning, but rather the inductive method by whose means we arrive at them.)

The initial justification of a method along the presently operative *faute de mieux* lines is accordingly something that can be developed with a heavy reliance on considerations of ignorance. Its assurance of practical necessity can be largely negative, with ostensible optimality = "no reason to think another method superior," and safety = "no reason to think any important objective is put to risk by its use." And insofar as something positive is required – namely *potential efficacy* = "some reason to think that is *may* work" – this imposes a very weak and minimal demand. After all, even mere *post hoc* success on some occasions will afford *some* grounds (albeit very weak ones) for attributing possible *propter hoc* efficacy.

Lost in a forest, the sensible man picks a given direction and walks steadily and persistently along its line.[6] He has no assurance that it will bring him to a safe destination. But what are the alternatives? To stay put and await developments; to wander about at random; to call for divine guidance; to sit down and hope for the best? The chosen course is clearly more promising than any of these. Therein, and therein alone lies its justification. It represents the route of practical necessity: if he can succeed at all, it will (within all human probability) be in

---

[5] Cf. D. Goldstick, "Methodological Conservatism," *American Philosophical Quarterly*, vol. 8 (1971), pp. 186–191.

[6] This is not altogether a hypothetical textbook example. Cf. Neville Henderson, *Water under the Bridges* (London, 1945), pp. 158–159.

this way. And it is this line of thought that underlies our present recourse to a methodological approach to the justification of induction by means of *faute de mieux* considerations.

The methodological perspective is accordingly of substantial and far-reaching advantage in the present context of justifying induction. For in this praxis-oriented domain, we are in a position to make effective use of the essentially negative consideration of there being no good reason to think that any rival to induction offers real promise of superior performance. And this, as it were, *initial* justification of induction calls for no preassurance of its actual efficacy – no prior guarantee that success must attend our recourse to inductive methods. No initial demonstration of actual effectiveness in point of success is needed. (Admittedly, one would only want to lean on the very weak reed of negativistic reasoning of this sort at the very outset, when the justification of a method first somes onto the agenda.)

5. THE SPECIAL CASE OF COGNITIVE METHODS

The preceding deliberations have proceeded with respect to goal-oriented methods in general. The present discussion will apply these general considerations of the justificatory situation in the practical sphere to the special case of our specifically *cognitive* praxis. Its methodological justification of induction is thus predicated on the fact that our cognitive methods, and specifically induction, can be regarded as just another case of methods in general. Induction, so we have argued, is, after all, nothing other than a *method*: is it a method of truth-estimation, a means for finding the "best available" answers to our questions that transcend the information at hand. As such, induction can, quite appropriately, be assimilated to the situation of methods in general in point of justificatory considerations. And this means that it can be justified – at any rate *initially* justified – by means of *faute de mieux* argumentation.

When the matter is viewed in this light, the initial justification of induction as a specifically cognitive, question-resolving method will (as we have seen) have to hinge on three considerations: (1) *Potential efficacy* – there is *some* good reason (however small) to think that induction can serve our cognitive purposes, (2) *Ostensible optimality* – there is no reason to think that some available alternative method for realizing our cognitive goals is more promising nor that some equally promising rival is more convenient, and (3) *Safety* – there are no indications that use of the method threatens any larger cognitive interests. And it is readily seen that all these requirements are clearly met in the special case of induction.

The respectable record of success of inductive inquiry in the sciences affords powerful indications of its *potential efficacy*. The fact that it has served us so well gives good augury for the prospect of its general effectiveness. And there is also the important effectiveness-indicative consideration (originally emphasized by Charles Sanders Peirce) that induction has the notable – though in itself feeble – theoretical virtue that if its aim is attainable at all (i.e., if nature incorporates regularities discernible to our inquisitorial gaze) then the persistent use of orthodox induction is able to bring them to light – over the long run, at any rate.

Nor do considerations of the comparative promise at issue with *ostensible optimality* indicate that any alternatives are serious rivals of induction. To be sure, it is certainly not a matter of there being no conceivable alternatives to induction as a question-answering mechanism. But while there are indeed alternatives to induction, there is no cogent reason to think that there are any *superior* alternatives. Consider some of the principal possibilities as to variant means for making predictions and in general answering our questions about the world:

(i) Special sources: oracles, sages, inspired guessers, self-declared "authorities," etc.
(ii) Occult methods: astrology, omen-interpretation, tea-leaf reading, etc.
(iii) Functional variants of inductivism: indifferentism (as to available alternatives), counter-inductivism, etc.

There is no good reason to think of any of these as serious rivals to induction as far as their initial merits are concerned; indeed there is little to be said on their behalf. As R. B. Braithwaite has put it:

It is not as if there were [efficient] competitors to the inductive policies in the predictive-reliability race so that it would be unreasonable to prefer the inductive policies unless we could depend on their swiftness in the race. The non-inductive policies are not starters. There is no general policy other than an inductive policy where there is good reason to believe has been effective in the past . . .[7]

There is simply no apparent reason to think any other alternative method to be more effective; *au contraire*, the superiority of induction over such alternative methodologies as have been tried in the historical course of events is altogether impressive.

Finally, the requirement of *safety* regarding induction comes down in our present cognitive context to the consideration that, in the words of C. S. Peirce, it should not "bar the path of inquiry;" that if there is indeed a better method, the use of induction will not blind us to it. Indeed, quite the contrary, rather than barring the path to inquiry, induction (as C. S. Peirce was wont to stress) has the important feature of being self-monitoring. We stand to lose little or nothing by its use. Its *modus operandi* is such that if some other method were more successful, our use of the inductive method would not only not preclude us from finding this out, but induction itself *can* presumably so operate as to reveal this.[8]

The upshot of these considerations, then, is that a methodological prejustification at issue in *faute de mieux* considerations – in terms of potential efficacy, ostensible optimality, and operational safety – is amply forthcoming with respect to our inductive methodology.

6. INITIAL JUSTIFICATION IS NONINDUCTIVE

It deserves emphasis that an initial justification of a method through *faute de mieux* considerations is itself free from any inductive involvements. This is perfectly clear with respect to

---

[7] R. B. Braithwaite, *Scientific Explanation* (Cambridge, 1953), p. 272.

[8] Note that one cannot, however, change this italicized *can* to *will*. For it is perfectly possible that we are simply not clever enough to perform the appropriate inductions.

the conditions of *ostensible optimality* and *safety*, both of which proceed wholly by a negative "no reason to think" line of consideration. (Ignorance needs no supportive grounding, and thus no inductive support.) But *potential efficacy* may seem to be a different matter. There is, after all, a positive claim present in the connection that "there is *some* good reason (however small) to think that a method *may* work." We must face the problem of how – other than inductively – such a claim could be substantiated.

The key here lies in noting that even the solely *post hoc* consideration of *merely seeming* success attendant upon some trial of the method can serve to ground the claim at issue with potential efficacy. Even the bare experience of having tried the method and finding that it worked out, to all appearances – even such merely *apparent* success – does actually afford *some* reason to think that the method may be effective (although it is, admittedly, a very slight and slender reason).

To be sure, it might still be asked: "Why take experience that is successful – or more accurately, just *seemingly* successful – to count favorably on behalf of a method's claims to at any rate possible efficacy? Is not some reasoning that is itself inductive at work here? The answer is negative. For a *this-or-nothing validation can be deployed to validate the step of according to its record of past apparent success some probative impetus towards the claim that a method may well actually work*. If we are not prepared to count past instances of its apparent success as having at least *some* tendency to show that a method may well be effective, then we can never obtain *any* supportive data to warrant this claim. The only kind of information that can ever be gleaned regarding the efficacy of a method is information relating to our proven experience in using that method. And it would be fundamentally irrational to preclude the sort of datum we can ever possibly get from counting as probatively relevant. But – and this is crucial – the issue is one of *presumption* rather than of *evidence*. *Post hoc* success is not here taken to afford *inductive evidence* for a substantive conclusion of potential effectiveness; it is merely taken to afford a procedural *presumption* whose role as such is to be justified as a matter of probative methology legitimated along this-or-nothing lines. (To be sure, if a substantive matter were at issue, rather than a merely procedural one, it would have to emerge inductively.)

Consider an additional objection:

> Surely there is no difference between "having grounds to think that the method *may* work" and "having some evidence (perhaps only a little) for thinking that the method *will* work" – which evidence will itself have to be of an inductive nature, so that potential efficacy cannot avoid inductive involvements.

The objection is flawed. The grounding of the claim that an eventuation *may* happen is by nature something different from – and far feebler than – the evidencing (even only weakly) that this *will* happen. If I buy a sweepstakes ticket, I have (*ex hypothesi*, as entrant in the competition) grounds for thinking that I may possibly win, but I still have no evidence (not even tenuous or weak evidence) to think that I will win. An illicit operator-switch occurs when the two issues are conflated: strong grounds for thinking that something *can* happen are something very different from *weak* grounds for thinking that this *will* happen.

Accordingly, the objection that our probative recourse to experience for establishing possible efficacy represents a fundamentally inductive move whose introduction into the justification of induction involves a circularity can be defeated. For what is happening at this initial stage of justification does not involve induction at all, but a course of this-or-nothing argumentation directed not at facts but at probative relationships.

One further issue. It might be asked: "Why not proceed *wholly* along negative lines? Why not simply determine potential efficacy along the *via negativa* of: *There is no good reason to think that the method will not (or: can not) work*?" The reply here is simply that this wholly negative approach is not sufficiently eliminative: there are, inevitably, zillions of imaginable methods that *might* work – it is conceivable and *theoretically* possible! Here, then, our methodological justification encounters the need for a positive probative element, slight though it may be, to cut the range of theoretically available possibilities down to manageable size. It is the merit of this-or-nothing argumentation that it can validate our recourse to this slight positive element without invoking inductive considerations of any sort.

7. LOOSE ENDS

The practical necessity at issue in *faute de mieux* considerations does indeed carry *some* justificatory weight: it gives the process a good start in providing the initial justification from which the argument proceeds. But it does not assure a potential for efficacy. The circumstance that the optimal prospect of success requires the method ($\sim M \to \sim S$) does not guarantee that use of the method affords optimal prospects of success ($M \to S$). And, of course, in the absence of such an assurance of actual effectiveness, the justificatory task is not brought to a satisfactory conclusion. To this end, we would require indications not only of necessity but of sufficiency as well, so that the ascertainment of actual efficacy is required.

The preceding account thus does not give the whole story. When all is said and done, *faute de mieux* justification is good but not good enough. On the methodological approach, the overall legitimation of induction will, in fact, have to proceed in two stages or phases: (1) an *initial* justification that proceeds with a view to its comparative PROMISE *vis-à-vis* such alternatives as lie to hand (as offering a relatively optimal prospect or potential of success), and (2) an *ultimate* justification that proceeds with a view to its actual EFFECTIVENESS. The *faute de mieux* reasoning of the present chapter does no more than address itself to the first of these issues. But an adequate overall justification cannot wholly evade this second, crucial issue of a method's *actual* rather than merely *potential* efficacy.

V

The Methodological Turn B: The Pragmatic Retrojustification of Induction

SYNOPSIS

(1) Initial justification of a method through *faute de mieux* considerations does not suffice for its proper validation: there must also be an eventual *retrojustification* in terms of its actual effectiveness in goal-attainment. (2) These considerations regarding methods in general also apply to cognitive methods – and to induction in particular. (3) An exploration of the issue of just how effectively induction achieves its goals thus becomes necessary. The Wheel Argument and the primacy of praxis in cognitive justification. (4) The Darwinian aspect of retrovalidation and the parallelism of efficacy and survival through rational selection within cognitive praxis. (5) How this pragmatic/evolutionary model of evolution through rational selection operates in the special case of induction. (6) A review of the overall structure of this method-ological/pragmatic approach to the justification of induction as an optimal process of truth-estimation. (7) Since induction is here operative in its own support, the fact that induction is legitimate – that we may rationally be confident that its use will prove effective – is thus in the final analysis contingent. This, however, is no occasion for appropriate complaint, since it is senseless to lament what cannot be otherwise. (8) The *potential* effectiveness of induction (in the conditional sense that if *anything* can realize its correlative goals, then it

has the capacity to do so in the long run) is a necessary feature, but its actual *efficiency* (its capacity to function successfully in the short run of *here and now*) remains an ultimately contingent issue that can itself be settled only by inductive means.

---

1. INITIAL JUSTIFICATION IS NOT ENOUGH

As long as we do not have grounds for expecting a method to be actually *successful,* the process of its rational justification is not carried through to a fully satisfactory conclusion. An initial justification of a method proceeds by establishing its superior *potential* with respect to alternatives, which is all well and good at the very outset. But eventually the question of its justification must face up to the issue of its superior *effectiveness* with respect to these alternatives.

Initial justification for adoption of a method on the basis of *faute de mieux* considerations clearly does no more than to make a good start at the justificatory enterprise. It is one thing for the method to be "the most promising-looking at hand" or "the best in sight," and something very different for it actually to afford good expectations of success. The *relatively* most promising or *comparatively* optimal method for doing something may be very bad indeed. Real merit is not just a matter of comparative merit, relative to alternatives that may, after all, make it the best of a bad lot, but of having some degree of actual effectiveness. It would not be reasonable to rest satisfied with "the best" of available methods when there is good reason to think that even this best is just no good at all.

Demonstrated effectiveness is clearly the ultimate standard of methodological merit. (In *this* regard, a pragmatic approach is patently appropriate.) To move beyond initial justification in assuring this desideratum for a method, the sensible thing to do is "to try it out and see." Clearly, the natural way to assess the merits of anything instrumental (tool, technique, method, etc.) is to put it to the test. Ultimately the question not just of *promise* but of *performance* becomes paramount – of seeing how the method really works out.

The justification at issue with efficacy is a pragmatic one to be developed in the light of experience. Practical necessity provides some initial *a priori* impetus to the justificatory enterprise. But only the attest of actual efficacy in the *a posteriori* light of experience can bring our justificatory project to full realization.

The overall legitimation of a method accordingly calls for more than an initial justification along the lines mooted in the last chapter. Specifically, it demands a retrospective rejustification upon due trial – a *retrojustification*, as one might call it. We need not demand a preguarantee of the success of our methods, but we certainly do want to take them "on approval," to be rejected if found wanting upon due trial. Initial justification does no more than establish a *presumption* in favor of using a method – a presumption which the course of subsequent events in regard to its utilization may either overthrow or make good.[1]

2. IS EXPERIENTIAL RETROJUSTIFICATION NECESSARY?

The preceding considerations regarding methodological justification in general will apply to cognitive methods in particular. Here, too, an experiential retrojustification of a method's actual efficacy – its applicative success – is ultimate unavoidable.

To be sure, one could simplify the justificatory process if it were possible to show *a priori* that induction *had to* succeed, that the world could not possibly be such that induction could fail to yield accurate information of its *modus operandi*. Just this was argued by C. S. Peirce in one (early) phase of his long-evolving thought on the issue of induction:

> If men were not able to learn from induction, it might be because as a general rule, when they had made an induction, the order of things would then undergo a revolution ... But this general rule would be capable of being itself

[1] For a discussion of the epistemology of presumption, see the author's *Dialectics* (Albany, 1977).

discovered by induction; and so it must be a law of such a universe that when this was discovered it would cease to operate. But this second law would itself be capable of discovery. And so in such a universe there would be nothing which would not sooner or later be known; and it would have an order capable of discovery by a sufficiently long course of reasoning. But this is contrary to the hypothesis, and therefore that hypothesis is absurd.[2]

But Peirce is barking up the wrong tree here. To be sure, the straw-man view that he criticizes clearly goes amiss. In projecting a picture of a world of which we could learn *inductively* that induction is *altogether* ineffective, it becomes mired in self-contradiction. But, nevertheless, there is no great difficulty in conceiving a world where *our* way of doing induction just doesn't work.

The crucial point is that there are alternatives to induction – to systematization with experience subject to the standard parameters of cognitive systematicity. For one thing, worlds are certainly imaginable where various non-systematic devices might work (blind guesswork or untutored intuition), while orthodox induction does not (say because of the malign operation of a deceitful demon). Moreover, worlds are also imaginable where *other* modes of systematization might well work whereas orthodox induction fails – a world, for example, where novelty of itself plays a significant role because things just get tired of going on in the same old way, or a world whose appropriate mode of cognitive systematization would not rest on the usual inductive parameters (simplicity, uniformity, regularity, etc.) but on essentially *aesthetic* parameters (symmetry, harmony, balance, etc.). (Of course, such worlds would have to exhibit a fairly complex design since the unorthodox standards at issue would have to operate in ways not smoothly amenable to inductive discernment.)

The efficacy of induction as we practice it is not something inevitable. Various alternative methodologies for determining "how things work in the world" are perfectly conceivable – witness the examples of such occult explanatory frameworks

---

[2] Charles Sanders Peirce, *Collected Papers*, ed. by C. Hartshorne and P. Weiss, vol. V (Cambridge, Mass.; 1935), sect. 5.352.

as those of numerology (with its benign ratios), astrology (with its astral influences), and black magic (with its mystic forces). To justify induction, we must therefore convince ourselves that the inductive procedures we actually employ are indeed effective as a cognitive instrumentality. The issue of a science-based retrojustification cannot be shirked; the initial and very general sort of justification that is given on the basis of *faute-de-mieux* considerations cannot be viewed as doing the whole job.

The balance between initial justification and eventual retrojustification is disturbed by the fact that it is actually not quite the same thing that is at issue in the two situations. For initial justification justifies a family of methods – the generic process of "systematization with experience." But the experience at work in pragmatic retrojustification exercises a feedback that exerts a formative pressure on the detailed character of our preferred modes of systematization.

3. INDUCTION AS THE SPECIAL CASE OF A COGNITIVE METHOD: THE WHEEL ARGUMENT AND THE PROBLEM OF EFFICACY

We must accordingly confront the key question of how effectively our standard inductive praxis accomplishes its methodological goals. Let us begin here by considering just what the goals of enterprise are. The teleology of inquiry is internally diversified and complex; it spreads across both the cognitive/theoretical and the active/practical sectors. Accordingly, our epistemic instrumentalities come to be endowed with a duality of objectives, and the relevant teleology of inquiry is both cognitive and practical.[3] Now the *immediate* goal of inquiry is, to be sure, purely cognitive, and relates to the securing of answers to our questions. But its *ultimate* or ulterior goal is practical and relates to the guidance of our action. The division between the theoretical and the practical dimension has a far-reaching bearing on the issue of cognitive justification.

How is one to determine that a fact-oriented inquiry pro-

---

[3] A fuller development of these considerations regarding the teleology of inquiry is given in the author's *Scientific Explanation* (New York, 1970).

cedure is adequate? What sort of monitoring process can be devised to assess whether the procedure is indeed "doing its job"?

On first thought, it might seem that one could simply employ here the standard quality-control strategy of assessing the adequacy of a process in terms of the merits of its product. Unfortunately, this will not do in the present, cognitively oriented case. For we immediately run up against the problem disputed in antiquity between the Stoics and the Academic Sceptics under the rubric of *the criterion* – the problem, that is, of the test-process that is to represent our standard of truth.

Let C represent the criterion we actually propose to use in practice for the determination of factual truth, whatever this criterion might be. Accordingly, one will be committed to classing a fact-purporting proposition P as a truth if and only if $C(P)$, that is, if and only if P meets the conditions specified in C. Now to all appearances the question of the appropriateness of C is simply this: *Does C yield truths?* But how could one resolve this question? Seemingly, in only one way: by looking on the one hand at C-validated propositions and checking on the other hand if they are in fact truths. But if C really and truly is our working criterion for the determination of factual truth, then this exercise becomes wholly pointless. We cannot judge C by the seemingly natural standard of the question whether what it yields as true is indeed *actually* true, because we *ex hypothesi* use C itself as our determining standard of actual truth.

This line of reasoning has been known from the days of the sceptics of antiquity under the title of the "*diallelus*" or Wheel Argument – a particular sort of *circulus in probandi* or "vicious circle." It is difficult to exaggerate the significance of this extremely simple argument. It shows in as decisive a manner as philosophical argumentation admits of, that our operative standard of factual truth cannot be validated by somehow exhibiting directly that it does properly accomplish its intended work of truth-determination.[4] The routine tactic of

---

[4] Clearly, if the issue were that of justifying a proposed *alternative* procedure C', the preceding methodology would work splendidly well. For we could then simply check whether the C-validated propositions are indeed truths – that is, whether they are also validated by C. But with respect to C itself this exercise is patently useless.

assessing process in terms of product is thus seemingly not practicable in the case of an inquiry procedure of the sort at issue: it is in principle impossible to make a direct check of this sort on the functioning of our truth-determining methods.

The lesson of this Wheel Argument is that there simply is no direct way of checking the adequacy of an inquiry procedure aimed at the substantiation of general claims. To be sure, we want correct answers to our factual questions, but if induction itself provides our standard of correctness, we cannot straightforwardly check if induction succeeds in this particular mission. It is thus necessary to explore the prospects of a different strategy of justification.

At this point, it becomes germane to recognize the tritely familiar but still fundamental fact of the amphibious nature of man as a creature of mind and body, intellect and will, reason and action, theory and practice.

In keeping with this duality, our knowledge serves to two distinct kinds of purpose, the theoretical and the practical, the pure and the applied. Its theoretical purposes relate to the strictly intellectual interest of man – the acquisition of descriptive information and explanatory understanding (to *what* and *why*) – whereas the practical relates to the material interests of man that underlie the guidance of human action: avoidance of pain, suffering, frustration, etc. – including that intellectual frustration which goes with disappointed expectations. The theoretical relates to correct belief, the practical to effective interaction with nature. The former operates in purely intellectual and cognitive regards, the latter affords a guiding standard for the practical conduct of life.

These two categories of purpose are inseparably interrelated. On the one hand, theoretical adequacy is a crucial factor in guiding the practice of specifically rational beings. And on the other hand, the arbitrament of praxis yields control over theory, and the correct canalizing of expectations in predictive contexts is itself a crucial aspect of that "control over nature" essential to the successful guidance of the practical affairs of a rational creature whose actions are determined by his beliefs. Taken as a whole, the inductive mission thus involves not only the theoretical-cognitive issues of information and understanding but also the practical-activistic issue of prediction and control – of the satisfactory alignment of our expectations with the course of events and, even more crucially, of our capacity to intervene in this course to bring about desired eventuations.

These pragmatic considerations bring to the fore the crucial monitoring role of the applicative dimension of prediction and control as the decisive factor in determining the "success" by which a cognitive method is judged. The index of such success does not operate just in the *theoretical* mode ("yields theses that state the truth"), but no less importantly in the *practical* mode: "yields theses that underwrite successful prediction and control." The ultimately appropriate testing-standard for our cognitive methods hinges on the efficacy of the praxis which the implementation of their deliverances underwrites.

4. THE DARWINIAN ASPECT AND THE PARALLELISM OF
   EFFICACY AND SURVIVAL THROUGH RATIONAL SELECTION

The question now arises of whether induction actually meets the practical tests of the preceding section. Have our inductive practices been all that successful? Let us approach this issue from an historical perspective.

The development of our methods of inductive inquiry is subject to the same sort of evolutionary pressures that John Dewey insisted upon with respect to the development of our methods of demonstration in logic and mathematics:

Some sorts of thinking are shown *by experience* to have got nowhere, or worse than nowhere – into systematized delusion and mistake. Others have proved in manifest experience that they lead to fruitful and enduring discoveries. It is precisely in experience that the different consequences of different methods of investigation and ratiocination are convincingly shown. The parrot-like repetition of the distinction between an empirical description of what is and a normative account of what should be merely neglects the most striking fact about thinking as it empirically is – namely, its flagrant exhibition of cases of failure and success – that is, of good thinking and bad thinking . . . . The more study that is given to empirical records of actual thought, the more apparent becomes the connection between the specific features of thinking which have produced failure and success. Out of this relationship of cause and effect as it is empirically ascertained grow the norms and regulations of an art of thinking . . . . [Our knowledge and its institutions are] a product of long historic growth, in which all kinds of experiments have been tried, in which some men have struck out in this direction and some in that, and in which some exercises and operations have resulted in confusion and others in triumphant clarifications and fruitful growths; a history in which matter and methods have been constantly selected and worked over on the basis of empirical success and failure.[5]

The standard conceptual machinery for structuring our view of reality – the intellectual mechanisms by which we form our view of "the way the world works" – are built up by an historic, evolutionary process in terms of "trial and error," exactly as with the bodily mechanisms by which we comport ourselves in the physical world. Our methods of inquiry are the product of an evolutionary pressure that assures the adaptation of our systematizing efforts to the real world in a course of trial and error subject to the controlling constraint of appli-

---

[5] John Dewey, *Reconstruction in Philosophy* (Enlarged ed.; Boston, 1957), pp. 136–137. Compare Max Black:

The inductive concepts that we acquire by example and formal education and modify through our own experiences are not exempt even from drastic revision. The norms may be usefully thought of as formal crystallizations into linguistic rules of general modes of response to the universe that our ancestors have, on the whole, found advantageous to survival, but the earlier experience of the race never has absolute authority. Piecemeal reform of the inductive institution can be observed in the history of modern science. [And] it remains important to insist that the inductive institution, precisely because its *raison d'être* is learning from experience, is intrinsically self-critical. Induction, like the Sabbath, was made for man, not vice versa. Thus, constantly renewed experience of the successes and failures of the specific inductive procedures permitted within the general framework of the inductive institution provides a sound basis for gradual reform of the institution itself, without objectionable circularity. (Art. "Induction" in *The Encyclopedia of Philosophy*, ed. by Paul Edwards, vol. 4 [New York, 1967], p. 179.)

cative success (pragmatic efficacy). This evolutionary process effects the due coordination of our cognitive systematizing with the "objective" workings of a nature that is inherently indifferent to our purposes and beliefs.

William James wrote:

> Were we lobstersor bees, it might be that our organization would have led to our using quite different modes from these [actual ones] of apprehending our experiences. It *might* be too (we cannot dogmatically deny this) that such categories, unimaginable by us to-day, would have proved on the whole as serviceable for handling our experiences mentally as those we actually use.[6]

Now the premiss of the first sentence is true enough. But the implication present in the "our" of the second sentence goes badly awry. The prospect that beings constituted as *we* are should function more effectively with the experiential modes of creatures constituted on different lines can be dismissed as simply untenable on Darwinian grounds. The serviceable handling of *our* experiences by *our* cognitive instruments is guaranteed – not by a preestablished harmony but by the processes of evolution.[7]

It is no more a miracle that the human mind can understand the world than that the human eye can see it. The critical step is to recognize that the question "Why do our conceptual methods and mechanisms fit 'the real world' with which we interact intellectually?" simply does not permit of any strictly aprioristic answer in terms of purely theoretical grounds of general principle. Rather, it is to be answered in basically the same way

---

[6] *Pragmatism* (New York, 1907), p. 171. (Georg Simmel had already proposed a comparable thought-experiment and James is presumably indebted to Simmel here.) Unlike most philosophers since Kant, James was prepared to consider the prospect of radically different conceptual schemes which dispense with our standard concepts of space, time, causality, the self, etc.

[7] The key point was already clearly perceived by C. S. Peirce around a century ago. Peirce saw man's evolutionary adaptation as an evolutionary product which endows his mind with a kind of functional sympathy for the processes of nature: under the pressure of evolutionary forces, the mind of man has come to be "co-natured" with physical reality. (For a fuller exposition of Peirce's views, see the author's *Peirce's Philosophy of Science* [Notre Dame, 1978].)

as the question: "Why do our bodily processes and mechanisms fit the world with which we interact physically?" Both are alike to be resolved in essentially evolutionary terms.

5. THE PRAGMATIC JUSTIFICATION OF INDUCTION AS A COGNITIVE METHOD THROUGH EVOLUTION BY RATIONAL SELECTION

A Darwinian legitimation along the previously envisaged lines of survival of the fittest clearly requires a standard of "fitness." Here, the governing standards of the Western tradition of human rationality are represented by the goals of *explanation*, *prediction*, and *control* over nature. (And thus not, for example, sentimental "at-oneness with nature.") Within the Western intellectual tradition, the ultimate standards of rationality are defined by a very basic concept of knowledge-wed-to-practice, and their ultimate validation lies in the combination of theoretical and practical *success*: i.e., success of theory in the effective guidance of action. In this tradition, Darwinian survival hinges on applicative efficacy.

It must, however, be stressed that the crux of cognitive evolution is not *biological*, but *social* – the process at issue is not biological evolution by natural selection, but cultural evolution by rational selection. As changes are entertained (under the pressure of necessitating circumstance), one methodological instrument may eventuate as more fit to survive than another, because it answers better to the range of relevant purposes. The crux is *what we see fit* to transmit.

A rigorously classical Darwinian model for methodological evolution thus goes too far. For what is basically at issue in this domain is a *rational* rather than a *natural* selection. Rational selection is a matter not of *biological* but of *rationally preferential* transmission – of historical survival owing to a reasoned preference on the basis of considerations relating to the whole spectrum of human needs and concerns. Our approach thus presupposes the picture of intelligent beings acting purposefully with reference to ends-in-view, with the controlling normative standard provided in the present situation by considerations of *theoretical adequacy and applicative practice*, and inherent in the use to which conceptual instrumentalities are put in the rational conduct of our cognitive and practical affairs.

Where rational selection is operative, pragmatism and evolutionism walk hand in hand. Our legitimation of the standard probative mechanisms of inquiry regarding factual matters accordingly began with the factor of pragmatic success and subsequently transmuted this into an issue of Darwinian survival. And, as this discussion has already foreshadowed at many points, it is clearly the inductive *method of scientific inquiry* that has carried the day here. The mechanisms of scientific reasoning clearly represent the most developed and sophisticated of our probative methods. No elaborate argumentation is necessary to establish the all-too-evident fact that science has come out on top in the competition of rational selection with respect to alternative processes for the substantiation of factual claims.

It is not difficult to give examples of the operation of Darwinian processes in the cognitive area. The intellectual landscape of human history is littered with the skeletal remains of the extinct dinosaurs of this sphere. Examples of such defunct methods for the acquisition and explanatory utilization of information include astrology, numerology, oracles, dream-interpretation, the reading of tea leaves or the entrails of birds, animism, the teleological physics of the Presocratics, and so on. There is nothing intrinsically absurd or contemptible about such unorthodox cognitive programs, even the most occult of them have a long and not wholly unsuccessful history. (Think, for example, of the prominent role of numerological explanation from Pythagoreanism, through Platonism, to the medieval Arabs, down to Kepler in the Renaissance.) Distinctly different scientific methodologies and programs have been mooted: Ptolemaic "saving the phenomena" *vs.* the hypothetico-deductive method, Baconian collectionism *vs.* the post-Newtonian theory of experimental science, etc. Thus the development of the means of inquiry and explanation invites a Darwinian account.

To repeat: the orthodox, scientific approach to factual inquiry is simply one alternative among others – it does not have an irrevocably absolute foothold on the very constitution of the human intellect, nor indeed any sort of abstract justification by purely "general principles." This being so, ought we not to examine the alternatives more seriously to assure ourselves of the relative success of induction? The answer is that we have already done so – since just this has been accomplished in historical evolution through methodological trial and error. The legitimation of science is not *a priori* and absolute, but *a posteriori* and relative. The merit of entrenched cognitive tools lies predominantly in their having established themselves in open competition with their rivals. It has come to be shown before the tribunal of bitter experience – through the historical vagaries of a Darwinian process of selection – that the accepted methods work out most effectively in actual practice *vis-à-vis* other tried alternatives. Such a legitimation is not absolute, but only presumptive – the product rather of a democratic struggle among rival candidates than of the divine right of a seventeenth-century absolute monarch. But it does, in its Darwinian aspect, give justificatory weight to the historical factor of being in *de facto* possession of the field. Science is not a matter of finished inspiration delivered from on high. The principles and processes through which we align our expectations with experience are themselves the subject of evolutionary development. We are compelled to recognize the ultimate emergence through rational selection of that body of inductive praxis that goes under the name of scientific method.

To be sure, there is no way of evading the fact that the success of science is certainly not an unqualified one. The range and the depth of our capacity to predict the eventuations of nature and – above all – to guide successfully our interventions in its doings are markedly limited. But as we have seen, such limitations are no impediment to justification. To validate a method, past successes need never be total, nor future successes guaranteed. What matters is that the method affords some real promise of goal-realization, and that this promise is relatively greater than that of the available alternatives. We learn from science itself about the failures of the scientific method. But we also learn of its successes – and of their relative predominance in comparison with the alternatives.

It is, of course, *theoretically* possible that induction might be less successful than some other way of reasoning about *a* world, but – given what we know and believe regarding its nature – it is unreasonable to think that some other way of reasoning about *the* world as it is actually constituted, this actual world of ours – the only one there is! – should be more successful. Admittedly we do not know, and certainly cannot establish *a priori*, that induction is the best (let alone the only) route to tenable claims and successful predictions: for aught we know there may well be better ways. But what we do know is that in the light of all those indications that we have at our disposal – inductive experience itself prominently included – there just is no more promising method of inquiry than to rely upon our standard inductive practices.

6. REVIEW OF THE PROPOSED JUSTIFICATION OF INDUCTION

It is useful to review briefly the overall course of supportive argumentation for the justification of induction that has been set out in the preceding pages.

Induction is *an ampliative method of reasoning* – it affords means for going beyond the evidence in hand in endeavor to answer our questions about how things stand in the world. Induction affords the methodology we use in the search for optimal answers.

Induction as a cognitive method proceeds by way of *the systematization of question-resolving conjecture with experience*, by fitting conjectural extensions sufficiently tightly into the overall setting of our other (generally tentative) commitments. Though induction always involves a leap beyond the information in hand, it only endorses these leaps when the fit is sufficiently close.

Why *systematization*? – because this affords our best rational resource for getting at the truth of things. (The Hegelian Inversion.)

Why *with experience*? – because this affords our only epistemic entryway into the domain of matters of fact and existence. (This or nothing.)

Accordingly, the induction becomes a process of plausible reasoning from the "data" of experience, with the parameters of systematicity themselves playing the role of standards of plausibility. All of the familiar modes of inductive inference can be fitted into this general pattern of reasoning.

What justifies induction – that is, what validates the specific way in which we use experience and the specific way in which we carry out inductive systematization? This question is best answered by noting that induction is a purposive instrumentality, a particular method for achieving a certain goal. It is a means for *doing* something – viz., filling in the gaps in our factual information. Its appropriate justification is thus a *methodological* justification – i.e., the justification of a method.

The present justificatory strategy now turns on the fact that method-justification is something very different from the establishment of a thesis, since in justifying a method one can quite appropriately be pragmatic and proceed via a two-tier process. This involves (1) an *initial justification* along the *faute de mieux* lines providing by noting (i) that it may succeed, (ii) that no more promising alternative lies to hand, and (iii) that its use is relatively risk-free. We can then move beyond such "*practical necessity*" to provide (2) an *experiential retrojustification*. This is a matter of trying the method out and finding that it indeed works (i.e., yields a record of success exceeding that of any other available alternative). And why let (successful) experience confirm us in the use of a method? Because if the method works then there is (all else equal) no reason to change it! The idea of a burden of proof – and of the sorts of considerations capable of shifting it in the practical domain – is crucially operative here. (See pp. 65–66 above.)

Such a two-tier justification achieves an important objective. It recognizes both that any truly satisfactory justification of a method must proceed with reference to its purposive effectiveness, and that – once we leave the secure domain of formal demonstration and mathematical operations – inductive reasoning from its established successes affords the only ultimately viable route to the establishment of the actual effectiveness of any method, the inductive method itself included.

This two-tier process thus rests crucially on the *methodological* nature of induction. It distinguishes sharply between (1) justifying *the use* of induction, and (2) establishing *the thesis* that induction is effective. The pragmatic strategy begins with this separation, realizing that in the end the two justifications must be reunited once more. It sets out from (1), moving at a level of wholly noninductive, *faute de mieux* considerations, but returns in the end to (2) – at a stage, however, when we need no longer proceed empty handed, without the availability of any inductive mechanisms at all.

The multi-stage structure of our justificatory reasoning is critical. For the initial part of the argumentation still goes no further than to maintain a justification through *ostensible* optimality with respect to the envisaged alternatives. The question of *actual* efficacy remains untouched, and to address this further issue – which is, of course, critical for the overall issue of justification – we have no alternative but to resort to a straightforwardly inductive argument from the experiential data, through induction with respect to the success of our inductive praxis. The fact is that no fully adequate justification of induction is accessible to someone who does not *already* in some modest degree accept its authority. And the key merit of a multistage justification that begins on an initial *faute de mieux* basis is that it makes such a process rationally available.

Note, moreover, how this two-tier process of justification for induction leads to a smooth dovetailing that retrovalidates at the end what we presume at the outset with the weak sort of "justification" at issue with *faute de mieux* considerations. For we set out from a negativity of "no good reason to think that some available alternative is better" and ultimately return with the positivity of "good reason to think that this is better than the available alternatives." Drawn to it initially on the basis of weak, noninductive *faute de mieux* considerations, we come to realize *ex post facto*, with the wisdom of inductive hindsight, that this course is more powerfully justified, and so arrive at a retrospective strengthening of the position. We come round in full cycle.

This sort of self-supportive systemic cycle fits smoothly into the overall structure of the model of rational legitimation in terms of cognitive systematization. Not only is the methodology of induction itself a matter of systematization (of conjecture with experience), but our justification of induction also emerges as a matter of appropriate systematization. Both in *using* and in *legitimating* induction we rely on the same basic equation:

justification (validation) = systematization

Cognitive justification, so we have argued (pp. 49–50, above), is by nature a matter of systematization – of fitting the item to be justified smoothly within its descriptive and explanatory context in the wider framework of our remaining cognitive commitments and inclinations. And in justifying induction our practice conforms to just this precept in proceeding to show how the standard mechanisms of our inductive praxis fit smoothly within the general framework of our epistemological predilections.

Moreover, as regards the issue of systematization *with experience* we also come round the full circle once more. Earlier (sect. 3 of Chap. III) it was argued that there is no alternative to having recourse to experience in the substantiation of factual knowledge. And now the present argumentation takes the comparably empiricistic line that one must also use experience as a basis for validating the methodology by which our factual knowledge comes to be established. If we view the inductively appropriate answer as more promising or probable than its conceivable alternatives (as we incline to do), this is not because of some essentialistic consideration about what induction *is*, but because of what induction itself ultimately teaches us about how matters stand in the world.

To the question "Will induction succeed?" we thus reply: It is reasonable by every applicable standard – induction itself included! – to maintain that it will. But to say this is not, of course, to say that we can *prove* that induction will actually succeed. This is something we cannot do, and cannot be asked to do, seeing that its realization is, in the very nature of things, impossible. Rather, our deliberations establish those considerations of potential efficacy on the basis of which the adoption and use of this cognitive method can be justified as constituting a rationally warranted step. Throughout, the course of justificatory argumentation remains fundamentally methodological in its orientation.

The desired justification is thus straightforward. The object of inquiry is to answer our questions about the world. In its interests we "play the inductive game" – we scan nature for regularities under the aegis of the parameters of cognitive systematization. But how can we be certain that the *local and apparent* regularities that these scanning efforts detect in our observational neighborhood are actually authentic – are *global and real regularities*? The answer is simple – we *cannot* be certain of this, nor indeed even establish it with high probability. How then can these efforts be justified? The answer lies in the consideration that the inductive method is – in the epistemic circumstances at issue – the one that *dominates* its alternatives by all the relevant standards of reasonableness we can bring to bear (inductive itself included): it is the cognitive method in whose favor the strongest argument can be marshalled, the one in which we can have the highest confidence given the rational standards and criteria we do and must employ. To complain about this is to say something like "Don't just assure me that there's jolly good reason to think that induction will work, assure me that it will actually do so." And this complaint is senseless – there is just no way of meeting the second requirement save by means of the first.

7. IS THE FACT THAT INDUCTION IS JUSTIFIED NECESSARY OR CONTINGENT?

Our justificatory strategy has encompassed two major components:

(1) the overarching idea that in the factual domain our question-answering must proceed by "triangulation from experience" – there simply is no real alternative here;

(2) the implementing thesis that this "triangulation" is properly a matter of systematization relative to the usual parameters of systematicity (simplicity, economy, uniformity, regularity, etc.)

The former point is, as we have argued, necessary – a matter of "this or nothing," there being no alternative to a recourse to experience and the "empirical data" we attain by its means. So much, then, is independent of the constitution of nature. But the second thesis is contingent, given the experiential basis of its supporting argumentation. The particular mechanisms of triangulating systematization – the specific *modus operandi* of our cognitive systematizing – could conceivably have been different. Here, then, the issue is indeed dependent on experience, and we must recognize it as a contingent fact that it is appropriate, effective and efficient to use certain particular yardsticks as parameters of systematization.

After all, our systematicity-implementing concepts of simplicity, uniformity, etc. are – as we have seen – rather abstract and schematic. They need to be filled in with determinative specifications that tell just *how* they are to be interpreted and applied in the context of particular lines of reasoning. Experience plays a significant role here: it teaches us not just about the facts of the world, but also about the cognitive devices by means of which we can effectively investigate those facts. In very substantial measure, the methods by which we learn from experience must themselves be a product of experience. The sort of "learning from experience" that is at issue *in* induction is also crucial *for* induction. How our systemic concepts work, and what sorts of considerations are or are not epistemically relevant in inductive praxis, are issues about which induction itself will have to inform us. Induction is thus not only a matter of learning from experience but of conforming our extrapolated expectations to experience with greatest systematic smoothness. For this very reason, it is self-critical, self-monitoring, and self-corrective in the face of expanding experience. (This is a crucial feature of any adequate means for obtaining information about the world.)

The unavoidable reliance upon retrojustificatory considerations means that the *overall* validation of induction – i.e. induction as we actually practice it, relative to the orthodox inductive parameters – is contingent. It is geared to the constitution of this world as experience best reveals it to us. No *a priori* assurance of its efficacy for every possible world is forthcoming. (The counter-inductivism of an evil-demon world remains a theoretical possibility.) To be sure, if we can learn about the world by any *method* at all (rather than say "insight" or "inspiration"), then we must learn from experience. So much is a necessary fact – i.e., it is a matter of necessity *that* we need certain ampliative methodological resources to learn from experience. (This or nothing!) But *how* we are to learn from experience poses a contingent issue that revolves around matters of experiential retrovalidation. This is something which our methodological-pragmatic justification of induction accepts and admits.

The methodological-pragmatic approach thus places the success of induction on a basis that is contingent, empirical, and itself accessible only inductively. A justification of a method in terms of its actual *success* is and must be an inductive justification because *any argument to methodological success is bound to be an inductive argument.* The *efficacy* of induction is not something that can be assured *a priori*; its establishment can only proceed at a level where inductive mechanisms are already in hand for our use, a level whose results are accordingly contingent.

Such a justification of induction – in which inductive reasoning itself plays a key part – places the overall justification of induction on an *a posteriori* basis. And in this context, it is worth pondering C. S. Peirce's contention[8] that any justification of induction which puts its appropriateness on a strictly contingent footing does not yield the kind of validity one would ideally want induction to have. For (so Peirce and others argue) our inductive proceedings are adequately justified only when their effectiveness in any and every possible world has been established. We must thus reconsider our own justification in the light of such an insistence on a necessitarian justification of induction that makes its validation wholly independent of the descriptive character of the world.

Does a contingent validation of induction fall short of what one would ideally wish to have? That depends. In particular, it depends on the answer we give to the question: Is there any appropriate ground for rational discontent?

The crux here is the Humean consideration that we cannot *demonstrate* that induction yields reliable results – any more than we can *demonstrate* that memory or sensation do so. F. P. Ramsey put the point well:

It is true that if anyone has not the habit of induction, we cannot prove to him that he is wrong; but there is nothing

[8] C. S. Peirce, *Collected Papers, op. cit.*, vol. 5, sect. 5.345.

peculiar in that. If a man doubts his memory or his perception we cannot prove to him that they are trustworthy; to ask for such a thing to be proved is to cry for the moon, and the same is true of induction.[9]

The most we can do is to rely on considerations of systematicity to extract information from memory, from perception, and from inductive reason. And since this is the most we can possibly do, it is the most that can be asked of us. (Recall the old Roman legal principle *ultra posse nemo obligatur*; and the issue has its Kantian aspect: "ought" implies "can" – so "cannot" implies "need not.") Since it transpires that no satisfactory justification of induction can possibly proceed on a wholly aprioristic basis, the Peircean complaint under discussion can be dismissed as an illicit hankering after the unattainable. That induction (as standardly practiced) is successful – that it is an efficient and generally effective way of answering our questions about the world – is an inevitably contingent matter. This conclusion is rendered inescapable by a consideration of what J. M. Keynes called "the fact that we can easily imagine a universe so constructed that [our] inductive methods would be useless"[10] or, even worse, would be *misleading*. And in view of this, the full blooded justification of induction – which will ultimately turn on the issue of its effectiveness (success, efficacy, etc.) will have to proceed *a posteriori*.

Precisely because of the cogency of the argumentation (of Hume and his followers) that we cannot justify induction *a priori*, it becomes necessary to strive for an *a posteriori* justification. The pivotal merit of the methodological approach is that it affords a way of doing this: it opens a door through which an inductive justification of induction can be made to work. Herein – as we shall see – lies its crucial advantage over alternative approaches.

8. MORE ON NECESSARY *vs.* CONTINGENT ASPECTS OF INDUCTION

It is worth examining in closer detail just exactly which specific

---

[9] F. P. Ramsey, *The Foundations of Mathematics and Other Logical Essays* (London, 1931), p. 1971.

[10] J. M. Keynes, *A Treatise on Probability* (London, 1921), p. 244.

aspects of the overall justification of induction are necessary and which contingent. Let us begin with the crucial potential-efficacy component of a methodologically based initial justification of induction which requires it to be shown that this method *may* work. How is this to be done?

To clarify this, we do well to ask: could the world (this world, or indeed *a* world) fail to be amenable to standard (orthodoxly systematicity-oriented) induction?

To be sure, nature might be so random that any systematization of its specific eventuations would prove impossible for us. But this *event*-randomness of nature itself constitutes a mode of *operational* order. And this facet of the *nomic* (rather than *contentual*) structure of the world is something that induction could indeed discover. An event-random world is thereby a lawful world and this lawfulness is – in principle, at any rate – accessible to inductive inquiry.

But nature might be random in a deeper sense. It might be geared to novelty and change in its nomic make-up so as to afford a world whose *laws* vary randomly (with randomly varying half-lives). Such a world – one that is *nomically* random rather than event-random – would not be accessible to induction. For one thing, beings capable of carrying on an orderly inductive praxis could (*ex hypothesi*) not exist and function in such a world. And if (*per impossibile*) they could, matters would so eventuate that none of its stable laws (save perhaps for that overarching metalaw of law-randomness itself) could possibly be discovered by induction, for the simple and sufficient reason that there just would be no such laws.

Still, the important fact remains that induction (orthodox, system-oriented induction) can work if any *method* of factual inquiry into the law structure of a world can work at all. The key aim of induction is to disclose regularities in nature. And it may cogently be argued that if *any* cognitive method *M* so operates as to reveal regularities in nature (be they universal or statistical), then orthodox induction itself CAN do so, because it can show that *M* so operates as to reveal such regularities. However, in the cognate argumentation of Peirce and Reichenbach, the emphasized *can* is altered to *will* (or *must*), leading to the dominance argument that induction will (or must) work if any method does. And this is quite incorrect: our conduct of the inductive enterprise may well never lead us to the method *M* that provides the crucial mediating link. All we can conclude on the basis of *a priori* considerations is that, if any method is effective, then it *may* turn out that induction is effective.

Here, then, we have an important *necessary* aspect of induction: if any method of empirical inquiry works – if any process cognitive systematization subject to certain (perhaps nonstandard) parameters can uncover regularities in the workings of nature – then this is itself something that we *could in principle* discover in the long run by the use of orthodox induction itself.

Nevertheless, it is perfectly possible – in theory – that the world (i.e. *a* world) could be so constituted that some substantially variant functional equivalent of induction would be vastly more efficient. That is, a world could be so constituted as to be congenial to *different* nonstandard parameters of inductive systematization. For example, we could have a world geared to *aesthetic* parameters – those of conceptual *beauty* rather than those of conceptual *economy*. Here the highest priority would be accorded to such parameters as harmony, balance, and equipose. Symmetries and cycles would predominate over economy and simplicity; variety over uniformity; novelty over normalcy, etc. In curve-fitting, for example, we would now prefer a symmetric mirror-imaging to an extrapolatively smoother uniformitarianism. And there conceivably could – to repeat – be worlds where such a nonstandard mode of "inductive" practice could be more effective. To be sure, this fact represents a facet of the structure of reality that we could in principle eventually discover by orthodox standard induction. But the course of "self-corrective" experience leading to such a discovery cannot be assured by any line of purely theoretical considerations whatsoever. We have to speak here of what induction *might* discover, and not of what induction *must* discover, nor even what it is plausible to suppose that it *will* discover.

In Section I, we espoused the principle of "practical necessity": "If a good prospect of success is to be realized, then the method at issue is to be used." At present, we are dealing with the even weaker thesis, "If a good prospect of success *can* be attained at all, then the method *can* (i.e., might possibly) attain it." Both of these conditionals move in the direction from success to method-use. But actual efficacy of course comes down to "If you use the method, you will (probably or presumably) achieve success." Its transit from method-use to success reverses the direction of motion of the earlier implications. A good deal more is required at this stage. A full-blooded justification of induction needs to establish not just that orthodox induction affords the prospect of realizing its goals not just *possibly in the inaccessible long run* but *promisingly over the workable short run*. To meet this requirement, we must, however, have recourse to factual considerations. Specifically, we can actually try the method in order to "see that results." And here the empirical – and inductive – factor of retrojustification comes to the fore. At this stage we must – and can – bring induction itself into operation.

To review: What is *necessary* about induction is (1) the fact that a method of inquiry must exploit experience and (*qua* method) do so subject to some family of stable parameters of systematization, and (2) the fact that the standard parameters (oriented towards systematicity and economy) offer us the *possibility* of success – i.e., that if any *method* can succeed, then induction as standardly conducted *can in principle* reveal this fact. Then, too, there is the negativistic *practical* necessity of the consideration that no superior-seeming alternative to induction lies within our cognitive range. On the other hand, what is significantly *contingent* about induction – and what alone serves towards its full-blooded justification – is the matter of its actual effectiveness. And for this ultimately decisive consideration – the contingent fact that induction is an *efficient* resource of inquiry – the inductive mechanisms of a pragmatic retrojustificatioan of induction are indispensably needed. However, the crucial point for our immediate purposes is that the necessaritarian aspects of the matter enable the endeavor to justify induction along methodological lines to get off to an unproblematically noninductive start.[11]

---

[11] Many of the ideas of this chapter are developed more fully in the author's *Methodological Pragmatism* (Oxford, 1977).

VI

The Straight Rule of Proportional Induction and its Justification

SYNOPSIS

(1) A consideration of Peirce's idea of using the "straight rule" of proportional induction as instrument for validating induction in general, subject to (2) the argument that the straight rule itself is *bound to succeed* in the long run in its intended mission of finding an inductively sought relative frequency, provided that this frequency exists. This argumentation fails because (i) we must operate in the short run, (ii) it is misleading to say that the rule enables us to *find* a limit, and (iii) there is no assurance that the limit towards which the rule leads is one we actually want. (3) However, viewed from the perspective of estimation theory, the rivals to the straight rule that have been mooted in the literature all exhibit serious defects. (4) The view of induction as a matter of providing a "best estimate of the real truth" is able to circumvent the difficulties of the Peirce/Reichenbach approach and provide the requisite initial (albeit methodological) justification of the straight rule. (5) The *a priori* considerations of such a methodological justification are *not* asked to accomplish the whole task of justifying induction, but only to give the process its initial impetus, subject to an eventual pragmatic retrojustification by inductive means.

1. THE PEIRCEAN STRATEGY FOR JUSTIFYING INDUCTION

The principal inductive instrument at work in the inductive retrojustification of induction is the process of straightforward sample-to-population projection – the "straight rule" of inductive generalization that underwrites the move from a record of established success (in a certain degree) to generic efficacy (to a comparable extent). The aim of the present chapter is to examine more closely the initial justification of the starting point for this inductive process – a justification which must, in the nature of the case, ultimately rest on wholly noninductive considerations.

A bit of historical stagesetting will prove helpful in this connection. C. S. Peirce, the founding father of philosophical pragmatism, produced a characteristically clever plan for justifying induction. He proposed to reduce the overall problem of justifying induction to that of justifying one of its particular modes, and then to use *this* mode of induction to provide an inductive justification of the rest of our inductive methodology.[1] Such a tactic is reminiscent of code-breaking. In cryptanalysis the main thing is to force an entry into the cypher at some one point. Once one has conquered even a small part of it, this can readily be exploited to gain mastery over the rest. As Peirce depicted it, the situation in the inductive case is analogous. Once one has made some entry into the inductive domain – even if at first only into a relatively modest sector of it – the area of justification can then readily be extended by inductive means.

This strategy obviously brings to the fore the problem of just where the entry-point is to be found. Here Peirce and, succeeding him, Hans Reichenbach, took the logical candidate to be the key principle of proportional induction – the principle which Peirce himself characterized as "quantitative induction," but which (following Reichenbach) is nowadays often referred to as "the straight rule" of statistical induction. This rule is formulated in the following precept:

---

[1] For a fuller description of Peirce's approach, see the author's *Peirce's Philosophy of Science* (Notre Dame, 1978).

When a certain percentage of a population *P* have in fact been observed to have a particular trait *T*, then adopt *this very value* as your answer to the question: "What proportion of the entire population *P* have the trait *T*?"

The rule is "straight" because straightforward – it simply enjoins one to take the sample-correlative frequency as the index of how things stand in the population as a whole.

Note that once this rule is adopted, we can readily use it to monitor the rest of our inductive praxis, because it can serve as a controlling principle for appraising our inductive methodology in point of its predictive and applicative success. Given the success-ratio of induction in past applications, we simply use the straight rule to project this degree of efficacy across the board. We can thus justify our inductive procedures by assessing their efficacy along these statistical/inductive lines.

But, of course, at this stage the problem of justifying the straight rule of statistical induction itself remains unresolved. Peirce (and Reichenbach later on) proposed to resolve this justificating problem by arguing that we know, *a priori* and by demonstration on the basis of general principles alone, that statistical induction *must inevitably succeed* in its intended mission and is consequently justified. As they saw it, a strictly necessitarian justification of the straight rule can be developed. Their position deserves close scrutiny.

2. THE PEIRCE/REICHENBACH JUSTIFICATION OF THE STRAIGHT RULE AND ITS SHORTCOMINGS

The basic idea of Peirce and Reichenbach is that the justification of the straight rule of statistical (or "proportional") induction inheres in the fact that it is "fated" to succeed in the long run – that it is demonstrably bound to lead us to the correct limit of the relative frequency of occurrence of the trait at issue, if such a limit indeed exists. For – so they maintained – what we are trying to get at in the inductive process is:

$$\theta^* = \lim_{t \to \infty} \theta_t$$

where θ^* is the relative frequency of the natural trait at issue in the whole of the *observable* population, while θ_t is the relative frequency of this trait in the actually *observed* subpopulation, our actual sample up to time t. Now if at the time t we take θ_t as our posit for the value of this limiting value, then we know that, in the long run, as $t \to \infty$, the difference between θ^* and θ_t is increasingly diminished. To all appearances, a strictly mathematical demonstration of the *ultimate* effectiveness of the inductive rule is thus at hand. If there is a limit at all – so they argue – then dogged adherence to θ_t across the reaches of time will eventually enable us to find it.

Peirce and Reichenbach viewed this fact as crucial; as they saw it, it affords a decisive reason for adopting the straight rule of proportional induction, and does so as a matter of unproblematic necessity. But, unfortunately, there are several cogent reasons why this otherwise attractive argumentation is not really satisfactory.

First of all, the crucial fact is that the consideration that statistical induction is "ultimately bound to succeed" in the long run does not underwrite any conclusion whatsoever about the appropriateness of its use here and now, in the short run in which we live, breathe, and have our being. Convergence in the eventual limit has no implications with respect to the present or the foreseeable future. After all, we have no choice but to live and do our cognitive work in the short run – seeing that, as Keynes remarked, in the long run we are all dead. And, unhappily, the long-run behavior of such a limit function is compatible with *any* short-run behavior whatsoever. There is thus no reason to regard the ratio θ_t, with $t = $ NOW, as foreshadowing or approximating the actual (long term) probability.[2] For no value of t, no matter how large, does θ_t bear any determinate relationship to the ultimate limit value – unless we are prepared to postulate *a priori* knowledge about the nature of the world. In itself, long-runism suffers the decisive defect of affording us with no differential reasons at all for preferring one inductive policy to another *here and*

---

[2] To be sure, these difficulties can be overcome by adopting a (problematic) metaphysical supposition to the effect that limits tend to be reached soon – that the world is in point of fact such that the near term situation has a tendency to approximate the situation at large.

now. Whatever the merits of the straight rule in the potentially infinite long run, they cannot by themselves substantiate Reichenbach's claim that this rule indicates the best wagers upon future contingencies that we can *presently* make.

Accordingly, there is nothing inherently rational (sensible, defensible) about our *present* use of induction to be derived from the fact that induction is bound to work out in the long run. Reichenbach himself was well aware of this fact:

> The case of convergence coming too late [given the finite duration of human life] amounts to the same thing as the case of nonconvergence, as far as human abilities are concerned.[3]

However, Reichenbach seems to have felt that in these cases where induction cannot do the job, no other epistemic *modus operandi* can possibly do any better. Unfortunately, his reasons for this view were never spelled out – understandably enough, since it is difficult to see how any such reasons could ever be forthcoming.

Secondly, it is not really appropriate to say the process of dogged θ-adherence enables us actually to find or even to approximate the limit – even if there actually is one (which, of course, there may not be). For *whatever* be the stage of t that we actually have reached, it is always entirely possible that θ_t should differ substantially from the limit-value: no matter what the time t is, we cannot ever guarantee that there is – then and there – any fixed relationship between θ_t and θ^*. We are never sure that we have actually found (or even approximated) the limit; and we can never be, no matter how large t becomes.

John Lenz has trenchantly formulated this mode of objection to the long-runist approach. Reichenbach, he says, has claimed "that, if there is a limit, it can be found in a finite though indefinite number of tries. . . . One need not be a devoté of ordinary language to insist that it is strange . . . to say that the method of induction will, if possible, *find* limits. At least this is a sense of 'find' in which one never knows [and never can know] that one has found that for which one looks."[4] No

[3] Hans Reichenbach, *Experience and Prediction* (Chicago, 1938), p. 361.
[4] John W. Lenz, "Problems for the Practicalist's Justification of Induction," in R. Swinburne (ed.), *The Justification of Induction* (Oxford, 1974), pp. 98–101 (see p. 100).

matter how much it may seem to us that "now at least we're getting to that ultimate limit" the prospect that the θ_t serves will wander off in some other direction can never be excluded.

It is clearly inappropriate to say that a process enables us to *find* something if we are not in a position to recognize this desired object even if, perchance, we should attain it. Suppose I instructed X to find Y. I send him to a room crowded with people and tell him: "Keep looking about – you're *bound* to find him sooner or later." He will surely complain: "Even supposing that I do actually encounter him, how am I to know that it's he? Until you give me a way of *identifying* him when I do come upon him, you've given me no way to recognize him. And so you haven't enabled me to *find* him at all. For all you've told me, not only can't I tell when I've got him, but I cannot even tell when I'm 'getting warmer' by coming closer to him." Here X's very proper complaint is a close analogue of one to which Reichenbach's theory is open. It too leaves us quite unable actually to "find" the desired limit in any save a Pickwickian sense of this term.

Thirdly, a further problem of θ_t-adherence is that $\lim_{t \to \infty} \theta_t$ relates to the limiting frequency of the trait at issue in the *observed* sector of the population P and this may be far removed from its true frequency in P because of biases operative within the observation process. Even if we do succeed in getting at the limiting frequency θ^* of the target-trait in the *observed* section of the population, we may not get to the limit we are really after, the actual value, θ, of the frequency in the entire population as a whole. How can we be confident our observational sampling of nature does not yield a biased upshot, so that the probability-determining limit process yields an altogether inappropriate result. To be sure, as $t \to \infty$, it must be that θ_t approaches the true value of the "frequency within the range of (actual) observation", $\lim_{t \to \infty} \theta_t$, if this limit indeed exists. But what assurance is there that this itself reflects the real object of our endeavors in inquiry, the *actual frequency in nature*, θ? As θ_t balloons out to approximate θ^* over the course of time, it may or may not happen that this value will itself afford a correct index of θ. The "ultimately observed" may fail to reflect the "theoretically observable".

The root problem of the Peirce–Reichenbach approach is that two rather different gaps need to be closed before its justificatory work is done:

(1) The potential gap between "the frequency indicated by the data in hand" (θ_t) and "the (ultimate) frequency in observation" ($\lim_{t \to \infty} \theta_t$)

and

(2) The potential gap between "the frequency in observation" ($\lim_{t \to \infty} \theta_t$) and "the frequency in nature" (θ)

Now the *a priori* argumentation offered by these theorists goes no further than to indicate that the former gap is (necessarily) closed *in the limit*; it does nothing whatever towards removing the second gap. This poses an obstacle that can only be overcome by means of problematic metaphysical assumptions (such as "the uniformity of nature").

Considerations of this sort indicate that if one is going to offer an *a priori* (noninductive) justification of the straight rule as an inductive principle, then it will have to proceed along rather different lines than those envisaged by Peirce and Reichenbach.

3. THE STRAIGHT RULE *VIS-À-VIS* OTHER PROSPECTS: THE PERSPECTIVE OF ESTIMATION

In seeking out a justification of the straight rule of statistical induction, it will be helpful to begin with a survey of some of the variant rules of statistical induction that have been mooted in the literature of the subject as affording *theoretically* available alternatives to the straight rule. Let us now regard these rules from our present point of view, as affording *estimates* of the actual frequency. They all thus take the form of claims to the effect that the *actual frequency in nature* (θ) of the trait at issue is (to be estimated as) a certain function (F) of the observed frequency to date (θ_t):

$$\theta = F(\theta_t)$$

Thus F affords the functional relationship through which we are to extract our estimate of θ on the basis of the relevant information actually at our disposal, namely θ_t. The straight rule itself of course takes the view that $F(\theta_t)$ is simply θ_t itself: $F(\theta_t) = \theta_t$. But various alternatives have been discussed,[5] and some of the main ones are set out in Table VI.1.

It is not difficult to see that none of the *alternatives* to the straight rule qualifies as a serious *rival*. Since what is at issue is

Table VI.1

ALTERNATIVE RULES OF FREQUENCY ESTIMATION

Observed Frequency (θ_1)	Estimated Frequency $F(\theta_1)^{(1)}$	Designation of the Inductive Rule
(1) θ_t	$\theta_t + c_t^{(2)}$	The Straight Rule modified by an additive "correction" factor[3]
(2) θ_t	$c_t \times \theta_t^{(4)}$	The Straight Rule modified by a multiplicative "correction" factor
(3) θ_t	$k = $ a constant[5]	The Indifferentist Rule
(4) θ_t	$1 - \theta_t$	The Counterinductive Rule

NOTES [1] F is the *estimator* at issue, i.e. the proposed estimating function by which we are to determine θ in terms of the data actually at our disposal (viz. the observed frequency to date, θ_t): $F(\theta_t) = $ our purported best estimate of θ [as of the time t].

[2] Here $0 < c_t < 1$ and $\lim_{t \to \infty} c_t = 0$.

[3] For some (unnecessary) worries about this rule, cf. Hans Reichenbach, *Experience and Prediction* (Chicago, 1938).

[4] Here $0 < c_t < 1$ and $\lim_{t \to \infty} c_t = 1$.

[5] Presumably $k = 1/n$, where n is the number of available alternatives. Hence the "indifferentism" at issue.

[5] For further deliberations regarding such pathologically variant inductive rules see Wesley C. Salmon, "The Pragmatic Justification of Induction" in R. Swinburne (ed.), *The Justification of Induction* (Oxford, 1974), pp. 84–97. Cf. also two other papers by this author: "Vindication of Induction," in H. Feigl and G. Maxwell (eds.), *Current Issues in the Philosophy of Science* (New York, 1961); and "On Vindicating Induction" in H. E. Kyburg, Jr. and E. Nagel (eds.), *Induction: Some Current Issues* (Middletown, Conn., 1963).

an *estimate* of a certain particular kind of thing – namely a relative frequency of a trait within a population – it is proper to regard the estimation function F as subject to two important requirements (among others no less relevant):

(i) *The character requirement* (cf. p. 24 above). This has the consequence that, since the trait at issue is (*ex hypothesi*) *present* with a frequency of θ, it must be *absent* with a frequency of $1 - \theta$. Thus we must have it that $F(\theta_t) + F(1 - \theta_t) = 1$. This is simply a consequence of the supposition that it is a relative frequency that is at issue. Our estimate of a thing must have the general character of the thing estimated.

(ii) *The coordination requirement* (cf. p. 24 above). This stipulates that divergences in the nature of our data-base of estimation must be reflected in appropriate differences in the estimates we base on them. Thus significant fluctuations in θ_t should be appropriately reflected in $F(\theta_t)$: If θ_t increases (or decreases), so should $F(\theta_t)$ increase (or decrease). The estimate should be appropriately sensitive to variations in the data on which it is based.

It is easy to see that all the rules at issue in Table VI.1 run afoul of these requirements. The condition of paragraph (i) is violated by Rules 1, 2, and 3, and the condition of paragraph (ii) is violated by Rules 3 and 4.[6] Accordingly, these variant non-standard rules all have the decisive defect of violating one or another constraint on the sort of estimate that is to be at issue. To be sure, this consideration, by itself, is nowise sufficient to justify the straight rule. The fact that some of its rivals are deficient does not mean that it is itself free from defects. If the rule is to be justified, one must therefore look to the positive side and examine its own claims and merits.

---

[6] Consider just one detailed example, that of Rule 1. Note that if the observed frequency of the trait T in the population P is now θ_t, then the observed frequency of the trait not-T is $1 - \theta_t$. Then by Rule 1 we estimate that T runs in the population as a whole with frequency $\theta_t + c_t$ and that not-T occurs with frequency $(1 - \theta_t) + c_t$. But by the character of what is at issue, the *sum* of these quantities must be identically 1, which it certainly will not be (unless $c_t = 0$, which would render this entire rule otiose). Accordingly, Rule 1 fails to satisfy the character requirement.

4. THE METHODOLOGY OF ESTIMATION AS BASIS FOR A
   SIMPLICITY-GEARED JUSTIFICATION OF THE STRAIGHT RULE

Notwithstanding the deficiences of the Peirce/Reichenbach approach, it is possible to develop a strictly methodological justification of the straight rule *as an instrument of estimation*. For a cogent *a priori* justification can in fact be provided for the straight rule of proportional induction along the methodological lines of our present approach. What is at issue from this perspective is that the task of induction is to furnish a method for question-resolving truth-estimation under the guiding aegis of considerations of systematicity in general and simplicity in particular. Let us trace out the implications of this line of thought.

(1) We must begin by recognizing a key idea of the general theory of methods (metamethodology). *In the absence of indications to the contrary, a METHOD cannot differentiate haphazardly – it must treat all cases alike.* Such a basic commitment to "consistency" in the sense of a fixed uniformity of process is built into the very idea of what a *method* is all about.

(2) The next consideration is that what is at issue in the present context is *a method of estimation on the basis of given data*. The method must accordingly provide for a fixed and uniform relationship between the proffered estimate and *the data* on which it is based. Now in framing our estimate the information that is actually at our disposal is merely $\theta_t =$ "the proportion of the P's that are T's *in the course of our experience to date* (i.e. up to the time t)." Thus given θ_t – as a summary of the situation regarding the data-in-hand to date, the method must proceed to determine a definite value $F(\theta_t)$, where F, the estimator at issue, represents some fixed and definite function of the data-parameter. This function specifies the manner in which the *estimated* frequency we are after is to be determined in terms of the *observed* frequency at our disposal. It specifies how we are to exploit our access to θ_t in the interests of the estimate we are endeavoring to make.[7]

---

[7] This approach treats the estimate as something independent of the *earlier* values of $\theta_{t'}$ (with $t' < t$). It takes the stance that, since the present evidence encorporates the past (in that the $\theta_{t'}$ data figure in our θ_t value), we need not take separate and additional cognizance of them. The position is that only the current (i.e. the latest) value of θ_t counts, and that the historical course of events by which we arrived at this

(3) Since it is a *relative frequency* that is to be estimated, we must of course have it that:

$$F(\theta_t) + F(1 - \theta_t) = 1$$

Clearly this condition – which follows from what we have designated as the *character requirement* – represents a fundamental structural feature of the estimand that must be preserved by any adequate estimate of it.[8]

(4) Finally, a very different set of considerations may be brought upon the scene, viz. those relating to systematicity – in particular, to simplicity and economy of means. In the interests of simplicity, we may presume the functional relationship F at issue to be one that is given by a polynomial:

$$F(\theta_t) = a_0 + a_1\theta_t + a_2\theta_t^2 + \cdots + a_n\theta_t^n = a_0 + a_1\theta_t + \sum_{i=2}^{n} a_i\theta_t^i$$

Such a polynomial is the simplest sort of candidate for a functional relationship of the general sort that is to be at issue. In seeking for the simplest solution for a function that can meet the various conditions of the problem, this is clearly where we would want to begin.[9]

Let us explore the consequences of these stipulations, which are all variations of themes already touched upon above.[10]

Note to begin with that:

$$F(1 - \theta_t) = a_0 + a_1(1 - \theta_t) + \sum_{i=2}^{n} a_i(1 - \theta_t)^i.$$

---

value – the specific path leading to it – is otherwise irrelevant. The justification of this procedure lies in methodological considerations. As always, *complicationes non multiplicandae sunt praeter necessitatem*, and where there is no good and apparent reason to bring certain factors upon the scene of consideration, we may safely omit them. The approach in question thus reflects our standard commitment to simplicity and systematicity (subject, as always, to eventual retrojustification through experience).

[8] By this same requirement, this must hold also for such other necessary features of θ_t, as, for example, lying in the interval between 0 and $1 : 0 \leqslant \theta_t \leqslant 1$.

[9] It is important to note that a polynomial of this sort always be fitted to any finite number of data-points. Since in the present case we can never *de facto* have more than a finite number of such points, a polynomial function F of the polynomial form at issue can *always* be found to fit the data we in fact have. Thus no very confining restriction is operative in this supposition.

[10] Observe that (1) relates to the uniformity requirement, (2) to the coordination requirement, (3) to the character requirement, and (4) to the effectiveness requirement as discussed at pp. 24–26 above.

Accordingly, the equation of paragraph (3) yields:

$$1 = F(\theta_t) + F(1 - \theta_t) = 2a_0 + a_1 + \sum_{i=2}^{n} a_i[\theta_t^i + (1 - \theta_t)^i]$$

Now this equation is an identity which must obtain *universally*, quite independently of the specific value of the parameter θ_t. The only way to guarantee this circumstance is to set $a_2 = a_3 = \ldots = a_n = 1$, and then have it that $2a_0 + a_1 = 1$. But clearly, if and when it happens that θ_t is and remains 0, there is no choice but to fix $F(\theta_t)$ itself at 0. (If we never, in any circumstances, encounter any P's that are T's, our "best estimate" of the appropriate answer to the question "What proportion of the P's are T's?" is clearly "None at all.") Thus we must have it that $F(0) = 0$. But, since the initial polynomial tells us that $F(0) = a_0$, this means that it must also be that $a_0 = 0$, and consequently that $a_1 = 1$. It follows that $F(\theta_t)$ will have the simple and straightforward structure: $F(\theta_t) = \theta_t$. And so Q.E.D. – we arrive at the straight rule of proportional induction.

It emerges that the function $F(\theta_t) = \theta_t$ is the *simplest* solution to the problem of finding an estimation function F that meets the various conditions at issue. The search for a *method* for providing data-based *estimates* that is maximally *simple* leads directly to the straight rule of proportional induction.[11] And note that this argumentation proceeds wholly *a priori* relative to the aims of the enterprise – on the basis of considerations of methodological suitability and simplicity alone.[12]

The straight rule thus results as an expression of the pursuit of systematicity (and especially simplicity) in estimation – it comes to the fore as a natural consequence of our view of induction as truth-estimation under the aegis of the para-

[11] It should be noted that all three italicized factors were appealed to in the course of the argument. A cognate albeit different argument to the same conclusion is presented in Wesley Salmon, "The Pragmatic Justification of Induction" in R. Swinburne (ed.), *op. cit.*, p. 95.

[12] The present argument accordingly resubstantiates along a somewhat more rigorous route the conclusion already arrived at by somewhat rough and ready means at pp. 42–44 above. There, however, our justificatory appeal rested on considerations of *uniformity* while our present argumentation rests on those of *simplicity*.

meters of systematicity. The "justification" of the straight rule is accordingly seen to lie – initially and in the first instance – in its affording the simplest, most natural, most *systematic* solution to the estimation problem at issue.

Such a subjection of the straight rule to considerations of systemic adequacy (accordingly themselves viewed as the more fundamental) will also condition its use in appropriate ways. Bertrand Russell, for example, worries about the apparent parallelism between:

(1) All the lightning I have ever seen has always been accompanied by thunder; therefore (particularly) all lightning is always accompanied by thunder

and

(2) All the cattle I have ever seen have always been found in Herefordshire; therefore all cattle is always to be found in Herefordshire[13]

But the parallelism disappears when further facets of systemic generality enter upon the stage. For the first case (unlike the second) survives the augmentation to "I *or as far as I know anybody* has ever seen." But the second case (unlike the first) involves a specific spatial limitation to one particular county that runs contrary to the whole of our systemic background information regarding the scientific irrelevancy of such political subdivisions. These two "applications" of the straight rule of induction are only seemingly parallel applications of inductive principles.

One further point deserves comment in this connection. Peirce and Reichenbach both see the aim of induction as a matter of determining the ultimate limit of the relative frequency of our observations:

$$\theta^* = \lim_{t \to \infty} \theta_t$$

[13] Bertrand Russell, *Human Knowledge: Its Scope and Limits* (New York, 1948), p. 455.

But this view is mistaken. As we saw above (pp. 103–104), the point of the inquiry is to determine not *this* quantity θ^*, the frequency in the *observed* population, but θ, the frequency in the population *as a whole* – it is not the frequency *in observation* but the frequency *in nature* that we want. But since it is the frequency in (indefinitely extended) observation that their analysis gives us, not the frequency in nature – because what it shows is that we have a certain (long-run oriented) warrant for using θ_t as evaluator of θ^* – both Peirce and Reichenbach become enmeshed in metaphysical argumentation. They have to argue that nature as such is irrelevant and that what matters for us is *perceived* nature. Peirce, for example, specifies it as the aim of inductive inquiry to determine "what would be found true in the usual course of experience, if it were indefinitely prolonged."[14] This simply gerrymanders the inductive realm in such a way that our *experience of nature* rather than nature itself becomes its object. It means (*inter alia*) that we are not to construe "All A's are B's" literally, but always as "All of the ever-observed A's are B's." All generalizations about nature itself have to be reconstrued as statements regarding our observations of nature.

Hans Reichenbach sought to meet the difficulty in much the same way:

> Let us introduce the term *practical limit* for a series showing a sufficient convergence within a domain accessible to human observations; we may add that we may cover by this term the case of a series which, though not

---

[14] Charles Sanders Peirce, *Collected Papers*, ed. by C. Hartshorne and P. Weiss, vol. 6 (Cambridge, Mass.; 1935), sect. 6.100. Peirce's doctrine that all reality will ultimately be known is not (basically) a thesis about the inevitable triumphs of inquiry, but one regarding the nature of "reality." See Chapter 2 of the author's *Peirce's Philosophy of Science* (Notre Dame, 1978), and cf. also the sympathetic presentation of Peirce's position in C. F. Delaney "Peirce on Induction and the Uniformity of Nature," in the *Philosophical Forum*, vol. 4 (1973), pp. 438–448 (Notre Dame, 1978). The Peircean tendency to equate *the domain of inquiry* (= nature as such) with *the domain of experience* goes back to Kant. "I do not by this argument at all profess to disprove void space, for it may exist where perceptions cannot reach, and where there is, therefore, no empirical knowledge of coexistence. But such a space is not for us an object of any possible experience [and so can have no objective reality *for us*]." (*Critique of Pure Reason*, A214 = B261.) Peirce's thinking of himself as a follower of Kant was no idle fancy.

converging in infinity, shows an approximate convergence in a segment of the series, accessible in practice and sufficiently long (a so-called "semiconvergent series"). We may then say that our theory [of induction] is not concerned with a mathematical limit but with a practical limit.[15]

Again, the problem is resolved only by gerrymandering the domain at issue.

It is a substantial advantage of an estimation-oriented approach that it does away with this sort of complexity. We are able simply to take the line that – of course and naturally! – what we perceive of it is our only *available guide* to nature itself ("this or nothing"). This therefore provides our best estimate. In the absence of counter-indications as to a gap between *perceived* and *actual* nature, we are perfectly entitled to base our "best estimate" of the latter on the former.

We need not argue (in Fox and Grapes fashion) that $\lim_{t \to \infty} \theta_t$

is itself what we really need or want, nor (*à la* Peirce) that it somehow must on metaphysical grounds lead us to what we need and want, but just that it affords the *best available estimate* of this desideratum. It is, of course, the quantity θ = "the proportion of the P's that are T's *in the whole of nature*" that we are after. But if the process of our experiential sampling of nature is sensibly contrived – if *there just is no* reason to think that nature presents a somehow distorted visage to us in the course of our interactive commerce with it – then we have adequate grounds for (and really no alternative to) accepting $\theta^* = \lim_{t \to \infty} \theta_t =$ "the proportion of P's that are T's *throughout the course of our experience* (that is, in the observed population)" as *the best available estimate* of θ. Without somehow giving up on θ itself, we simply recognize that θ^* is – inevitably – the very best we can do towards its realization.

Accordingly, our recourse to estimation does the whole job for us. A two-stage process of estimation is at work:

(1) At t, θ_t is our "best available estimate" of $\theta^* = \lim_{t \to \infty} \theta_t$.

[15] Hans Reichenbach, *Experience and Prediction* (Chicago, 1938), pp. 361–362.

This emerges from the preceding argumentation in support of the straight rule, and is also underwritten by the condition of Fisherian "consistency".[16]

(2) $\theta = \lim_{t \to \infty} \theta_t$ is in turn our "best available estimate" of θ, realizing that what we actually need and want in inductive inquiry is not θ^* itself (the frequency in observation) but the frequency in nature.

Putting these two pieces together, we arrive at the result that θ_t is our "best available estimate" of θ. The gap between θ and $\theta^* = \lim_{t \to \infty} \theta_t$ is closed not by metaphysics but simply by the consideration that a matter of estimation is at issue. And since $\lim_{t \to \infty} \theta_t$ itself is not something we can lay our hands on, it, too, is something we must perforce merely estimate, with θ_t providing the optimal estimator. The aspect of estimation is the key that unlocks the difficulties. The model of induction as a method for question-resolving truth-estimation through cognitive systematization easily and naturally bypasses the sorts of philosophical difficulties that enmesh the Peirce/Reichenbach argument for justifying the straight rule.

5. THE ROLE OF *A PRIORI* AND *A POSTERIORI* CONSIDERATIONS IN A METHODOLOGICAL-PRAGMATIC JUSTIFICATION OF INDUCTION

Let us review the theoretical advantages of practical and methodological provenience that militate *a priori* for the straight rule of proportional induction. They are primarily two, namely (i) that the method has the merit of affording the simplest viable solution to the estimation problem at issue (as per Sects. 3–4), and (ii) the method has the merit of being

[16] The consideration at issue is simply R. A. Fischer's "criterion of consistency" to the effect that, when applied to the population as a whole, our statistical estimator should yield a result *demonstrably* equal to the estimandum (the parameter-value being estimated). See p. 25 above.

bound (though, alas, only in the long run) to approximate to $\lim_{t \to \infty} \theta_t$, the actual frequency of the trait at issue within the ultimately total *observed* population (*à la* the argumentation of Peirce and Reichenbach).

This second finding is of more than trivial importance. The fact that the straight rule *does* accomplish a significant part of the inductive mission in the long-run suggests that it *may* work in the short-run (though this merely possibilistic claim stops far short of affording any basis for claiming that it *will* do so). But even such a very feeble consideration suffices to establish the weak sort of potential efficacy at issue in the initial stages of methodological justification.

The Peirce/Reichenbach point regarding ultimate limit-approximation can thus be allowed to carry *some* weight within a methodological line of legitimation. But only very little. We do not ask of the *a priori* argumentation of the sort with which the Peirce/Reichenbach approach is concerned that it should in and of itself justify our use of the straight rule. Like considerations of simplicity and systematicity themselves, this argument is merely invoked to provide some scintilla of initial justification, some element of favorable presumption. The defect of the argumentation of Peirce and Reichenbach lies in its treating the satisfaction of this one particular theoretical desideratum as altogether decisive – as being able to carry the whole weight of justification at issue in and of itself. And this is clearly asking more of these theoretical *a priori* considerations than they could possibly deliver. On the present argumentation, however, they need only be asked to help in providing the basis on which a methodological *faute de mieux* justification can have some small initial foothold: they are not asked to accomplish the whole justificatory task, but only to give the process some minuscule initial impetus. From there on in, the remaining justification can – as we have seen – be accomplished by (inductively laden) retrojustification. But of course at *this* later, inductive stage, when we already have *some* inductive mechanisms available for use, we can resort to the Peircean strategy of using one inductive mechanism to justify the others (and indeed also to retrojustify itself).

The fact that a methodological/pragmatic justification

along these lines can be provided for the straight rule of proportional induction is critically important in the present context, because it is clear that this rule must itself be called on to provide the inductive mechanism that has to bear the main brunt in any inductive justification of induction. For, as we have seen, any argument to the actual *efficacy* of our inductive methods will have to extrapolate from the historical record of established success. And, to this end, the straight rule – or some close functional equivalent thereof – is an indispensably needed tool. Fortunately, the methodologico-inductive approach to the justification of induction is able to render this tool available at this early stage at which the most critical need for it exists.

VII

The Charge of Circularity

SYNOPSIS
(1) A methodological justification of induction as pragmatically successful appears circular because it maintains the success of induction by inductive means in arguing from experienced success to general efficacy. But there is nothing viciously circular or question-begging about our present course of argumentation. Thanks to the two-phase character of the overall justificatory argument, we *already* have in hand, through an initial, noninductive stage in the justificatory reasoning, the inductive tools that are needed at the later, retrojustificatory stage. (2) The weight of actual justification can thus be born by essentially inductive techniques without impropriety, given the overall structure of a methodological-pragmatic approach. (3) That induction stands validated on its own telling is not a basis of complaint, but a crucial aspect of its adequacy as a cognitive method. For the adequacy of our cognitive methods requires that they be *self*-substantiating, and form part of a systematic ensemble of cognitive commitments. The fundamentally inductive character of the proposed justification must be admitted, but can nevertheless be seen to be not merely harmless but actually helpful. (4) Still, it is not inherently circular to invoke *experience* in a justification of induction, seeing that induction is itself the very method by which we learn from experience? The answer is negative – no damaging circularity need arise here since an initial prejustification can proceed *noninductively* to put at our disposal those inductive instrumentalities by whose means an inductive justification of induction can then be developed.

1. THE CHARGE OF QUESTION-BEGGING AND ITS AVOIDANCE

A justificatory recourse to methodological success calls for exploiting the "lessons of experience." But since induction is itself our experience-exploiting method, it turns out that an experiential justification of induction actually uses induction in justifying induction. The *experiential retrojustification* component of the methodological justification of induction, which involves the element of learning by experience, is clearly inductive in nature. By its means, induction is validated by a justification that moves from the experiential basis of a record of established success to the conclusion of presumptive *efficacy* – the promise of *general* success. Can such a selfjustificatory use of induction possibly be appropriate?

The fundamental idea of providing an inductive justification of induction is an attractive one that has been mooted by many writers.[1] Yet such an approach has never managed to make much headway because of its vulnerability to the objection that it is circular. "Surely," it is always urged by way of objection, "you cannot validate the general policy of appealing to experience by an appeal to experience. Since this very sort of 'appeal to the experiential record' is itself the *object* of justification – the process whose legitimacy is *sub judice* – a justificatory argument that appeals to experience moves in a circle to beg the very question at issue." This line of objection must be overcome by any acceptable inductive justification of induction.

Some have contended that a straightforwardly inductive

[1] See Richard B. Braithwaite, *Scientific Explanation* (Cambridge, 1953), Ch. 8, "The Justification of Induction," pp. 255–292. But see also Abner Shimony's severely critical "Braithwaite on Scientific Method," in *Review of Metaphysics*, vol. 7 (1953–1954), pp. 644–660. And compare H. E. Kyburg, Jr., "R. B. Braithwaite on Probability and Induction," in *British Journal for the Philosophy of Science*, vol. 9 (1958–1959), pp. 203–220. A defense of the soundness of self-supporting inductions can be found in Max Black, "Inductive Support of Inductive Rules," pp. 191–208 in *Problems of Analysis* (Ithaca, NY, 1954), and "Self-supporting Inductive Arguments," pp. 209–218 in *Models and Metaphors* (Ithaca, NY, 1962),, as well as in Black's article on "Induction" in P. Edwards (ed.), *The Encyclopedia of Philosophy*, vol. 4 (New York, 1967), pp. 169–181 (see esp. pp. 173–174). For criticism of Black's views, see Peter Achinstein, "The Circularity of a Self-supporting Argument," in *Analysis*, vol. 22 (1961–1962), pp. 138–141. See also Black's reply in the same journal, vol. 23 (1962–1963), pp. 43–44, and Achinstein's rejoinder, *ibid.*, pp. 123–127.

justification of induction is feasible because *explicit* circularity can be avoided. Alice Ambrose, for example, has tried to meet the charge of *petitio principii* by arguing that the principle of induction is not a *premiss* of inductive arguments, but a *principle of inference* according to which inductive inferences are made.[2] What is one to make of this line of defense?

A *deductive* analogy may help to clarify the issue. Consider the following argumentation:

 - All arguments that do no more than place a special case under a general rule are valid. [This is the so-called *dictum de omni*.]
 - *Barbara* syllogisms do no more than place a special case under a general rule [= "*Barbara* syllogisms instantiate the *dictum de omni*."]

∴ Barbara syllogisms are valid

It is clear that two things must be done to establish the conclusion at issue by means of this argument: we would need (1) to assure the truth of the premisses, and (2) to assure the validity of the argument-form. But, as regards this second point, it is important to observe that the argument is itself a *Barbara* syllogism. Thus to establish the truth of the conclusion by this argument – to establish by its means the validity of Barbara syllogisms – we would need *already* to have established the validity of a (typical) syllogism of this type.[3] The argumentation at issue thus fails us – on grounds of circularity – as a useful route towards establishing the required conclusion. Observe, however, that this circularity-induced failure does

[2] Alice Ambrose, "The Problem of Justifying Inductive Inference," *The Journal of Philosophy*, vol. 44 (1947), pp. 260ff. Cf. also R. B. Braithwaite's argumentation to the same effect:

[T]he proposition 'presupposed' in the predictionist justification of an inductive inference does not function in the inference as an additional premiss. The inductive inference to the proposition that induction by simple enumeration is an effective policy in the *petitio principii* sense of professing to infer a conclusion from a set of premisses one of which is the conclusion itself. (*Scientific Explanation* [Cambridge, 1955], pp. 275–276.)

[3] Lewis Carroll's well-known paradox of Achilles and the Tortoise is a variant of this reasoning.

emphatically *not* lie in the presence of the conclusion among the explicit premises of the argument. Rather, it inheres in the no less vitiating fact that the inferential principle whose validity is at issue is being used within the argumentation through which its validity is purportedly forthcoming. This variant mode of circularity – let us call it "rule-circularity" – is none the less problematic for avoiding inclusion of the conclusion among the premises.

Viewed at closer range, the argumentation envisaged by Ambrose would look somewhat analogous. Its pivot is an inductive rule akin to the following:

Rule R: To argue from "most have" to (probably) "most
will"

The question at once arises: How do we justify Rule R and validate the belief that this rule will (probably) guide us aright? Consider the contention that we can show this by Rule R itself as per the argument:

Use of Rule R has for the most part guided us aright

— Rule R

Use of Rule R will (probably) guide us aright in general
[and its use is thus justified]

Patently, this argument will establish the acceptability of its conclusion only if we *already* have in hand an adequate (and thus noncircular and Rule-R-independent) justification of Rule R. That is, the argument is only cogent if it is probatively *redundant*, and is thus pointless because it can accomplish its task only if it is altogether *dispensable*.

As these considerations indicate, circularity is also bound to arise when a process of argumentation is used in its own support – when the very argument-form at issue is question-beggingly invoked for its own substantiation, be it explicitly or tacitly.

Now it is important to note that this is certainly not the

case with our present justification of induction. For we emphatically do *not* argue along the lines of the following
inference:

- By induction itself (with reference to the success of our
  past inductive endeavors) we establish that induction
  is a generally successful method of reasoning
- A generally successful method of reasoning is *eo ipso*
  rationally justified (i.e., its deliverances merit acceptance)

∴ Induction is rationally justified (i.e., its deliverances
  merit acceptance)

Such a line of argumentation would clearly be improper in that
it invokes – in its first premiss – the validity of the very process
of argumentation whose legitimacy the argument is desired to
establish. The key fact, however, is that the present methodological justification of induction is altogether free from this
sort of problem. Let us examine this important consideration
more closely.

Our course of justificatory reasoning envisages a two-stage
process: (i) an *initial justification* that is wholly noninductive
but is developed through *faute de mieux* argumentation, and
(ii) an *experiential retrojustification* that proceeds inductively
on the basis of applicative success. Now the crucial point is
that the use of induction in the course of its own validation
occurs only at stage (ii), where we do indeed argue from experienced successes to generic efficacy, staking a strongly committal, positive knowledge-claim as to facts about the effectiveness of induction. There is, however, no begging the question here. When it comes to the substantiation of this positive
knowledge-claim at issue in the second phase of argumentation, where our initial recourse to the inductive method is
duly *retrojustified*, it fortunately transpires that the results of
the initial phase of justificatory argumentation are already
available to meet our needs. At this later stage of its actual use
we *already* have induction in hand, duly endowed with its
initial justification – a justification which, albeit weak, does
carry a legitimate weight sufficient for this early stage of the
discussion. (Just this was, after all, the very reason for being

of the initial justification – to render the use of induction a reasonable proposition even in advance of its further justification through demonstrated efficacy.)

There is no escaping the fact that the linkage between the *rationality* of inductive method on the one hand, and its *efficacy* (its prospects or promise of success) on the other, can only be provided *ex post facto* through experience – that is to say, *inductively*. The trick is to render this sort of self-reliance probatively viable. And this is exactly what our two-phased argumentation makes possible.

2. THE INDUCTIVE ASPECT OF THE PROPOSED JUSTIFICATION

The present methodological-pragmatic approach to justifying induction accordingly resembles the Peircean tactic of using some sectors of inductive reasoning to justify others, while yet insisting on an *a priori*, noninductive starting point for the justificatory enterprise. But it differs from the justificatory strategy of Peirce (and Reichenbach) in one very fundamental respect. For on our approach, the question of the *actual success* of any inductive method is seen as crucial for an effective justification, and yet is something that can only be determined empirically (and thus inductively). This means that *a priori* considerations cannot of themselves bear the sort of justificatory weight that Peirce and Reichenbach accord to them.

Let us review the legitimating resources invoked in the course of the argumentation. Our invocation of noninductive methodological considerations is never asked to do more than provide a starting point. We begin by counting upon them to carry a very modest burden of justificatory argument: on the positive side, that the method has certain – themselves indecisive – purely theoretical advantages (with reference to simplicity, systematicity, etc.); on the negative side that there is no reason (at this stage of the matter) to think any other method superior. This first, purely theoretical stage is one of mere *faute de mieux* argumentation.

We next move to another stage of the justificatory argument – one which is already empirical – with the claim that there is some reason to think that the method is successful in that its use is (to all appearances) attended by some success. Now all we can observationally determine is that success *follows upon* implementation of the method, but not that it is *due to* it: *post hoc* is not *propter hoc*. The attribution of success to method-implementation thus also involves an inductive step. As the argumentation proceeds, we move ever more deeply into the empirical, inductive domain, first to the method's being "more successful than alternatives" and finally to its being "at least somewhat successful *per se* (noncomparatively)." But throughout these later, inductive stages we already have some pre-validated inductive machinery in hand – fortunately so, since this is what we need. (For example, the move from "somewhat successful in the sample of observations" to "somewhat successful *per se*" clearly requires the straight rule of proportional induction.)

The whole methodologically justificatory process is one of pulling ourselves up by the bootstraps. Initially, at the very outset, *a priori* considerations are put to work. They give us not full-blooded justification, but mere *protojustification* for certain inductive processes. But once these are available – however tentatively – they can be used to retrojustify themselves, and they are thereupon available to justify inductively still other sectors of the inductive method. Step by step, the feedback cycle of this argumentation enables us to develop a more and more ample retrojustification of our *a priori* starting points. But throughout these later phases of the process we use – and cannot help but using – inductive mechanisms whose use is already validated (in some measure) by earlier phases of the argument. And the methodological justification of induction is so structured as to underwrite the legitimacy of such a process.

In the end we are brought back to a crucial reliance upon initial, induction-independent, *faute de mieux* considerations which, though weak, are to be welcomed as useful and indeed necessary just because they are at bottom *inevitable*. For the division of labor between initial justification and ultimate retrojustification means that we do not come empty-handed to the latter, inductive task. The aim of the division of justificatory labor between initial and ultimate is just exactly to provide a noninductive basis for building up what is – and unashamedly can be – a fundamentally inductive justification of induction, along the lines set out in Figure VII.1. There is no vicious or vitiating circularity here, but a systematic feedback process of sequential *self*-substantiation supervenient on an initial *other*-substantiation. A cyclic process of this sort makes it possible without viciousness to validate a method by use of its own products.

Figure VII.1

THE PROBATIVE STRUCTURE OF THE
METHODOLOGICAL JUSTIFICATION OF INDUCTION

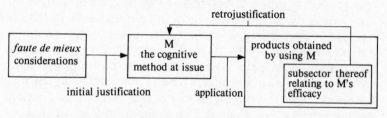

There is good reason for envisaging such a multi-stage procedure. A cognitive method, just like a person, can only *establish* credit by being *given* credit. That first step of trust must be taken – however small or tentative it might be. To become credited – or discredited – a method must be given enough rope to hang itself. Consider an example. A deliverance of memory can only be checked and refuted by some other item drawn from memory. Here, too, we can show (by this-or-nothing argumentation) that only an experiential-inductive substantiation can be provided. Now how could such an inductive argument proceed? Clearly it must take the form of arguing from the premiss that "memory has generally proven reliable in the past" to the conclusion that "memory will generally prove reliable." But how could this premiss possibly be secured? Obviously only by memory! Whatever self-reliance there is here is clearly unavoidable, and for that very reason cannot be condemned as vicious. One cannot reasonably regard as a shortcoming what cannot be helped in the very nature of things. And this holds for induction as well. Once induction is given initial approbation – however tentatively and provisionally – it can grow apace, feeding on its own resubstantiation.

3. SELF-SUBSTANTIATION

The present inductive justification of induction does not rest on any fine distinction between good and bad circularity. Rather, it manages to avoid circularity altogether through its specifically methodological orientation.

It is certainly true that a *thesis* must never be employed in its own probative support. And this – as we have seen – holds also for a *particular* rule of reasoning or inference as well. But this is not true of something as general as a *method* – and certainly not of a cognitive method. In showing the propriety of our cognitive tools we may have no alternative but to put them to work in their own behalf.[4] There is no circularity here – nothing vicious or vitiating; it is simply a part of that systemic self-supportingness which is a requisite of any adequate cognitive instrumentality. A defense of reasoning must use reasoning. What we have here is not a vicious circle, but an essential feedback mechanism that reflects the ultimately systemic aspect of all justificatory argumentation. There is thus no viciousness here because one would expect – and indeed demand – that any rationally warranted process of reasoning emerge as justified on its own telling. Any fact-oriented verification-method of a sufficiently broad scope can always be turned upon itself and its performance evaluated from its own point of view. For if it is capable of serving as a test of general factual theses, then general claims about *its own* performance will also fall within its scope.

To clarify this recourse to systematic coherence and self-substantiation, let us consider the worthwhile contrast-case of an admittedly artificial (and even perverse) inquiry procedure, that of *counterinductivism*. The counterinductivist adapts the following policy of validation for empirical generalizations:

If a generalization has been applied *un*successfully (sic) in

---

[4] Some of the lines of thought in this discussion are developed at greater length in the author's *Methodological Pragmatism* (Oxford, 1976).

prior applications, one is to infer its (probable) success in the application presently in hand; and if it has been applied successfully in prior applications, one is to infer its (probable) failure in the case in hand. (Cf. p. 25 above.)

This counterinductivist approach to inquiry *appears* to be thoroughly self-sustaining; given its manifest failures in the past, we would be led – by the standards of the principle itself – also apply this method in present cases. Yet in a somewhat deeper sense this method is not self-sustaining. For our interest in any *method* is always systematic: we care not simply about *this* application (or the next or the next two or three), but at least about the whole sequence of applications in the near term – if not about the long run as well. (A procedure to be applied in one special case hardly qualifies as a *method*.) And from *this* perspective, the method of counterinduction does not really qualify as self-sustaining. For consider the question: "What would lead the counterinductivist to feel increased confidence – by the standards of his own method – that this method is effective in its future application beyond the next two or three cases?" The obvious answer is its *failure* in the near term cases – specifically including its *present* application. We thus reach the paradoxical result that the best support this "method" can provide for itself lies in its failure to work in the case at hand. The very fact that this method realizes its goals in a given case counts *against* its future employment. For if the counterinductivist is to have warrant – by his own standard – for the continued use of his method in cases beyond the horizons of the present moment, then he must refrain from endorsing the application of his method in the present case (*any* present case!) because its actual effectiveness in this case would only count against its effectiveness in further applications. Thus, the counterinductivist method fails to achieve self-sustainingness in the *systematic* sense and thereby emerges as ultimately incoherent.[5]

As we have seen, our principles of inductive systematization have the feature that they are themselves monitored by con-

---

[5] Compare also A. Öfsti, "Some Problems of Counter-Inductive Policy as Opposed to Inductive," *Inquiry*, vol. 5 (1962), pp. 267–283.

ditions of systematic order. This aspect of fit, of conformation, of a closing of the cycle of retrovalidation, is itself an aspect of systematicity. For it is inherent in the conception of the "appropriateness" of a principle that is must be of *general* applicability. The principles by which we do our "ground floor" inductions regarding the empirical facts of nature must thus be the same as those by which we do "higher order" inductions regarding our methods and procedures – including our cognitive methods. Our inductive methods should be self-sustaining in this way. Inductive self-substantiation is thus not a matter of vicious circularity, but is itself an aspect of that systematicity through which alone cognitive adequacy can be determined.

The sort of methodological self-substantiation that is at issue in these deliberations is simply a matter of that smooth systematic dovetailing of our cognitive resources that is the hallmark of their rational adequacy. The argumentation is *comprehensively systematic*, placing its several elements into a coordinative framework which unites them within one overall nexus of mutual substantiation.

As C. S. Peirce stressed a century ago, self-correctiveness is a requisite for any cognitive method by which we claim to learn from experience. If a cognitive method does not work, this fact is something that the method itself should not block from our view but, rather, should itself enable us to discover. And if the specific way in which we are using the method is deficient and capable of improvement, this too is something the method should be able to bring to our notice. An adequate method of learning from experience must be self-monitoring – it must be such that even the way in which we use it can be improved upon by its own means. The sort of self-monitoring at issue in the inductive monitoring of induction is a token of adequacy rather than a defect of circularity, precisely because of its capacity to set in motion a feed-back cycle of self-conformation and self-improvement.

The important point deserves stress that in methodological justification self-resort is bad only when this procedure commits the fallacy of question-begging (*petitio principii*) so as to preempt the prospect of error-discovery and correction. A methodological justification of induction certainly avoids this defect. Its self-recourse is harmless precisely because it is compatible with defeasibility – the potential discovery of mistakes in the wake of actual experience. What is critical is corrigibility – and *self*-correctiveness will (if genuine) serve perfectly well.

4. WHY ALLOW EXPERIENCE TO COUNT?

Why allow our favorable experience with induction to count in its behalf? The reply here is that the adequacy claims of any cognitive method must be capable of control and that experience is, in the end, the only *available* sort of controlling monitor we can have in this domain. The complaint that such a course would be circular, since induction is itself our experience-exploiting method, is to be met by the observation that we simply have no alternative – this or nothing! If you are *not* prepared to let our experience with induction count in its favor, then you cut yourself off immediately and *a priori* from developing the only course of reasoning along which a fully adequate – and thereby efficacy-oriented – justification of such a method of inquiry could ever be developed.

The literature of the justification of induction affords various instances of the following line of thought:

> Hume has shown decisively that we cannot establish that any predictive method – such as induction – will be successful. It follows that we must sever the question of establishing the *rationality* of the use of induction from the question of establishing its *efficacy*. Accordingly effectiveness and rationality must be treated as altogether separate issues.[6]

Such a position is ultimately untenable. With induction – as with any method – we cannot sever the issue of rationality of employment from that of task-realizing efficacy. It would be

[6] This position underlies P. F. Strawson's contention that while the "success of induction" is (at best) a contingent fact about this world, the "rationality of induction" is a matter of conceptual necessity. Cf. *Introduction to Logical Theory* (London, 1952), pp. 261–262.

foolish to adopt a method whose effectiveness could not be presumed, and asinine to employ one whose effectiveness is counter-indicated. But there is only one way in which the actual efficacy of the inductive method can be established – namely, through an appeal to the tribunal of experience. (As Hume and his followers have rightly insisted, the success of induction is not *and cannot be* guaranteed *a priori* and in advance.) This being so – necessarily and as a matter of the general principles of the case – it is absurd to require that it should be accomplished (*ultra posse nemo obligatur*; "ought" implies "can"). So we must be content to establish this important aspect of the justification of induction through the only effective means at our disposal for doing so, namely inductive ones. And there is no harm in this, no vitiating circularity as long as, at the eventual stage at which the relative success of the inductive method is inductively argued for, we already have in hand some *preliminary* noninductive justification. (The crucial merit of a methodological justification of induction is that it provides for such an essential prejustification possible by *faute de mieux* means.)

These considerations show how a consistent empiricism becomes possible in the face of argumentation by Bertrand Russell and others that empiricism cannot provide a justification of induction:

> The inductive principle, however, is . . . incapable of being *proved* by an appeal to experience. . . . . All arguments which, on the basis of experience, argue as to the future or the unexperienced parts of the past or present, assume the inductive principle; hence we can never use experience to prove the inductive principle without begging the question. Thus we must either accept the inductive principle on the ground of its intrinsic evidence, or forgo all justification of our expectations about the future.[7]

The situation in which we are left by Russell is one of a Hobson's choice between the unworkable rationalism of a wholly *a priori* validation of induction on the one hand, and the emptiness of radical scepticism on the other. The

---

[7] Bertrand Russell, *The Problems of Philosophy* (Oxford, 1912), pp. 106–107.

methodological-pragmatic justification of induction has the important merit of enabling us to evade the horns of this dilemma. It manages to provide us with a justificatory starting point that avoids dubious rationalistic presuppositions and proceeds to an inductive validation of induction in a way that manages to avert vitiating circularity

VIII

Humean Issues

SYNOPSIS
(1) A methodological-pragmatic justification of induction seemingly runs afoul of Hume's barrier in arguing from "has been successful in the past" to "is successful in general" (and thence to "is justified"). (2) But this appearance of transtemporal argumentation is misleading. As we have seen, the basic grounding of the justification is (in the first instance, at any rate) not of this temporal and inductive sort at all; it is a matter of *faute de mieux* argumentation. (3) A consideration of the sceptical objection that: "A methodological-pragmatic justification of induction does no more than to show that inductive reasoning is legitimate with respect to *practical* matters, but does not show that such inferences are legitimate from the *theoretical* point of view." The fact is that all the legitimate requirements on the theoretical side can in fact be satisfied through the practical deliberations of a methodological justification.

1. HUME'S PROBLEM

A pragmatic justification of induction seemingly runs afoul of Humean considerations. For the direction of its overall argumentation is that of a transition from success to justification, from "is successful" to "is justified." And here the question at once arises: how is one to establish the antecedent part of this implication – how can one show that induction is an effective method? To all appearances, there is no choice but to establish this claim itself by inductive means, arguing through the transition from "has been successful in the past" to "is successful in general." But any such course of argumentation from the past to the future is precluded by Hume's insistence that the past just does not offer failproof cognitive guarantees for the future. This reentry of Hume's problem appears to put a serious obstacle in the way of any experientally pragmatic justification of induction of the sort at issue in the present methodological approach. This must – and fortunately can – be overcome.

2. THE STRUCTURE OF EXPERIENTIAL JUSTIFICATION: THE CENTRALITY OF *FAUTE DE MIEUX* REASONING

In confronting this Humean difficulty, it is crucially important to realize that the course of the present pragmatic argumentation does *not* take the line of the transition from "has succeeded in the past" to "succeeds in general" and then to "is justified." Rather, our argumentation turns on a *faute de mieux justification for continuing to rely on a (relatively) successful method*, an argument which proceeds

– There is *some* reason to think that the method is effective
– There is no reason at hand to think that any alternative
method will work better

∴ We are rationally justified in using the method in view.

To be sure, the establishment of the first premiss will turn on the contention that we must allow a record of experienced success with a method to bear *some* weight towards establishing its general efficacy – experienced success qualifies as an index of adequacy to at least some extent. And so the following objection may be pressed: "This pragmatic line of approach to justification could not do its justificatory task if facts about working in the past are devoid of probative weight *vis-à-vis* success in the future." But this objection misses its mark. The crucial issue is one regarding the mechanics of justificatory argumentation in the practical sphere. The point is simply and atemporally: Why should a method's having *some* success constitute grounds towards its promise of proving successful in general? As we have seen, the answer to this pivotal question lies in a fundamentally this-or-nothing argument that proceeds on the following lines:

> If you are prepared to let *anything* in the way of conceivably available information count towards rationalizing a claim of actual effectiveness for a practical precept or method (that is, if in this practical context you are going to play the rationality game of giving grounds and reasons at all), then you simply have no alternative to letting "it works in some cases as best we can tell" count, because it is true *as a matter of principle*, that in the case of a practice or method rooted in the contingent sphere of empirical fact, this is the only sort of "evidence" of actual efficacy that one can ever hope to have in hand.

Such a this-or-nothing argument can provide the basis for validating the step of giving at least *some* probative weight to the experiential data in such practice-justifying cases. And, as we have seen, even a weak grounding of this sort can render good service in the context of praxis. For it establishes a presumption which – in the practical domain – is quite sufficient as a basis for acceptance (acceptance, to be sure, of a *method*, not of a *thesis*). The consideration that rationalizes – under *faute de mieux* conditions – the practical policy of *continuing* (in the absence of any specific and sufficiently weighty indications to the contrary) to use a method (procedure) that has, to all appearances, succeeded in the past is just this very fact of its apparent success. This weak consideration exerts a practical impetus in and of itself; no more ambitious claims need be made for it.

We thus have no quarrel with Hume here: Our methodological argumentation does not ask the past to give cognitive guarantees for the future. No transtemporal *inference* is at issue at all – no theoretical argumentation from past-oriented premises to some future-oriented conclusion. Of course, success in the past does not assure continued success. But the mere fact of apparent efficacy in certain cases does, after all, serve to

afford *some* reason or ground – however tentative and incon-
clusive – for thinking that the procedure may work in general.
In the practical sphere, instances of apparent success must be
allowed to carry *some* justificatory (or at any rate
presumption-establishing) weight in point of general efficacy.
And if there is no ground for thinking that any other, alternative method at hand will do better, then we do, after all, here
have adequate rational warrant – based on *faute de mieux*
considerations – for the continued use of our present method.
The justification we obtain is that of the essentially practicalist
consideration of having done the very best that it is possible to
do in the circumstances in which we find ourselves.

Do we really know that arsenic will continue to poison and
bread to nourish? It is, of course, perfectly true that, as sceptical philosophers so cogently argue, no firm theoretical guarantee can possibly be given here. What has been characterized
as "Hume's problem" by some philosophers – viz., that of
demonstrating the efficacy of induction– is a pseudo-problem.
The very fact that it is in principle unsolvable on its own terms
shows its illegitimacy. Its underlying argumentation asks for
what, in the nature of things, cannot be vouchsafed – a failproof guarantee of invariable or at any rate general future
efficacy. But given the fact of its unattainability, the demand
for such a guarantee is itself unwarrantable and irrational.[1]
Indeed, we may take Hume to have shown with all the lucidity
that philosophical arguments admit of that there simply can be
no "justification of induction" by way of a demonstrative
proof that induction must always or indeed even generally succeed. This is not only true, but true as a matter of the theoretical general principles of the case. And the important lesson to
be drawn from this is that it is irrational to ask for one. It is
senseless to make demands or impose conditions which cannot
in the very nature of things be satisfied, and absurd to require
the performance of a task whose accomplishment is manifestly
impossible.

What legitimates our conviction that we should plan for the
morrow, on the basis of our belief that there will continue to be
a world in times to come? The answer is simply "It's this or

[1] This contention represents the main thrust of Jerrold Katz's *The Problem of
Induction and its Solution* (Chicago, 1962).

nothing." To act, to plan, to survive, we must anticipate the future, and the past is the only guide to it that we have. Imperfect as it is, and misleading though it may often be, we've got to rely on it as best we can: its guidance is all we've got. We are a cognitive creature that must use the past to divine the future. We cannot guarantee that we will not be mistaken – it is possible, nay likely, that we will be wrong much of the time. No Cartesian deity has made a cognitive covenant with us to assure the successful issue of even our most rational contrivings. We cannot give what we do not have, and so can issue no guarantees of the future. We simply have to do the best we can, and this is exactly what induction is all about: it is our methodology for doing what we can. There is not – and cannot be – any assured *guarantee* that rationally guided action will be successful. Even the best laid and most rationally contrived plans can misfire. Reality is not always and inevitably on the side of our strongest arguments and best theoretical contrivances. All we can do – and all we can rationally be asked to do – is the best we can.

We do not, we cannot, and we need not argue that the future is like the past. We do not, we cannot, and we need not argue that recourse to the inductive method will be attended by success.[2] Indeed, if induction from the history of science indicates any conclusion, it is that the scientific method leads us astray, that our science is wrong, that scientists two or three generations hence will think of our own science as shot through with errors of omission and commission.[3] Sceptics throughout the ages have always maintained – quite rightly – that inductive inferences may prove mistaken and fail to yield us the actual facts. Yet this sort of contention, albeit correct, misses its mark. For when used to counter the justification of induction, it commits an *ignoratio elenchi*. A justification of induction need not issue in any *preassurance* of its success. Initially and in the first instance, it is a matter of *faute de mieux* argumentation: insofar as we have reason to think that the job

[2] Already Sextus Empiricus argued (*Outlines of Pyrrhonism*, Bk. II, §195) that induction is not reliable since by induction we would conclude that all animals eat by moving the lower jaw, a conclusion falsified by the crocodile.

[3] C. S. Peirce wrote: "Why, according to my estimate of probabilities there is not a single 'truth of science' upon which we ought to bet more than about a million of millions to one." (*Collected Papers*, vol. I, sect. 150.)

can be done at all, we have reason to think that induction can do it. And *ultimately* we have recourse to retrojustification – a revalidation which again does not guarantee success but only offers us some assurance of efficacy and of relative optimality – the systematic dominance over the envisaged rivals.[4]

The challenge of the Humean sceptic runs roughly as follows: How is it that you can, on inspecting part of the whole, claim to know what holds of it in entirety, or by examining the past claim to secure knowledge of the future? The response is that this sort of thing is just what empirical knowledge is all about – that no exaggeration, no fallacy, is at work here. The concept of "knowledge" so operates that such knowledge-claims are wholly appropriate, that such claims are made – and received – in full understanding that a realistic, and not hyperbolically unattainable standard is at work in the groundrules that govern our knowledge-claims.

A sceptic will doubtless protest: "But how, given your concessions about the fallibilism of our inductive processes, can you possibly claim your inductive conclusions as true?" The answer lies in the consideration that in the interests of uniformity we must apply *to* our science the same methods of reasoning that we apply *within* our service. And this leads back to the systematist's procedure of inference to the best explanation. Clearly the best explanation of the successful praxis that our science underwrites is that its methods do actually

[4] The only sort of justification of induction capable of effective development thus falls into the family generally known as "vindications":

> The type of justification . . . called "vindication," as Herbert Feigl termed it, . . . resolves Hume's problem by bypassing it. We know for certain that what Hume desired – namely, certification of the soundness of inductive argument by the standard of demonstrative reasoning – cannot be supplied. But . . . by conceiving the practice of induction as the adoption of certain policies, applied in stoic acceptance of the impossibility of [deductively] assured success in obtaining reliable knowledge concerning matters of fact, we are able to see that such policies are, in a clear sense, preferable to any of their competitors. (Max Black, article "Induction" in *The Encyclopedia of Philosophy*, ed. by P. Edwards, vol. 4 [New York, 1967], p. 176.)

To be sure, the crucial difference among the various sorts of vindication-justifications of induction can differ drastically as regards the "clear sense" in which they see induction as superior to its alternatives. Here the characteristic aspect of our own methodological pragmatic justification that it permits this superiority to be viewed itself in a specifically inductive light – and yet manages to do this without any vicious or vitiating circularity.

achieve a fairly good job at truth-estimation. Retro-justification at the methodological level thus provides a reasonable basis for the truth-claims consequent upon our use of these methods. Here too the answer to the sceptic lies in assuming the systematists' perspective that has been at work throughout these deliberations.

3. THE HUMEAN SCEPTIC'S CHARGE OF *IGNORATIO ELENCHI*

One critically important facet of this *faute de mieux* aspect of our pragmatic-methodological justification deserves comment. It is a *method-pragmatism* and not a *thesis-pragmatism* that is at issue. What we do through *faute de mieux* reasoning is to commit ourselves to a certain method, which, since it is a *cognitive* method, in turn serves to determine belief or acceptance. We do *not* underwrite any thesis *directly* through *faute de mieux* deliberations. Hence, we are *not* concerned with what Kant calls "pragmatic beliefs" and which he characterizes as follows:

> The physician must do something for the patient in danger, but does not know the nature of his illness. He observes the symptoms, and if he can find no more likely alternatives, judges it to be a case of phthisis. . . . Such contingent belief, which yet forms the ground for the actual employment of means and certain actions, I entitle *pragmatic belief.*[5]

What Kant has in view here is a matter of the best-bet adoption of a maxiprobable thesis for the sake of guiding action under the pressure of necessity – a kind of inferior, "merely practical" quasi-knowledge. But our present theory does not take this line: its pragmatism is oriented towards the adoption of an optimal *method* and not towards beliefs or theses.

To be sure, it is a *belief-determinative* method that is at issue, a method of high-estimation via the choice of a "best alternative." But we construe this *alethically,* as "most promising for being true relative to validated norms" – and not *pragmati-*

[5] Immanuel Kant, *Critique of Pure Reason*, B852.

cally, as "most promising in point of (probable) goal attainment." We are concerned with *alethic* and not *pragmatic* optimality, despite the fact that, on our theory, it is through pragmatic optimality (at the methodological level) that alethic optimality (at the thesis level) is ultimately determined.

A practicalist vindication-justification of the reasonableness of induction along these pragmatic lines seemingly still leaves it open for the Humean sceptic to invoke the ancient (indeed Platonic) division between what is valid for practice and what is valid for theory:

> Your argumentation commits the fallacy of *ignoratio elenchi*. It argues to the wrong conclusion. What one wants to know is not that adoption of inductive method is "reasonable" (in some pragmatic, praxis-oriented sense), but rather that we are entitled to expect that induction will deliver the goods – that there are good *theoretical* reasons for expecting that our inductively based beliefs will in general turn out to be correct, that as a matter of substantive fact induction *is actually effective*.

The best reply to this objection is to press the question of just what it is that the sceptical objector actually requires. His own argumentation is designed to show that a certain sort of "theoretical" justification of our inductive praxis is in principle unrealizable. But this is clearly self-defeating as a prelude to asking for just such a justification.

Philosophical sceptics generally set up some abstract standard of absolutistic incorrigibility and then proceed to show that no knowledge-claims in a given area (sense, memory, induction, etc.) can possibly meet this standard. From this, they infer that such a category of "knowledge" is impossible. But this inference is altogether misguided. For surely what actually follows is simply the inappropriateness or incorrectness of the standard at issue. If the vaunted standard is such that knowledge-claims cannot possibly meet it, the appropriate moral is not "too bad for knowledge-claims," but rather "too bad for the standard." For it is senseless to impose conditions which cannot in the very nature of things be met. To repeat: obligation does not exceed the limits of the possible. Once all

that is reasonably possible – i.e., all that can *appropriately* be
expected – has been done to assure some knowledge-claim, it is
unreasonable, nay *irrational,* to ask for more.

A certain irony emerges here. To the extent that the sceptic
"proves" his case by a clever deployment of considerations
regarding the theoretical general principles of the matter, he
thereby destroys it. For one would naturally reply:

> Let it be even as you say, that it is not possible to de-
> monstrate the general correctness of our inductive claims.
> Then this fact *itself* shows the impropriety, indeed the
> absurdity, of such absolutistic demands. It makes no
> sense to ask for what is *in principle* not to be had: one
> cannot demand the impossible.

To the extent that the sceptic's argument succeeds, his conception of "validated inductive knowledge" is untenable in
imposing on our inductive reasoning conditions that cannot in
principle be met.

The present analysis has its own characteristic way of avert-
ing the thrust of the sceptic's complaint that our inductive
reasonings are "merely good enough for practice, but not
adequate to the demands of theory," that the results they yield
are merely "pragmatic beliefs" in the Kantian sense considered above. This objection, too, is turned aside by the methodological orientation of our argumentation. For the methodological approach is so designed as to look on theorizing as
itself constituting a mode of practice. Its basic strategy is to
assimilate the question of cognitive methods to the the case of
methods in general. It seeks to validate our *cognitive* methodology along generically methodological (i.e., *pragmatic*) lines
through recourse to the ground-rules for the justification of
our practical tools and instruments in general. We thus argue
against the sceptic that he must also be prepared to apply with
respect to our *cognitive* practice in the domain of factual inquiry what he is prepared to accept as "good enough for
practice in general." Insofar as the demands of praxis are able
to exert a legitimative force – as the sceptics (Hume himself
included) have generally been prepared to grant – this legitimative force can be invoked on behalf of our *cognitive* praxis

as well, and can thus also be invoked in support of our subscription to those contentions that this praxis authorizes. The option of the sceptical philosopher of antiquity who, disdaining to engage in what he could not justify, simply ceased *talking* and just went along *doing* is not ultimately coherent. Our assertoric and cognitive activity is itself a mode of praxis. If one is prepared to allow a practicalist justification for other departments of our praxis, one cannot properly stop short of allowing it for our *cognitive* praxis as well – induction included.

When all is said and done, the present methodological-pragmatic justification of induction is accordingly not all that far removed from Hume's own position. It endorses fully his emphatic insistence that our inductive reasonings cannot be validated by any theoretical argumentation proceeding from grounds of general principle. And it, too, accepts Hume's inference that this incapacity means that our reliance on induction must be justified in terms of considerations not of the theoretical but of the practical sphere. The point in which we do diverge from Hume is in taking the burden of validation to rest not on the operation of a practical *instinct*, but on the probative weight of deliberations of practical *reason* in relation to the legitimation of our cognitive methods.[6]

[6] Some of the lines of thought of this chapter are worked out more fully in the author's *The Primacy of Practice* (Oxford, 1973), *Methodological Pragmatism* (Oxford, 1977), and especially in *Scepticism* (Oxford, 1980).

IX

Induction and Communication

SYNOPSIS

(1) Inductive *reasoning* is broader than inductive *inference* in also encompassing our *categorical* factual judgments whose inductive basis also needs to be justified. (2) The existence of an "evidential gap" here entails that the assertive content of any statement of objective fact outruns the evidence we ourselves ever do (and can) have in hand about it. (3) This gap is only to be crossed by an *imputation* that transcends the available information, and so involves the characteristically inductive "leap beyond the evidence in hand." Since *judgment* is not *inference*, this imputational process indicates that the realm of inductive *reasoning* is larger than that of inductive *inference*. (4) The validation of such inductive imputations is ultimately pragmatic, and so their justification of our inductive imputations runs parallel to that of our inductive inferences.

1. INTRODUCTION

Any satisfactory justification of induction must come to grips with the fact that the range of *inductive reasoning* is larger than that of inductive *inference*. Inference is *hypothetical* – it has an if-then structure in moving from the data that furnish given or assumed *premisses* to the correlative *conclusions* that they underwrite. Reasoning, however, can be *categorical* as well, operating to establish certain unconditional claims or contentions. And induction is operative in this categorical sphere also wherever our categorically asserted theses outrun their supportive grounding. Our justification of induction will be inadequate if, in failing to address this categorical sector of inductive reasoning, it fails to do the whole of the justificatory job that must be done.

2. THE EVIDENTIAL GAP

It is necessary to distinguish from the very outset between objective factual assertions that make descriptive claims about "the real world" and those contentions that are merely subjectively phenomenological and appearance-oriented. Objective assertions deal – or purport to deal – with how things actually and objectively stand; phenomenological assertions merely deal with how things appear to people, or with what people think about them. (The relevant range of locutions here includes such qualifying expressions as "it seems to me," "it strikes me as," "it appears to me that," "I take it to be," "it reminds me of," etc.) This distinction between subjective and objective judgments underpins the very far-reaching fact that the *assertoric content* of objective factual claims is always so extensive as to render them inherently data-transcending. Let us explore more closely the ramifications of this present sort of "evidential gap," which pertains to induction in its categorical rather than hypothetical mode.

All discourse about real things as they actually exist in the world accordingly involves an element of *experience-transcending* commitment to claims that go beyond the acquirable information, but yet claims whose rejection would mean that we would have to withdraw the thing-characterization at issue. To say of the apple that its only features are those it actually manifests is to run afoul of our very conception of an apple. To deny – or even merely to refuse to be committed to the claim – that it *would* have such-and-such features *if* these and these things were done (e.g. that it would have such and such a taste if eaten) is to be driven to withdrawing the claim that it is an apple. A real apple must, for example, have a certain sort of appearance from the (yet uninspected) other side, and a certain sort of (yet uninspected) subcutaneous make-up. And if anything goes wrong in these respects, my claim that it was *an apple* I saw (rather than, say, a clever sort of apple-substitute, or something done with mirrors and flashes of colored light) must be retracted. The claim to see *an apple*, in short, cannot achieve a *total* (logically airtight) security on the basis of evidence-in-hand. Its content is bound to extend beyond the evidence that is actually – or even potentially – in our possession, and does so in such a way that the claim becomes vulnerable to defeat by further evidence. If, on the other hand, one "goes for safety" – and alters the claim to "It *seems to me* that I see an apple" or "I *take myself* to be seeing an apple" – this resultant claim in the language of appearance is effectively immune from defeat. Security is now assured. But such assertions purchase this security at the price of content. Pure phenomenal subjectivity as such is objectively vacuous.[1] No volume of claims in the language of subjectivity and appearance – however extensively they may reach in terms of how things "appear" to me and what I "take myself" to be seeing, smelling, etc. – can ever establish what *is actually the case* in the world. While they themselves are safe enough, appearance-theses – like theses about one's thoughts, beliefs, wishes, etc. – will thus inevitably fall short on the side of objective content.

Accordingly, objective factual claims are quite in general such that there is a wide gap between the data we do (and ever can) actually and specifically have at our disposal to make a claim warrantedly and the *substance* of this claim. The evidence-in-hand transcendence that is the hallmark of induction will accordingly also play a pivotal part throughout this objective, factual domain. Throughout this sphere, judgment – the intentional endorsement (making, propounding, accepting, etc.) of factual assertions – is a rational process of thought that is fundamentally inductive in character in that its informational claims and commitments outrun the evidential grounding on which they rest.[2] Induction thus lies at the very root of

---

[1] As C. S. Peirce put it,

Direct experience . . . affirms nothing – it just *is*. There are delusions, hallucinations, dreams. But there is no mistake that such things really do appear, and direct experience means simply the appearance. It involves no error, because it testifies to nothing but its own appearance. For the same reason it affords no [objective information]. (*Collected Papers*, vol. I, sect. 1.145.)

[2] It would, however, be very ill advised – indeed mistaken – to formulate the pre-

man's communicative use of language, since only on the basis of inductive processes of thought does it become possible to convey information about matters of objective fact. One must accordingly recognize the ubiquity of inductive mechanisms throughout the entire domain of our thought and discourse about the real world.

3. CROSSING THE EVIDENTIAL GAP: IMPUTATIONISM AND THE ROLE OF LANGUAGE – USE-CONDITIONS *vs.* TRUTH-CONDITIONS

All of our thinking about the real world – not only in scientific contexts but in the most ordinary circumstances of everyday life – takes place in a framework where the claims at issue go beyond the evidence actually at our disposal. An inevitable "evidential gap" separates the *assertoric content* of an objective claim – the range of what we become committed to in making it – from the *supportive data* we ever actually obtain for it. This "evidential gap" represents a fundamental fact of epistemic life. It is (clearly) not closed by information at our disposal, but by a *fact-transcending imputation*[3] – a claim of a postulational or conventional nature that steps beyond the probative resources at our command. Observation does not provide an *inferential* basis for making an "inductive leap" over the gap at issue, but merely inductive *cues and clues*.

Now the important point here is that imputation is not *inference*. It is not a matter of a move from given premises to a resulting conclusion elicited from them by the extraction of implicit commitments. We do not somehow *derive* or extract "objective theses" from "observed data"; to speak in such terms would be gravely misleading. The actual situation is one of exploiting cues and clues on the basis of which, given the

---

ceding point by saying: "Our objective factual statements always *say* more than we can actually *know*." For this prejudices the issue quite improperly in a sceptical direction. It is important in this context to recognize that the sphere of *knowledge* far exceeds that of the "actually and specifically verified." For a fuller treatment of the relevant issues, see the author's *Scepticism* (Oxford, 1980).

[3] Compare the author's *The Primacy of Practice* (Oxford, 1973), pp. 65–68.

assertion-norms that govern language-employment (its use-conditions), certain claims are appropriate and in order.

It thus emerges that the range of inductive *reasoning* is larger than that of inductive *inference*; for inductive reasoning embraces a domain of imputation-laden objective *judgment*, in which the extractive process of standardly premiss-relative *inference* has no part.

Such imputing is not, however, reckless, baseless, unfounded. It is a *warranted* imputation that has a suitable rationale of legitimation. But just what is it that underwrites the legitimacy – the warranting *rationality* – of an imputational process which involves cognitive commitments that outrun the evidence in hand? The answer is straightforward: it is *language* that does the job. The imputation at issue is not personal and idiosyncratic. Its ground-rules are a matter of public property: it is not a personal act but a public resource built into a social framework, based upon a communally available linguistic praxis. Such imputations are not a matter of human psychology (this is where Hume's resort to habit goes wrong), but rather are built into the conceptual scheme codified in language.

Clearly, the question of whether or not we are entitled to apply particular elements of our language in a certain way turns on the question of the established conventions that govern such usage. A language is governed by built-in conventions of various different sorts. Truth-conditions and inference rules are familiar from logical and semantical discussions.Such semantical rules of a language govern the truth-conditions of its statements by specifying what range of the *objective* circumstances (actual or possible) must obtain if these statements are to be made *correctly*. However, the *warranting conventions* or *use-conditions* that underly our standard practice in verbal communication are less familiar. In contrast to truth-conditions, the warranting conventions fix the governing norms of assertibility of its statements, and specify the *epistemic* circumstances (actual or possible) in which these statements can be made appropriately (or defensibly). The truth-conditions of a statement determine its assertive content, the consequences that can be derived from it (the set of all *ontological* circumstances in which what it says is true). And the use-conditions delineate the range of its evidential warranting (the set of all *epistemic* circumstances in which its assertion is warranted). Use-conditions established the norms of assertibility. They specify the circumstances under which certain claims are in order – including what sorts of further circumstances abrogate such entitlements.[4] They encompass, *inter alia*, the ground-rules of plausibility and presumption that indicate the standard bases on which our factual claims rest "in the absence of counter-indications" and determine the paradigmatic moves that can defeat such claims.

Given the *modus operandi* of language, these two issues of declarative content and use-authorizing data – of what follows from its application and what proceeds it, so to speak – cannot be equated with one another.[5] The fact that the *content* of an objective claim always far *outruns* our *evidence* for it means that the use-conditions of assertion-entitlement – the evidential warranting conventions – will encompass only a modest sector of the range envisaged by the truth-conditions correlative with content-determinations.

The data-transcendence of *all* factual discourse makes it inevitable that the reach of truth-conditions should extend beyond the verificational resources at issue in the use-conditions.[6] There will, of course, generally be *some* fairly intimate relationship between the truth-conditions of an objective functional statement and its use-conditions: the authorizing conditions for its warranted assertion. (After all, the realization of the use-conditions affords presumptive grounds for the range of claims at issue in truth-conditions.) But the

---

[4] See Ludwig Wittgenstein, *On Certainty* (Oxford, 1969), sect. 18.

[5] But which is it that determines the "meaning" of a statement – its truth-conditions or its use-conditions? This question is misguided in its either-or form. The term is sufficiently diffuse to encompass both issues.

[6] Recognition of the importance of use-conditions for objective factual concepts can be traced back to Immanuel Kant, who insists that in the absence of such conditions the concept at issue would be a pointless verbalism devoid of serious purport:

> We demand in every concept . . . the possibility of giving it an object to which it may be applied [i.e., a possible epistemic circumstance where it may come into operation]. In the absence of such [a potential] object, it has no meaning and is completely lacking in content. . . . Therefore, [objective] concepts . . . relate to empirical intuitions [i.e., conditions of potential, real-life applicability], that is, to the data for a possible experience. Apart from this relation they have no objective validity. (CPuR, A.239 = B.293; Kemp Smith.)

warranting conventions or use-conditions of our claims can – and indeed in the case of all objective claims *must* – fall short of exhausting their truth-conditions.

It is crucial to the very viability of language that the truth-conditions for its sundry assertions should embrace much more than the conditions of appropriate usage can manage to assure. As we have seen, "evidential gap" at issue with objective factual claims means that the *content* of every such claim involves such a variety of implications and ramifications that it would be in principle impossible to check them all. And since omniverification is *impossible*, it becomes through this very fact an irrational demand.

It is thus important to avoid confusing the evidential issue of use-conditions with the semantic issue of truth-conditions or assertive content. With respect to objective factual claims, the latter (truth-conditions) are so ramified that we could never establish complete epistemic control item by item over the whole of their extent. The task of monitoring them *in toto* would be unending. Were the use-conditions not something more manageable, any and all prospects of the assertoric use of language in the objective domain would be aborted at the outset. These two sets of conditions do not and – in the nature of things governing communication – cannot be made to coincide. To identify them would make demands that automatically render the warranted assertion of factual claims impossible, and do so *a priori*, on the basis of the general principles of the matter. One must accordingly resist any temptation to equate truth-conditions with warranting conventions or use-conditions, an identification which would be fatal to the capacity of language for accomplishing its proper work.[7]

These warranting conventions are intrinsic components of

---

[7] The ideas at issue have entered into recent philosophy at many points. Thus conditions of use and assertibility are presumably at issue where Wittgenstein speaks of "criteria." (Cf. Rogers Albritton, "Wittgenstein's Use of the Term 'Criterion'," *The Journal of Philosophy*, vol. 56 (1959), pp. 845–857.) Rudolf Carnap distinguishes between truth-criteria (= truth-conditions) and confirmation-criteria (= assertibility conditions). (See his "Truth and Confirmation" in H. Feigl and W. Sellars (eds.), *Readings in Philosophical Analysis* [New York, 1949], p. 120.) Cognate ideas are at work in Michael Dummett, *Frege: Philosophy of Language* (Oxford, 1973). Compare also Chap. I, "The Criteriology of Truth" of the author's *The Coherence Theory of Truth* (Oxford, 1973). The issues are dealt with at greater length in the author's *Scepticism* (Oxford, 1980).

the language – a part of what every child learns about the use of his native tongue "at mother's knee." For a crucial part of learning what a word *means* is to learn how it is *used* – i.e., to get a working grasp of the types of conditions and circumstances under which its use in certain ways is *appropriate*. And it deserves stress that the imputational processes operative here involve an "inductive" component based on an implicit view of "the way in which things work in the world."[8] The language of our descriptive discourse regarding the matters of objective fact is in its very nature a vehicle for evidence-transcending imputations.[9]

To be sure, it would be misleading to speak of use-conditions in terms of assertibility-*rules* so as to invoke the idea of "rules" in this connection. For the "rules" at issue are not, strictly speaking, *rules* at all; they are not formulated and codified; and doubtless they are not even codifiable, any more than are the "rules" for hitting a forehand in tennis. What is at issue is a matter of the characterizing conditions of a practice, of how-to-do-it guidelines, of tricks of the trade or skills, of what is learned largely through observation, imitation and practice rather than through mastery of and adherence to explicitly specifiable rules. The warranting conventions at issue are a constitutive aspect of the praxis of language-use.

But consider the following objection:

An assertibility condition takes the implicative form that if a contention P meets a certain epistemic condition C, then it is to be asserted:
   If $C(P)$, then $\vdash P$
Suppose now that P entails $Q: P \rightarrow Q$. Then we must clearly have:
   If $C(P)$, then $\vdash Q$
Thus $C(P)$ must suffice to assure the assertibility of each and every implicit consequence of P. Does this not preclude the prospect of any sort of epistemic gap between $C(P)$ and P?

The answer here is negative. To be sure, in asserting P, we are

---

[8] Cf. Chapter VI of the author's *The Primacy of Practice, op. cit.*, pp. 107–123.
[9] Compare the author's *Conceptual Idealism* (Oxford, 1973), pp. 86ff.

committed to asserting Q when (*ex hypothesi*) $P \to Q$ holds. But this emphatically does not mean that we are entitled to assert P only if $C(P)$ establishes epistemic control over each and every component of P – i.e., that we are to assert P only if both $C(P)$ and $C(P) \to P$ obtain. The point is that the authorizing implication

If $C(P)$, then $\vdash P$

is part of the "practical politics" of the epistemic life, and does not inhere in a logico-conceptual necessitation of the form $C(P) \to P$.

It is perfectly possible – and not only logically but realistically possible – that one should play the game correctly by all the epistemological rules and still come to a result that fails to be true.[10] For the truth of our objective claims hinges on "how matters really stand in the world" and not on the (inevitably incomplete) grounding or evidence or justification that we ourselves have in hand. The epistemic gap between the apparent and the real is *theoretically* unbridgeable in this imperfect world, whatever twists and turns we may take. We cannot cross it by logically failproof means, but only by imputation.

To repeat, the circumstances under which use-conditions become operative are not such as to issue in a necessitating guarantee for the truth-conditions. To say that the gap between $C(P)$ and P itself is crossed by an "inductive leap" of sorts is emphatically not to say that this gap is filled – at each and every juncture – by *ad hoc* evidence that fills up the hiatus.

A basis for imputation is thus built into the conceptual scheme reflected in our use of language. Our *concepts* are designed to work in such a way that what is – from the logical aspect alone – a seemingly unwarranted claim is in fact rationally warranted because "that's what's being said": the conceptual scheme embodied in the language incorporates a "theoretical" stance towards the world that embodies certain factual (and inevitably data-transcending) imputations. An

[10] Cf. Hilary Putnam, "Realism and Reason," *Proceedings and Addresses of the American Philosophical Association*, vol. 50 (1977), pp. 493–498 (see p. 485). Putnam argues that it is incoherent to suppose that a theory that satisfies all our epistemic criteria might be false. It is not made clear, however, why we should differ from others in this regard.

inductive component is thus involved in all of our factual statements about real objects. In making the inductive leap, we at the same time stand committed to what we have leapt over: we are always committed to more than we have in hand (epistemically speaking) by way of actually secured data. We always assert more than we have a strictly logical authorization for saying relative to the actual evidence actually at hand – and that is where assertibility conventions come in. An inductive commitment is at issue throughout the linguistic framework we employ for organizing and conveying our thought about the objective condition of things. And this inductive aspect of our categorial judgments of fact renders induction a larger topic than the domain of inductive inference alone.[11]

4. THE QUESTION OF LEGITIMATION

As the preceding considerations suggest, the authorizing basis for the imputational component of our objective categorical judgments ultimately roots in the purposive teleology of language-use – successful communication. The information that I myself have about a thing at first hand is always personal and egocentric – based upon the contingencies of what I "happen to have experienced" about it and what I "happen to have gathered" about the experience of others. In making objective assertions about something, it is thus crucial that I *intend* to discuss "the thing itself" rather than "the thing just precisely as I conceive of it" relative to the body of information I have about it. Only the former is something that somebody else can get hold of; the latter certainly is not. We could never establish communicative contact about a common objective item of discussion if our discourse were geared to things conceived of as corresponding just exactly with our own specific information about them. If our assertoric commitments did not go beyond our own data we would never be able to "get in touch" with others about a shared objective world.

There is – there can be – no demonstrable *proof* of the correctness of our experientially grounded but yet experience-transcending factual claims; there is simply the provision of *appropriate rational warrant* for accepting them as such.

[11] The ideas of this section are more fully developed in the author's *Scepticism* (*op. cit.*).

Accordingly, what we have here is not a *demonstration* that the rationally appropriate exploitation of experience does always or indeed even generally yield authentic knowledge. Rather, we have a probatively weaker argument to the effect that it is rationally warranted and appropriate to take the stance that it indeed does so. This line of reasoning is purpose-relative. It turns on the issue of the potential efficacy of means to ends. It does not demonstrate the correctness of our experience-transcending factual claims. Rather, it recognizes that the best we can do is to argue that in the purpose-relative context of our cognitive aims and objectives it is rational to accept them as true. This, to be sure, is not a conclusive demonstration of the thesis but a pragmatic defense of it. However, there is no warrant for any rational dissatisfaction here. For we must face the fact that, in the circumstances, this sort of argumentation is the strongest that can reasonably be asked because it is – in the very nature of the case – the strongest that can possibly be had.

The quintessentially inductive move beyond the evidence in hand is called for by any step into the domain of the publicly accessible objects in whose absence interpersonal communication about a shared world becomes impossible. The teleology of communication provides the ultimate warrant for the imputational information-in-hand transcendence of our assertions regarding matters of objective fact. In the absence of inductive commitments we lack an indispensable precondition of communication in the factual domain: without our imputational praxis of making evidence-in-hand transcending assertions, all communication about matters of objective fact would become impossible. The work of inductive *reason* is to enlarge the sphere of what we can communicate about (the range of the information we can convey); but the work of the imputational processes of inductive *judgment* is to put us into a position to communicate at all.

Yet just what validates the linguistic mechanisms that underpin the evidence-transcending imputations reflected in our objective factual judgments? The pragmatic aspect comes once more to the fore at this juncture. For the legitimation of the evidence-transcendence of our linguistic mechanisms is rooted in the demands of effective praxis. The evolutionary development of symbolic processes and conceptual schemes provides the key to rational validation here: they are *entrenched on Darwinian grounds and validated through pragmatic considerations*. The success of our inductive proceedings must be considered at least partly responsible for some of its accepted connections with our use of terms like "rational" and "justified". Indeed, induction's most dramatic and least understood success is its role in our acquisition of the rules governing our objective discourse in whose terms we learn to link terms to the world in such a way as to communicate with others about our personal experiences within the setting of a community-wide, shared set of empirically based commitments concerning what kinds of things there are and how we are to speak of them. In this intricate fabric of relations between the structural features of our discourse, its practical efficacy, and the inductive aspect of our use of language, the question of cognitive justification reasserts its complexity. But in the end, lines of thought parallel with those articulated in the preceding discussion of the pragmatico-evolutionary justification of our methodology of inductive inference also come into play here. They articulate an evolutionary pragmatism able to justify a conceptual framework whose concepts have a semantical meaning-content that goes beyond what the evidential basis of their application is or indeed could possibly be.

A closer look at the precise character of the justification of our evidence-transcending imputations is warranted. It was suggested above that this is simply a matter of this-or-nothing – that if we wish to achieve answers to our questions about the world and if we wish to communicate with one another about matters of objective fact, then we simply have no alternative but to undertake such evidence-transcending commitments. But we now see that this focus in this-or-nothing considerations is by no means the whole story. For the consideration that we *must* proceed in this way – the fact of *practical necessity* that there just is no alternative if our objective is to be reached – stops well short of achieving full adequacy in its justificatory force. It does not offer us any assurance that we actually will succeed in our endeavor if we do not proceed in this way; it just has it that we won't if we don't. The issue of actual effectiveness remains untouched. And here we have no choice but to proceed experientially – by the simple stratagem of "trying and seeing." Practical necessity remains a matter of *a priori* considerations, but efficacy – actual sufficiency – is again a matter of *a posteriori* experience. The justification at issue with efficacy emerges through pragmatic retrojustification – a retrospective revalidation in the light of experience. The pragmatic consideration that our praxis of inquiry and communication does actually work – that we can effectively and (by and large) successfully communicate with one another about a shared world, inquiry into whose nature and workings proceeds successfully as a communal project of investigation – is the ultimately crucial consideration that legitimates the evidence-transcending imputations built into the use-conditions of language.

In answering the question of what justifies our recourse to evidence-transcending imputations we thus proceed at two levels. On the negative side we confront the realization (1) that we *must* accept them; it is this or nothing, given the goals of the enterprise. (2) On the positive side, we rest in the fact of pragmatic retrojustification based on the fact that our proceeding in this way underwrites an actually effective praxis.

The warranting of the process of inductive *imputation* which underlies our objective factual discourse accordingly proceeds by a line of reasoning that parallels in its essentials that given for inductive *inference* in our earlier discussion. To begin with, there is an initial justification which proceeds with reference to practical necessity in noting that we must (inescapably) move beyond the "evidence in hand" if we wish to communicate about publicly accessible objects. In due course, the initial justification of this-or-nothing argumentation is supplemented and rounded off through pragmatic retrojustification. Once the imputational praxis is "in place" so to speak – i.e., once its use has some initial standing of credibility – then we can (without circularity) employ it in the course of its own support, through an appeal to "the record of experience." Once again, the prospect of an inductive justification of inductive reason becomes workable.

The present deliberations are important to the overall viability of our pragmatic-methodological justification of induction. In their absence, someone might well object: "Your proposed line of justification works only in the hypothetical and not the categorial case. It is all very well as far as the legitimation of inductive *inference* is concerned. But it leaves the no less important issues of inductive (i.e., data-transcendent) *judgment* unaccommodated." The aim of the present discussion is to avert this sort of objection.

X

Does Induction have Metaphysical Presuppositions?

SYNOPSIS

(1) Does induction require for its justification an *a priori* assumption of the uniformity of nature or some comparable metaphysical presupposition? (2) No, because our inductive systematicity-preference in the cognitive domain rests on considerations of methodology and does not call for any metaphysical presuppositions. Induction as a facet of the regulative drive for system is at bottom a methodological device of inquiry and can be justified on this basis. (3) The aim of the proposed metaphysical assumptions is to underwrite an advance guarantee of the success of induction, whereas its appropriate justification does *not* require any sort of advance guarantee of success. Insofar as our warranted confidence in the effectiveness of induction is a part of its justification, this is something that is, and quite properly can be, a retrospective result of our use of induction. (4) Induction thus need not presuppose the systematicity of nature. Its reliance on systematicity is not a recourse to a substantive position regarding the nature of the world, but to a methodological process that is as such devoid of ontological precommitments. (5) A refutation of the contention that metaphysical presuppositions are needed to rule out the *a priori* prospect of a plurality of alternative but equally eligible inductive systematizations of the data.

1. THE QUESTION OF METAPHYSICAL PRESUPPOSITIONS

It is often said that induction cannot be justified save on the basis of a metaphysical presupposition regarding the constitution of the world – the uniformity of nature, the finite complexity of nature, and lawfulness of nature as assured by a principle of causality, or some such substantive ontological thesis.[1] The validity of induction is thereby tied to some descriptive feature of the world. Any such view at once poses a king-sized problem. For how – save inductively – could we ever establish the substantive premiss at issue. And not only are such ontological principles hard to come by, but there is always the question of whether they could do the requisite job even if we had them. The uniformity of nature, for example, will not automatically do the trick itself. For there is nothing to prevent nature from being uniform in such a way as to defeat systematically all of our inductive endeavors. And, of course, it would not be very helpful to adopt as a variant the claim that nature in *appropriately* uniform (i.e., induction-supportively uniform). For while such a claim would (*ex hypothesi*) support induction, its reading of "Since nature is uniform, induction is effective" is vacuous and thereby unable to perform any useful justificatory labors because the issue is now put on a question-begging basis.[2] Moreover, one must not argue *ad difficilem per difficilius*, justifying the difficult by what is yet more so. It seems plausible enough that we should reason inductively. But to claim the uniformity of nature – or some comparable blockbuster principle of metaphysics – seems highly problematic.

The standing of such a metaphysical supposition is in-

[1] Bertrand Russell, for example, launches into a quest "to discover the minimum principles required to justify scientific inferences" and proceeds to enumerate five rather complex substantive "postulates required to validate scientific method." One of these, for example, is a thesis to the effect that: "Given any event *A*, it happens very frequently that, at any neighboring time, there is at some neighboring place an event very similar to *A*." See *Human Knowledge, its Scope and Limits* (London, 1948), pp. 487–496.

[2] Even Hume did not question the contention that induction will work if nature is appropriately uniform. The problem, clearly, is to determine whether or not nature is, in fact, so uniform. Compare Max Black's discussion in *Problems of Analysis* (Ithaca, NY, 1954), pp. 179–187.

variably questionable – no matter how we twist and turn, we can never feel altogether comfortable about its use. One does not relish being put into a position of having to support something so natural and plausible as our particular inductive arguments by something as relatively far-fetched and questionable as such metaphysical postulates. No very satisfactory justification of induction is to be found down this ontological road.

To be sure, *if* it were essential for a "justification of induction" to provide in advance – prior to and independently of any and all use of induction – an *a priori* guarantee that induction will succeed (always or generally or by and large), *then* we would indeed require a metaphysical thesis along the indicated lines as supporting premiss for our justificatory reasoning. And at this point, the justificatory program would become enmeshed in difficulties. Given that we have no telephone line to the recording angel, we clearly can give no validation to such a principle *a priori*, independently of the inductive exploitation of our experience of the ways of the world.

Fortunately, however, such metaphysical supports can be dispensed with. A methodological-pragmatic legitimation of induction requires no such substantive assumptions, but can – as we have seen – be articulated along very different practicalist lines that involve no resort to any such metaphysical presuppositions. On such an approach, what justifies our inductive proceedings is *initially* the consideration that there is *some* reason, conceivably a very scanty one, to think that this method may succeed (at reasonable cost), while yet no more promising alternative is available; and then, *ultimately*, that experiential retrovalidation which is forthcoming in the wake of actual trial. On such a justificatory strategy that unfolds along methodological-pragmatic lines, no prior guarantees of methodological success are required – most fortunately so, since none are forthcoming.

2. ONTOLOGICAL *vs.* METHODOLOGICAL FACTORS

But cannot induction be validated wholly *a priori* on grounds of theoretical general principles alone and in a manner quite free from experiential involvements? A good place to begin here is with the oft-invoked example of a maze or labyrinth:

> The methods of reasoning about the unknown could be compared to the methods by means of which we find our way out from a complicated labyrinth. . . . We might just run ahead and [try to] guess the right course at each turn. Or we might determine the course to be chosen according to a fixed rule. One of such rules holds a peculiar position. It is the determination *consistently to keep to the same hand,* either to the right or to the left. Of this rule it can be proved that it must finally lead us out of the maze. It is very likely that the employment of some other rule, or even mere guessing, will lead us more quickly out of the labyrinth, but the employment of any such method *may* also never attain this end. The determination to keep to the same hand is the only method of which we can be sure that, if persisted in consistently, it will lead to the goal.[3]

In trying to find the way out of a maze or labyrinth, the first choice that confronts one is that between selecting one's turns by *fiat* (guesswork, that is, or inspiration, or "feelings") or by *method.* It is clear that important advantages accrue to the latter alternative, seeing that a method offers a plan or procedural design that is codifiable and learnable. Moreover, it is possible to furnish a general demonstration that the tactic of always turning right (or left) at every opportunity is *bound* to lead out of the maze eventually. To be sure, another plan, say that of alternating the turning direction, may possibly work (and indeed will work much more efficiently in *some* cases), but it certainly need not; and so that no comparable *a priori* assurance can be extended. Accordingly, in the maze/labyrinth situation the indicated policy is rationalizable *a priori*, on considerations of general principle alone.

Given these considerations regarding the maze/labyrinth problem, one might (as Peirce and Reichenbach and others have done) adopt the position that orthodox induction repre-

[3] G. H. von Wright, *The Logical Problem of Induction*, 2nd ed. (Oxford, 1957), pp. 158–159.

sents an altogether analogous situation. It could then be argued that induction is rationalizable on the *a priori* basis that it is demonstrably bound to succeed in the end. But this would be a grave mistake. For a good deal of metaphysics lies hidden away in the dim background of the analogy. In the maze/labyrinth situation, after all, we know what it is that we are (*ex hypothesi*) dealing with: the constitution of the "world" at issue is given *a priori* by the supposition that it is a maze or labyrinth that is at hand. No such comfortable situation obtains on the inductive side of the analogy.

To set a proper analogy afoot we would have to change the conditions of the problem from ontological to methodological terms of reference. We must suppose that we find ourselves emplaced within what merely *looks* like a maze in our own cognitive neighborhood – the part that we have been able to see and explore. We have no *a priori* assurances about "the big picture," and, specifically, we don't know if the thing really is a maze at all; beyond our horizons it may turn out to be . . . God knows what – perhaps a wholly closed, exitless structure. The analogy thus breaks down. In the inductive case we have no preguarantee that the maze-analogous strategy will actually work. The needed metaphysical preassurances about "the nature of the world" are not in hand.

Nevertheless, the maze analogy is not wholly bereft of justificatory lessons. For there is, after all, *some* reason to think that the maze-appropriate strategy may succeed – the situation is (*ex hypothesi*) maze-like as far as we can tell. And at this stage, *faute de mieux* considerations become operative. No more hopeful option for realizing our ends lies within sight – there simply is no more promising-looking alternative method at hand. Such a line of thought extricates us from substantive (ontologically constitutive) presuppositions regarding inductive systematicity and shifts the issue of justificatory reasoning here onto a strictly methodological basis.

Just such a methodologically oriented approach underlies the practicalist justification of induction. It insists that the rationale of our inductive praxis – based, as it is, on a certain mode of systematicity preference – does not invoke metaphysical presuppositions along the substantive lines of the old Aristotelian dictum that "God and nature create nothing that has not its use,"[4] but, initially at any rate, rests on purely regulative considerations regarding the methodology of inquiry and its objectives. It cannot be emphasized too strongly that this essentially methodological-pragmatic legitimation of the pursuit of systematicity on the cognitive side involves no substantial prejudgment of the substantive question of the systematicity of nature on the *ontological* side. The character and the extent of the systematicity of nature are interesting empirical issues that await investigation by inductive means, but which have no decisive bearing on the issue of the justification of induction in the first instance. Cognitive systematicity roots in the methodological or regulative principles of plausibility and presumption that govern how we are to proceed in the transaction of our cognitive business. It must *not* be construed as prejudging – let alone preempting – the issue of the ontological systematicity of nature.

3. A METHODOLOGICAL-PRAGMATIC APPROACH TO JUSTIFYING INDUCTION AVOIDS METAPHYSICAL PRESUPPOSITIONS

The difficulties encountered by most of the familiar approaches to justifying induction arise in effecting with the transition from inductive systematicity to truth. For how – save by induction – could one possibly legitimate contentions like the scholastic precept that simplicity is the hallmark of truth (*simplicitas sigillum veri*), with its commitment to the whole gamut of traditional ontological precepts of the type "Nature abhors complexity," etc.? The methodological turn circumvents this range of problems altogether. It is able to operate in the procedural arena, where opting for various modes of economy of operation can be validated – initially, at any rate – on a basis of operational advantageousness, without recourse to suppositions about the nature of the world.

Ultimately, to be sure, our use of induction also stands validated on substantive, success-oriented grounds, but at this later stage, the situation is transformed, since prevalidated

---

[4] *De Caelo*, I, 4, 271a34.

inductive mechanisms are already in hand. And this is fortunate. For insofar as we are in a position to validate the claim that the inductive enterprise as we actually conduct it is indeed successful with respect to its correlative aims, we can only do this inductively. It emerges that we are well advised to abandon the whole project of looking for general principles to issue advance guarantees of the success of induction, and with it to abandon reliance on metaphysical presuppositions.

Such a course is not only desirable, but wholly possible – given a methodological approach to the justification of induction. Induction, as we have seen, is the search for order, and our processes of inductive inquiry into nature are geared to instill as much order into our cognitive commitments as is possible in the circumstances. When fishing, a net whose mesh has a certain area will catch fish of a suitably larger size *if* any are present. Use of the net indicates a *hope*, perhaps even an *expectation* that such fish will be there, but certainly not a preassured *foreknowledge* of their presence. Nothing in the abstract logic of the situation guarantees *a priori* that we shall find order when we go looking for it in the world. (Our cognitive search for order and system may conceivably issue in a finding of disorder and chaos.)

J. M. Keynes wrote:

> If every configuration of the Universe were subject to a separate and independent law, or if very small differences between bodies – in their shape or size, for instance – led to their obeying quite different laws, prediction would be impossible and the inductive method useless.[5]

The question of whether the world is such that in the final analysis our knowledge of it can be inductively systematized is ultimately a *contingent* question, whose answer must itself emerge from our actual endeavors at inductive systematization. It is a contingent fact accessible only *a posteriori* through actual experience that inductive systematization as we practice it actually works in "the real world." And so, when we first cultivate induction we do so relative to what is, at that stage, a merely hopeful supposition that we are dealing with an

---

[5] John Maynard Keynes, *A Treatise on Probability* (London, 1921), p. 249.

"inductively normal" world – a world in which induction is an actually efficient mode of inquiry.[6] Then we ultimately retrovalidate this presumption by showing (by inductive means) that the world actually is such that its stipulations are indeed satisfied. The argumentation thus closes in a smoothly self-supportive cycle of systematic reasoning where an initial presumption is ultimately retrovalidated by the course of subsequent inquiry.

This approach to the justification of induction is best appreciated in the light of a contrast between an *ontologically* based rationale for systematicity-preference and a *methodologically* based one. In the days of the medieval Schoolmen and of those later rationalistic philosophers whom Kant was wont to characterize as dogmatists, systematicity (simplicity, etc.) was viewed as an *ontological feature of the world*. Just as it was held that "Nature abhors a vacuum" – and, more plausibly, "In nature there is an explanation for everything" – so it was contended that "Nature abhors complexity." Kant's "Copernican Revolution" shifted the responsibility for such desiderata from *physical nature* to *the human intellect*. Kant acutely observed that what was at issue was not a facet of the teleology of *nature*, but one of the teleology of *reason*, responsibility for which lay not with the theory but with the theorizers. Simplicity-tropism, uniformity-tropism, etc., accordingly became features not of "the real world," but rather of "the mechanisms of human thought." The subsequent Darwinian Revolution may be viewed as taking the process a step further. It abolished the teleological element of ontological purposiveness in nature. Given the workings of a cognitive Darwinism of *rational* (rather than *natural*) selection, neither nature nor man's rational faculties are now thought to function as the locus for a systematicity-preference. Rather, the rationale is now placed on a *strictly methodological* basis. Responsibility for simplicity-tropism lies not with the "hardware" of human reason, but with its "software" – i.e., with the procedural and methodological principles which we ourselves employ because

[6] In more traditional terms, one would speak here instead of a world whose structure is such that one can *demonstrate* that the orthodoxly "inductively valid" modes of reasoning will predominantly yield true conclusions from true premisses. A "universe as cosmic urn" model of induction as "random sampling of nature" underlay the classical approaches to induction.

we find simpler theories easier to work with and more effective. It is not that *nature* avoids complexity, but that *we* do so insofar as possible.

Our justification can thus initially content itself with methodological considerations of convenience and potential efficacy; all those more deeply substantive issues of success, efficacy and attunement to "the real world" can be left for later consideration by way of eventual *retrojustification*. Such a methodological line of justificatory argumentation can (fortunately) avoid any resort to metaphysical presuppositions. We can dispense altogether with the position of old-school metaphysicians along the lines of Newton's celebrated dictum "Nature is pleased with simplicity and effects not the pomp of superfluous courses,"[7] accepting, in the first instance at any rate, the essentially Kantian insight that systematicity (or rational intelligibility) is not a descriptive feature of nature, but a methodological or regulative aspect of our approach to inquiry.

The methodological justification of induction accordingly does not move from metaphysics to epistemology, but moves entirely within the epistemological domain, and proceeds wholly without resort to any presuppositions of metaphysical fact.

4. INDUCTION AND THE SYSTEMATICITY OF NATURE

Consider the following argument:

> Induction is only justified once the uniformity, simplicity (etc.) of nature is given or presupposed. For if nature were not uniform and simple (etc.), if it were so disorderly or chaotic that our systematicity-geared cognitive gapfilling almost inevitably failed, then induction would not be successful, and so would not be justified.

This reasoning draws an inappropriate conclusion from a correct premiss. To be sure, it is quite right that for induction to *succeed* (sufficiently) nature must be (sufficiently) uniform and

---

[7] Isaac Newton, as quoted in *Newton's Philosophy of Nature*, ed. by H. S. Thayer (New York, 1953), p. 71.

simple (etc.). But as we have stressed, it would be quite wrong to confuse justification with a preguarantee of success – to see in such a guarantee the only basis of the rational validation of induction. The overall justification of induction does indeed require the issue of its success to be broached. The key question is, however, not *whether* this must be done, but *when*. And as we have argued time and again, it certainly need not be done initially, at the very outset, and in advance of any recourse to induction itself.

It deserves stress that the connecting linkage between cognitive and ontological systematicity must not be drawn too close. An intellectually incompetent workman can present information regarding even a simple and regular (etc.) configuration of objects in complex, disorganized form; and a clever workman may be able to describe a disorganized chaos in relatively simple and systematic terms. Ontological systematicity on the part of the objects of knowledge is *not* a requisite for the cognitive systematicity of our knowledge about them: things need not *be* systematic in order to admit of systematic study and presentation. (Knowledge need not share the features of its objects: to speak of a sober study of inebriation or a dispassionate analysis of passions is not a contradiction in terms.) The systematicity at issue in induction is a matter not of the ontological structure of the world, but of the *conceptual* structure of our knowledge of it. And this is fortunate because the ontological systematicity of nature is something we certainly cannot demonstrate *a priori* – and perhaps not *a posteriori* either.

Accordingly, one need not prejudge that the world *is* a system in order to set about the enterprise of striving to know it systematically. The finding of ontological systematicity (orderliness, lawfulness) in nature – to whatever extent that nature *is* systematic – is a substantive product of systematizing inquiry, rather than a needed *input* or *presupposition* for it.

To be sure, one qualification is in order. Ontological systematicity relates to the orderliness and to the lawfulness of nature – its conformity to *rules* of various sorts. Now if nature were not rulish in exhibiting manifold regularities – if it were pervasively "unruly" (say because its laws changed about rapidly and randomly) – then anything approaching a scientific study of the world would clearly be impossible. In this case the whole machinery of induction would be useless. If the world were not orderly (both in itself and as concerns the *modus operandi* of inquiring creatures), then there would be no uniformity in information-gathering, information-storage, etc., and consequently there would be no avenue to the acquisition of knowledge of the world – or indeed even putative knowledge of it. If the attainment – nay even the pursuit – of knowledge is to be possible for us, the world must be at any rate sufficiently orderly to permit of our cognitive functioning – it must be sufficiently systematic (orderly, regular) to permit the orderly conduct of rational inquiry, and thus, *a fortiori*, the existence of intelligent beings capable of it. The aims of science – the description, explanation, prediction, and control of nature – would clearly be altogether unrealizable in a world that is sufficiently badly asystematic. A significant degree of ontological systematicity IN the world is (obviously) a causal requisite for the realization of codificational systematicity in our knowledge OF the world.[8]

Thus the ontological systematicity of the world while not a *conceptual presupposition* for the legitimacy of systematizing inquiry, is nevertheless – at least in some degree – a *causal precondition* for its success. But these are very different issues that must not be run together. Moreover – and this is the important point – a discussion of the legitimation of the penchantly cognitive systematicity operative in the workings of induction can afford to leave aside the question of the ontological systematicity of nature.[9]

In the context of induction, the mistake of doctrinaire empiricism lay in its misguided conception of the *tabula rasa*, its idea that we begin the process of inquiry empty-handed. This is quite false: for while we do not, to be sure, begin with *theses*, we do and must start out with methods – and with the re-

[8] To be sure, a world that admits of knowledge-acquisition need not be a *total* system, *partial* systematicity will do – merely enough to permit orderly inquiry in our cosmic neighborhood by beings constituted as we are. For example, various thinkers (from Plato in the *Timaeus* to Herbert Spencer and C. S. Peirce) have viewed the ontological systematicity of nature in evolutionary terms as a developmental process that is as yet largely incomplete.

[9] For further discussion of the relationship between cognitive and ontological systematicity, see the author's *Cognitive Systematization* (Oxford, 1979).

gulative and methodological principles for the conduct of inquiry through which we arrive at the theses that represent acceptable answers to our questions. The mistake of traditional rationalism, on the other hand, was to think that a substantive presupposition is called for – a commitment to a somehow preestablished metaphysics of nature. In taking the methodological turn we can, fortunately, steer a middle course between these two flawed approaches.

5. METAPHYSICS AND THE PROBLEM OF SYSTEMIC UNIQUENESS

The following line of argumentation must also be considered in this present context of induction's supposed need for metaphysical presuppositions:

> Truth is One, but systems are (potentially) Many. The prospect of divergent but equally advantageous inductive systematizations arises and cannot be excluded without recourse to metaphysical considerations. Only through metaphysical presuppositions can systemic uniqueness be assured.

This argumentation has a simple and cogent structure: the Truth as pictured in our inductive systematizations must of necessity be unified; *ergo*, reality must be such that the unity of Truth is assured; *ergo*, metaphysics is needed to establish this character of the real, and to do so *a priori*.

It will not do to reply that the prospect of systemic pluralism need not worry us because the data of experience and experiment are so complex that the prospect of even *one* smooth systematization – let alone *several* alternatives ones – is so remote as to lie beyond a reasonable hope of realization. For the considerations at work here are essentially factual, a matter of the observed realities, so to speak, whereas what the objection clearly demands is an assurance of systemic uniqueness on grounds of theoretical principles alone. The objection must thus be met on a different basis. Fortunately, two distinct alternatives are available.

One route of reply lies in arguing that systemic uniqueness

can indeed be assured as a matter of *conceptual*, rather than *metaphysical*, necessity. The parameters of inductive systematicity, so it would be contended, are themselves such as to enforce uniqueness. (Consider a mathematical analogy: that of curve-fitting. Given *n* points there is, demonstrably, only one maximally simple curve – i.e., polynominal of lowest degree – to link them.) It would accordingly be maintained that the concept of optimization (or maximization) carries sufficient uniqueness-enforcing weight in the inductive case, the relevant parameters of systematicity being such that while there can indeed be several alternatives for systematizing a given body of data, only one unique alternative can ever be *optimally* systematic.

A second, very different line of response is also open, one so radical that it is tempting to dismiss it at first sight as a matter of "thinking the unthinkable." It consists in rejecting the fundamental premiss of the premiss of the objection: the principle that the Truth is One – that if all the data were in, then there is but one unique well-proportioned manifold of propositions capable of embracing the whole in a tightly coherent and smoothly consistent inductive synthesis. This traditional view of the systemic unity of truth is met by the challenge: What deity has made a compact with us to assure that the Truth is One – that the picture of the real that we obtain through inductive inquiry cannot possibly be internally complex and diversified to the point of inconsistency?

The preservation of consistency is, to be sure, one of the prime tasks of the systematizing enterprise. For often it is "experience" that presents inconsistencies and "theory" that *restores* harmony rather than destroying it. Think of the old sceptics' example of sight telling us the stick is bent while touch informs us it is straight. Each eye presents a somewhat different picture of the world: the brain alone enables us to "see" it consistently. To assert the consistency of nature is to express one's faith that the mind will be able ultimately to impress consistency upon the results of inductive inquiry. But this confidence may in the final analysis prove to be misplaced.

A consideration of the disputes initiated among quantum theorists in the 1920s and 1930s, involving such issues as the fact that light quanta can be looked upon *both* as particles *and* as waves, should pave the way towards a frame of mind that grants at least the *possibility* – the *theoretical* prospect – that such a state of affairs might conceivably prove *final*. There is no guarantee that science – as far and as best as we humans can cultivate it – must issue in an account of nature and its workings from which all elements of inconsistency have been excluded.

There is no decisive *logical* (i.e., purely theoretical) impediment to the contemplation of systems purporting to characterize an inherently inconsistent nature. A steadily growing sector of recent logical theorizing has so evolved as to indicate that a pervasive diffusion of contradiction need not result in general, but only in the setting of the particular framework of the logical machinery now generally characterized as "classical." Over this past generation, logicians are increasingly chary of the view that one may distinguish between pervasive inconsistency (of the disastrous, "anything goes" form) and merely logical anomalies, isolable incompatibilities whose logical perplexity is confined to within a small, localized region of a wider system.

The idea that one unique member from among incompatible alternatives must in the end prevail embodies what might be called *the myth of the God's-eye view* – that all such discordancies are ultimately unreal appearances that only appertain to us beings of limited cognitive capacities. They can arise on the epistemic side but cannot possibly characterize reality itself. Different and discordant perspectives may obtain for imperfect knowers, but a perfect knower would resolve these into one unique – and uniquely correct – alternative. This condition may represent a plausible hope but is certainly not an established fact.

At this point, then, the prospect of an "Averroism" which maintains that the Truth is *not* One, that reality may be even embrace inconsistency, would appear as a possibility that cannot be rejected out of hand. And in entertaining this possibility, we obtain yet another way of meeting the objection that it is necessary to have recourse to metaphysical presuppositions to rule out the prospect of a plurality of discordant but equally advantageous systematizations. For the stance at issue puts at our disposal the prospect of simply combining such a plurality of "incompletable alternatives" in such a way as to treat them as so many distinct components of one single, internally diversified macrosystem. On such an approach, then, we do achieve a guarantee of uniqueness, but only by accepting the possibility of an internal diversification of the most radical sort – a superposition of what would ordinarily be thought of as logically discordant alternatives.[10]

Either one of these two envisaged approaches of consistency-forcing or inconsistency-toleration would make it possible to deal with the prospect of a plurality of alternative systematizations without any recourse to metaphysical principles.

[10] The themes of this section are developed more fully in *Cognitive Systematization* (*op. cit.*), and in Nicholas Rescher and Robert Brandom, *The Logic of Inconsistency* (Oxford, 1980).

XI

The Regulative Rationale of Systematicity-Preference

SYNOPSIS

(1) The rationale of inductive systematicity-preference consists of purely regulative or procedural considerations regarding the methodology of inquiry. These regulative considerations center about the desideratum of *economy* of operation in the cognitive domain. (2) The case study of curve fitting illustrates how this issue of economy and convenience plays a decisive role here. (3) The pursuit of simplicity, uniformity, and inductive systematicity in all its forms is a matter of economy – of the avoidance of needless effort and complication. A Principle of Least Effort is at work with respect to inductive systematicity. The crucial point is that systematicity is a *regulative* ideal for the methodology of inquiry whose espousal certainly does not prejudge, let alone preempt, any substantial part of the question of ontological systematicity. (4) The proper legitimation of systematization as a valid cognitive ideal is accordingly teleological – it lies in the efficacy of a methodology geared to the pursuit of system in facilitating realization of the goals of inquiry. To be sure, the establishment of this efficacy is itself a matter of inductively laden retrovalidation. And here evolutionary pressures operate to assure the coordination of methodological convenience with operational effectiveness.

1. THE METHODOLOGICAL STATUS OF SYSTEMATICITY-
    PREFERENCE

As has been stressed throughout, the systematicity-preference
that lies at the base of induction is the product not of an
ontological position, but of adopting a certain methodological
stance. The aim of this chapter is to explore more fully the
regulative dimension of this methodological approach.

Galileo wrote:

> When therefore I observe a stone initially at rest falling
> from a considerable height and gradually acquiring new
> increases of speed, why should I not believe that such
> increments come about in the simplest, the most plausible
> way?[1]

Why not indeed? Subsequent findings may, of course, render
this simplest position untenable. But this recognition only
reinforces our stance that simplicity is not an inevitable hallmark of truth (*simplex sigillum veri*), but merely a methodological tool of inquiry – a facet of the standard process of
inductive systematization.

We need not presuppose that the world is systematic
(simple, uniform, etc.) to validate our penchant for the systematicity of our cognitive commitments. To be sure, our
theories regarding nature should not *oversimplify* – they should
not picture the world as simpler, more uniform, etc., than
it indeed is. But our striving for cognitive systematicity in its
various forms persists even in the face of complex phenomena.
The ontological systematicy of nature is ultimately irrelevant
for our regulative concerns: the commitment to inductive
systematicity in our account of the world remains a methodological desideratum regardless of how complex or untidy the
world may turn out to be.

Henri Poincaré has observed that:

> [Even] those who do not believe that natural laws must be

[1] Galileo Galilei, *Dialogues concerning Two New Sciences*, tr. by H. Crew and A. de
Salvo (Evanston, 1914), p. 154.

simple, are still often obliged to act as if they did believe it. They cannot entirely dispense with this necessity without making all generalisation, and therefore all science, impossible. It is clear that any fact can be generalised in an infinite number of ways, and it is a question of choice. The choice can only be guided by considerations of simplicity. . . . To sum up, in most cases every law is held to be simple until the contrary is proved.[2]

These observations are wholly in the right spirit. As cognitive possibilities proliferate in the course of theory-building inquiry, a principle of choice and selection becomes requisite. And here economy – and its other systematic congeners, simplicity, and uniformity and the rest – are the natural guideposts. Whether the direction in which they point us is actually a correct one is something that "remains to be seen." (This is where retrovalidation comes in.) But they clearly afford the most natural and promising starting point.

E. H. Gombrich has written:

Whatever the fate of the Gestalt school may be in the field of neurology, it may still prove logically right in insisting that the simplicity hypothesis cannot be learned. It is, indeed, the only condition under which we could learn at all. To probe a hole we must first use a straight stick to see how far it takes us. To probe the visible world we use the assumption that things are simple until they prove to be otherwise.[3]

This perspective seems profoundly correct, and can indeed be extended from simplicity to systematicity in general. The systematically smoothest resolution of our questions is patently that which must be allowed to prevail – at any rate *pro tem*, until such time as its untenability becomes manifest.

Discovery and learning can only take place against a background of established expectations. (The man whose maxim is *nil admirari* – "To be surprised at nothing" – has nothing to

[2] *Science and Hypothesis* (New York, 1914), pp. 145–146.
[3] E. H. Gombrich, *Art and Illusion* (Princeton, 1960), p. 272.

learn.) Expectations can only be formed through projections of prior experiences: what *else* could possibly shape and canalize an expectation? And so the urge to systematize experience is a crucial requirement of the whole process of learning and inquiry. Our systematicity-preference is not a *result* of this process but a regulative *precondition* of it, because without the formative guidance of a determinative principle such as this systematicity-tropism provides, the process of learning and inquiry could not go into effective operation at all. In such perspective, induction is seen as a fundamentally regulative and procedural resource in the domain of inquiry, proceeding in implementation of the injunction: "Maximize the extent to which your cognitive commitments are smoothly systematic." In the absence of such a principle – or some functional equivalent of it – the venture of rational inquiry could not get under way at all.

But just what is the essential nature of the methodological factors that militate *a priori* for our inductive systematicity-preference? The reply is straightforward: they are considerations of economy and convenience of operation. The simplest answer is (*eo ipso*) the most economical one to work with. We do not presume simplicity, uniformity, normality,[4] etc., because we know or believe that matters always stand on a basis that is simple, uniform, normal, etc. – surely we know no such thing! – but because it is on this basis that we cannot conduct our cognitive business in the most advantageous, the most *economical* way. Complexities, disuniformities, abnormalities, etc., are complications that exact a price, departures from the easiest resolution that must be motivated by some appropriate benefit, some situational pressure. An invocation of Charles Sanders Peirce's concern for the economics of inquiry may be helpful in this regard.[5] The parameters of inductive systematicity – simplicity, uniformity, regularity, normality, coherence, and the rest – all represent principles of

---

[4] Note that in explaining the behavior of people we always presume normalcy and rationality on their part – a presumption that is, to be sure, defeasible and only holds "until proven otherwise."

[5] For fuller information regarding C. S. Peirce's theory of the economic aspects of inquiry – "the economy of research" as he called it – see the author's *Peirce's Philosophy of Science* (Notre Dame, 1978). Cf. also John Dewey, *Reconstruction in Philosophy*, Enlarged Edition (Boston, 1957), pp. 154–155.

cognitive economy.[6] They are labor-saving devices for the avoidance of complications in the course of our endeavors to realize the objects of inquiry.

Induction is seen – from this point of view – as operating so as to organize our cognitive commitments most economically. The initial justification of induction in the methodological-pragmatic mode pivots crucially on this economic perspective. To justify induction is to validate systematicity-preference – the concession of priority to simplicity, regularity, and all the other forms of "economy" of operation in the cognitive sphere. Accordingly, the rationale of our inductive praxis is a fundamentally economic one, subject to the regulative injunction: *Resolve your cognitive problem in the most economical possible way compatible with an adequate handling of the epistemic situation at hand.* The penchant for systematicity is a matter of striving for economy in the conduct of inquiry. It is governed by an analogue of Occam's razor – a principle of parsimony to the effect that needless complexity is to be avoided. Given that the inductive method, viewed in its practical and methodological aspect, aims at the most efficient and effective means of question-resolution, it is only natural that our inductive precepts should direct us always to begin with the most systematic, and thereby economical, device that can actually do the job at hand. Our systematizing procedures pivot on this injunction always to adopt the most economical (simple, general, straightforward, etc.) solution that meets the conditions of the problem. The root principle of inductive systematization is the axiom of cognitive economy: *complicationes non multiplicandae sunt praeter necessitatem.*

This methodological approach to the rationalization of cognitive systematicity on grounds of economy embodies no claim, tacit or otherwise, to any sort of *ontological* linkage between simplicity, uniformity, etc., and (probable) truth. In the first instance, at any rate, the thesis that nature is a system is seen as a regulative principle for its cognitive rationalization. The basis of the principle is epistemologico-conceptual rather

---

[6] These considerations explain how we are to proceed in situations where the parameters of cognitive systematization stand in apparent conflict with one another; when conformity seems at odds with cohesiveness or the like. Reconciliation is to be effected here in terms of the demands of overall economy.

than ontological.[7] On such a view, inductive systematicity is best viewed as an aspect, not of *reality* as such, but of our procedures for its conceptualization and accordingly of *our conception* of it, or, to be more precise, of our manner of conceptualizing it. Simplicity-preference (for example) is based on the strictly method-oriented practical consideration that the simple hypotheses are the most convenient and advantageous for us to put to use in the context of our purposes. There is thus no recourse to a substantive (or descriptively constitutive) postulate of the simplicity of nature; it suffices to have recourse to a regulative (or practical) precept of economy of means. And in its turn, the pursuit of cognitive systematicity is ontologically neutral: it is a matter of conducting our question-resolving endeavors with the greatest economy. The principle of least effort predominates – the process is one of maximally economic means to the attainment of chosen ends. This amounts to a *theoretical* defense of inductive systematicity that in fact rests on *practical* considerations.

2. CURVE-FITTING AS A CASE STUDY

An example will help to show how considerations of economy bear upon our present problem of the validation of inductive reasoning. It is recognized by theoreticians on all sides that *simplicity* must play a prominent part in the methodology of science. There is as widespread agreement as there ever is on philosophical matters on the principle that simple hypotheses enjoy a preferred status in point of plausibility and credibility in inductive contexts. But on the other hand, when one pushes

---

[7] Kant was the first philosopher clearly to perceive and emphasize this crucial point:

> But such a principle [of systematicity] does not prescribe any law for objects. . . ; it is merely a subjective law for the orderly management of the possessions of our understanding, that by the comparison of its concepts it may reduce them to the smallest possible number; it does not justify us in demanding from the objects such uniformity as will minister to the convenience and extension of our understanding; and we may not, therefore, ascribe to the [methodological or *regulative*] maxim ["Systematize knowledge!"] any objective [or descriptively *constitutive*] validity. (CPuR, A306 = B362.)

Compare also C. S. Peirce's idea that the systematicity of nature is a regulative matter of scientific attitude rather than a constitutive matter of scientific fact. Charles Sanders Peirce, *Collected Papers*, vol. VII, sect. 7.134.

the issue back to first principles and presses the question of legitimating the rationale of this simplicity-preference, one meets with a wavering note of indecisiveness in the literature. Discussions of this issue are replete with indications of queasiness about the acceptance of a principle that seems less congenial to tough-minded scientific analysts than to old-school metaphysicians with a penchant towards quasi-theological ideas like the principle of the simplicity of nature.

It is difficult to justify simplicity-preference on grounds either of informativeness or of falsifiability,[8] but it is easy to justify on grounds of economy. If one claims a phenomenon to depend not just on certain distances and weights and sizes but also (say) on temperature and magnetic forces, then one must operate a more complex testing apparatus and contrive to take readings over this enlarged range of physical parameters. Or again, in a certain curve-fitting case compare the thesis that the resultant function is linear (Figure XI.1A) with the thesis that is it linear up to a point and sinusoidally wave-like thereafter (Figure XI.1B).

Figure XI.1

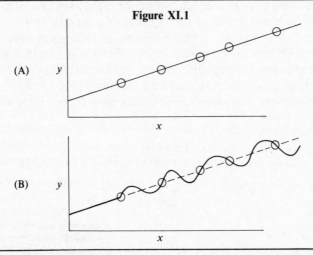

(A) y

x

(B) y

x

---

[8] It is dogma among the Popperians that a simple theory is more readily falsified than a complex one. But this is far from clear. It is a simpler theory that "The number of constellations is *odd*" than that "The number of constellations is *prime*" but it is no easier to falsify. It is a simpler theory that "All in nature happens naturally" than "The events of nature depend on the inscrutable will of a powerful spirit." But the former theory is not the more easily falsified.

Now think of writing a set of instructions for checking whether empirically determined point-coordinates fit the specified function. This is clearly a vastly less complex – and so more economical – process in the linear case as compared with its more convoluted cogener. And comparable considerations of operative economy attach to simplicity on the side of utilization as well as that of substantiation, rendering simpler alternatives more advantageous to select, both for *adoption* and for *investigation*.

On this approach, simplicity-preference is based on the strictly practical ground that simple hypotheses are operationally cheaper, and hence the most advantageous for us to put to use. There is no need for recourse to a substantive (or constitutive) postulate of the simplicity of nature; it suffices to have recourse to a regulative (or practical) precept of economy of means.

But just how does systematicity operate in this inductive context – how is "simplicity" (for example) to be construed here? As already noted (p. 92), our parameters of inductive systematicity are highly schematic ideas that have to be fleshed out in concrete detail in the context of concrete applications. And just how are we to make the choice that arises here? This issue itself becomes a matter of economic considerations. For there are clearly very different ways of construing simplicity, uniformity, and the rest. For example, why take (as we do) the *smoothest* curve in these curve-fitting situations – why not the

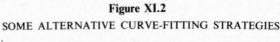

Figure XI.2

SOME ALTERNATIVE CURVE-FITTING STRATEGIES

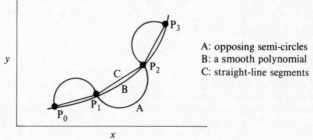

A: opposing semi-circles
B: a smooth polynomial
C: straight-line segments

shortest, or that which uses only (opposing) semi-circles? (See Figure XI.2.)

What we are trying to do in such cases is to fit a continuous curve $y = F(x)$ to a number of specific points $P_i = (x_i, y_i)$. The curve-fitting process can be viewed as a matter of *estimating* the "correct" function on the basis of such data.

We may begin with a basic principle of the theory of estimation:

> In estimating a point-value, we automatically also estimate all of the single-valued function-values of it, so that in estimating X, we also arrive at an estimate of $\theta(X)$.

> In estimating a function, we automatically also estimate all of its hyperfunctions, for any prespecified hyperfunction: for example, in estimating θ, we also estimate θ^2, $\sqrt{\theta}$, θ^{-1}, etc.

Thus an estimation-method must satisfy what R. A. Fischer characterizes as "the need for invariance in respect to functional transformations," a requirement which he describes as follows:

> A primary, and really very obvious, consideration is that if an unknown parameter θ is being estimated, any one-valued function of θ [such as θ^2, for example, or $\sqrt{\theta}$] is necessarily being estimated by the same operation. The criteria used in the theory must, for this reason, be invariant for all such functional transformations of the parameters.[9]

This precept may be characterized as "Fischer's Principle." It enjoins a certain uniformity of approach upon us in the interests of methodological consistency of operation. Our methods of estimation must be of the widest possible applicability. They must accommodate the fact that a method is not even really a *method* if it does not treat like cases alike in the absence of explicit counter-indications.

Now in estimating the curve we *eo ipso* estimate all its derivatives. But the only policy we can apply here uniformly,

[9] R. A. Fischer, *Statistical Methods and Scientific Inference* (London, 1956), p. 140.

across the board, is that of "opting for the smoothest," in contrast with the sorts of alternatives mooted above (the shortest, the most semicircular). For in smoothing the curve we *eo ipso* smooth all its derivatives, whereas in, say, shortening (linearizing) or in circling the curve we do not at all accomplish the same sort of thing for its derivatives. The fact is that smoothing is the only *uniform* estimation policy in these interpretative cases that satisfies the requirement of Fischer's Principle. Accordingly, if this is at all possible within the constraints of the problem, the curve (function) should be linear (since this resolution meets all the desiderata at issue in the simplest possible way), but in any case it must be as mathematically uniform as possible.

Again, in estimating the curve (function) throughout an interval from x_1 to x_2, we also thereby automatically estimate this curve for every subinterval from x_1' to x_2' [where $(x_1 \leqslant x_1' \leqslant x_2' \leqslant x_2)$]. Thus Fischer's Principle can also be applied here: such a function has among its hyperfunctions the *partitive* function which cuts it down to one of its subdomains. In estimating a function (curve) we also estimate all of its constituent component parts. And so our manner of proceeding with the whole must be homogeneous with our procedure in relation to its parts. Accordingly, the principle in view enjoins us to proceed with respect to our estimate for (any) subinterval $x_1' - x_2'$ in exactly the same way as with respect to the interval $x_1 - x_2$. And so the curve (function) that we determine must be determined *homogeneously* – that is, every part of it must (insofar as possible) have the same mathematical character as the whole. This aspect of uniformity accordingly also means (*inter alia*) that the curve (function) should be continuous and smooth.

The principles of uniformity, simplicity (etc.) which operate in this curve-fitting situation thus all emerge as aspects of systematicity in its key role as a vehicle of intellectual economy.

3. SYSTEMATICITY, ECONOMY, AND THE PRINCIPLE OF LEAST EFFORT

Hans Reichenbach has written:

> Actually in cases of inductive simplicity it is not economy which determines our choice ... [W]e make the assumption that the simplest theory furnishes the best predictions. This assumption cannot be justified by convenience; it has a truth character and demands a justification within the theory of probability and induction.[10]

This perspective is gravely misleading. There is no need to resort to the supposition that "the simplest theory gives the best predictions" – for such a belief would simply be foolish. What on earth is its basis? Induction with respect to the history of science itself would soon undermine our confidence that nature operates in the way we would deem the simpler: *au contraire*, the history of science is an endlessly repetitive story of simple theories giving way to more complicated and sophisticated ones. We opt for the simplest adequate alternative just because *there is* (*ex hypothesi*) *then and there no preponderating reason* for resorting to a more complex possibility. At any particular stage of the inquiry we allow considerations of economy of means to play the determinative role. (Why on earth not!?) The rationale of our simplicity-preference is of the purely procedural sort – it has and need have no admixture of ontological precommitment. It *is* indeed economy and con-

---

[10] Hans Reichenbach, *Experience and Prediction* (Chicago and London, 1938), p. 376. Compare:

> Imagine that a physicist ... wants to draw a curve which passes through [points on a graph that represent] the data observed. It is well known that the physicist chooses the simplest curve; this is not to be regarded as a matter of convenience ... [For different] curves correspond as to the measurements observed, but they differ as to future measurements; hence they signify different predictions based on the same observational material. The choice of the simplest curve, consequently, depends on an inductive assumption: we believe that the simplest curve gives the best predictions. ... If in such cases the question of simplicity plays a certain role for our decision, it is because we make the assumptions that the simplest theory furnishes the best predictions. (*Ibid.*, pp. 375–376.)

venience that determine our regulative predilection for simplicity and systematicity in general. In the first instance, at any rate, we do indeed opt for them just on the basis of considerations of methodological and procedural rationality.

This present approach in effect combines the commonsensical precept "Try the simplest thing first" with a principle of burden of proof: "Maintain your cognitive commitments until there is good reason to abandon them."[11] It clearly makes eminent sense to move onwards from the simplest (least complex) available solution to introduce further complexities when and as – but *only* when and as – they are forced upon us. Simpler (more systematic) answers are more easily codified, taught, learned, used, investigated, etc. The regulative principles of convenience and economy in learning and inquiry suffice to provide a rational basis for systematicity-preference. Our penchant for simplicity, uniformity, and systematicity in general, is now not a matter of a substantive theory regarding the nature of the world, it is a matter of search strategy – of cognitive methodology. In sum, we opt for simplicity (and systematicity in general) in inquiry not because it is truth-indicative, but because it is teleologically effective in conducing to the more efficient realization of the goals of inquiry. We look for the dropped coin in the lightest spots nearby, not because it is more likely to be there than in the shadows, but because this is – in the circumstances – the most sensible strategy of search: if it's not there we can't find it at all.

From this perspective, systematicity-preference emerges as a matter of *simplification of labor*, a matter of the "intellectual economy" of the cognitive venture. Why use a more complex solution where a simple one will do as well? Why depart from uniformity – why use a new, different solution where an existing one will serve? The good workman selects his tools with a view to (1) their *versatility* (power, efficacy, adaptability, etc.) and (2) their *convenience* (ease of use), and other suchlike factors of functional adequacy to the task in hand. On this basis, the pursuit of systematicity em-

---

[11] Some issues revolving around this principle are discussed in D. Goldstick, "Methodological Conservatism," *American Philosophical Quarterly*, vol. 8 (1971), pp. 186–191.

erges as a *regulative* matter of intellectual economy of operation.

In the context of an interesting analysis of tool-use, George K. Zipf has observed that the intelligent workman solving his immediate problems will view these against the background of his probable future problems, as best he can foresee them. Moreover he will strive to solve his problems in such a way as to minimize the *total work* that he must expend in solving *both* his immediate problems *and* his probable future problems. This in turn means that the person will strive to minimize the *probable average rate of his work-expenditure* (over time). And in so doing they will be minimizing his *effort* – least work and least effort being two different sides of the same coin.[12]

There is no reason to withhold application of this principle of the economy of tool-use in general to the special case of our cognitive tools. And so, we opt for simple tools of the highest potential versatility and generality with a view to future applications and the resolution of comparable issues. The simplicity of our conceptual machinery is thus bound to march hand in hand with the generality of its application and thus with the frequency of its use. (The view of effective *explanation* as "reduction to the familiar" is closely bound up with this – familiarity is clearly determined by use-frequency, and simplicity is coupled to explanatory power because of its greater versatility.) The less intricate and specialized our conceptual instrumentalities – the fewer assumptions and complications they involve – the wider their reach is bound to be.

In the selection of tools we naturally avoid recourse to the complex or the esoteric save under the pressure of necessity. The parameters of systematicity play an analogous role. It is our prime motivation to get by with a minimum of complication: to adopt strategies of question-resolution that enable us (*inter alia*) (1) to continue with existing solutions unless and until the epistemic circumstances compel us to introduce changes (uniformity); (2) to make the same processes do insofar as possible

---

[12] George K. Zipf, *The Principle of Least Effort* (New York, 1965), p. 5. The discussion of the economy of tool-use in the opening chapter of this work is highly suggestive for the purposes of our present deliberations.

(generality), and (3) to keep to the simplest process that will do the job (simplicity).

Our inductive systematicity-preference thus emerges as a means towards implementing the precepts of economy of operation in the intellectual sphere. Its initial advantages are not theoretical/ontological but methodological/pragmatic in orientation. Insofar as the issue of success and efficacy and "furnishing the best predictions" comes upon the scene (and admittedly it cannot be wholly left out), we can and do proceed inductively, letting the process of induction itself teach us about the relative efficiency of our inductive proceedings and monitoring the *modus operandi* of our inductive praxis by inductive considerations.

4. THE ASPECT OF RETROVALIDATION

It is perhaps tempting to think of systematicity-preference as telling the whole story about the justification of induction – to think of our commitment to inductive systematicity (simplicity, uniformity, etc.) as in and of itself providing a sufficient basis for the justificatory job. But this is not so. It is, in theory, perfectly conceivable that lessons learned in the "school of bitter experience" would lead us to shift from this most appropriate of starting positions. Our choice of economy reflects a procedural (regulative) stance that needs retrovalidation. The issue of efficacy – of an appeal to actual trial and the arbitrament of praxis – cannot be dispensed with. A closer look at this aspect of the matter is in order.

The justificatory process we have characterized as "retrojustification" has for its aim not to underwrite *ex post facto* the substantive conclusion that the world is simple or uniform or the like, but to show that a methodology of inquiry geared to systematicity-preference is *efficient* – that it accomplishes the ends at issue in the cognitive enterprise with due economy of means. For the salient fact is *not* that (as Reichenbach puts it) "we make the assumption that the simplest theory furnishes the best predictions" – an assumption obviously ill-advised in the light of experience – but because *experience shows that a process of inquiry that proceeds on this basis is comparatively efficient* in the realization of our cognitive goals. The point is not that the simplest alternative demonstrably affords (or is more likely to afford) successful predictions of and interventions in nature, but that a policy of inquiry that embodies simplicity-preference emerges as relatively effective as an epistemological policy. The crucial fact is that systematicity-preference is a cognitive policy recommended by considerations of *cost-effectiveness*: in the setting of the cognitive purposes at issue it affords a maximally advantageous search-strategy in the context of empirical inquiry.

Induction, as we have seen, is a matter of the pursuit of system in the cognitive sphere. Systematicity here represents a regulative ideal of inquiry correlative with the procedural injunction "So organize your knowledge as to impart to it as much systematic structure as you possibly can!" But does not the prospect that its objective may well be unattainable destroy the validity of this ideal? Surely not. The validation of this cognitive ideal does *not* lie in the fact that its realization can be guaranteed *a priori* from the outset on the basis of considerations of general principles alone. We may in fact never realize this ideal. But this possibility should not be allowed to impede our efforts to press the project of systematization as far as we possibly can. Here, as elsewhere, the validity of an ideal does not call for any prior guarantee of its ultimate realization. (What ideal is ever validated in this way?) To be sure, a hope of its eventual realization can never in principle be finally and totally demolished. But this feeble comfort is hardly sufficient to establish its propriety. This is something that emerges from the circumstance that while we have no *a priori* assurance of ultimate success in the quest for systematicity, what began as an initial presumption in favor of this ideal ultimately re-emerges as rationally legitimate because of its demonstrated furtherance of the inherent aims and objectives of the cognitive venture.

This point is critical for the recourse to what we have characterized as the inductive retrovalidation of induction. Its task is not to show, *ex post facto*, as it were, that the world is indeed an ontological system (via a principle of the uniformity of nature or some other such metaphysical presupposition). Rather, its task is *to show that a process of inquiry geared to systematicity-preference is relatively efficient*. This crucial point cannot be overstressed. It affords the Archimedean fulcrum on which the whole of the methodologico-pragmatic justification of induction pivots.

To reemphasize: cognitive systematicity functions throughout as a regulative ideal governing the conduct of inquiry – an ideal whose implementation along economy-governed lines, while at first merely hopeful, is ultimately retrovalidated by the fact that its pursuit enables us to realize more efficiently the fundamental aims and purposes of the cognitive enterprise. Initially, the pivotal issue is simply the matter of *our convenience* in doing what must be done to serve our purposes. The whole ontological question of the systematicity of nature can safely be left to await the results brought in by the actual *use* of the inductive processes. No prior presuppositions are needed in this regard: initially the outcome here is largely irrelevant from the standpoint of justificatory considerations.

Our inductive systematicity-preference finds its final justification in the fact that it affords an effective search-policy for serviceable truth-estimates regarding answers to our questions, rather than in providing an index of truth. The task of the retrovalidation at issue is not to establish that nature is systematic, but to show that a methodology of inquiry geared to systematicity-preference is relatively successful. The justification of systematicity as a regulative ideal in the pursuit of our cognitive affairs must thus be seen in essentially instrumental terms: "Design your cognitive procedures with a view to the pursuit of systematicity!" This is a regulative principle of inquiry whose legitimation ultimately lies in its being pragmatically retrovalidated by its capacity to guide inquiry into successful channels. We are to prefer the optimally systematic (simple, uniform) alternative in the first instance because this is the most economical, the most *convenient* thing to do, and ultimately because experience shows that the utilization of such economical methods to be efficient – i.e., as optimally conducive (relative to *available* alternatives) to the realization of the task.

The following objection will doubtless be made:

Such a methodological-pragmatic justification does not establish that induction will actually succeed. In pivoting the justification of induction on "the conveniences of our epistemic situation," the position invites the question: What reason is there to think that nature obliges man?

The answer here is simple: It doesn't and it doesn't need to. To repeat the key point once more – a prior guarantee of success just is NOT needed to justify our recourse to inductive procedures. Insofar as the factor of *success* is a legitimate justificatory consideration – as in the final analysis it is bound to be – it is also something that can be fashioned "in due course" rather than "in advance," a fact that can – quite appropriately – be allowed to emerge as a product of induction itself.

The evolution of our cognitive methods through rational selection plays a key role in this connection. For (as we saw in Chapter V) it so unfolds as to assure *the coordination of convenience with effectiveness*. This coordination is not a miracle inserted into the scheme of things from without by a benign *deus ex machina*; it is a matter of evolutionary conformation between nature itself and the cognitive apparatus (sensory or discursive) of a creature that must make his way in the world by its wits. The fact *that* inductive systematization, as we employ it, actually works is no mere "brute fact," because *why* it works is something we can explain quite satisfactorily in strictly evolutionary terms.[13] A process of *rational* selection is at work to support the retention, promulgation, and transmission of those cognitive resources that prove themselves effective in operation.

To sum up: *Economy and convenience* play the crucial pioneering role in the initial justification of our systematizing praxis on procedural and methodological grounds. But, in its turn, the issue of *effectiveness and success* comes to predominate at the subsequent stage of ex-post-facto retrojustification. And the question of the seemingly "preestablished harmony" of the coordinatiaon of these two theoretically disparate factors is ultimately resolved on the basis of evolutionary considerations.[14]

[13] Charles Sanders Peirce's idea of the inquiring mind as "co-natured with reality" through evolution is relevant here.

[14] A wide spectrum of considerations relevant to these issues is canvassed in the author's *Methodological Pragmatism* (Oxford, 1977) and *Cognitive Systematization* (Oxford, 1979).

XII

Advantages of the Methodological Approach

SYNOPSIS

(1) Any even halfway plausible justification of induction is preferable to the scepticism engendered by having none at all. But the methodological-pragmatic validation has substantial advantages over the various other familiar approaches to the justification of induction such as: (2) necessitarian apriorism, (3) conditional apriorism in its principal version of long-runism, (4) uniformitarian deductivism, (5) probabilism, (6) intuitionism, (7) inductivism, (8) analytical rationalism, and (9) falsificationism. (10) In view of the significant shortcomings and defects that characterize each of its rivals, the methodological-pragmatic validation of induction deserves consideration as a promising strategy for the solution of this much-disputed problem.

1. PRELIMINARIES

This concluding chapter offers what diplomats would call a *tour d'horizon* of recent attempts at the justification of induction. Such a survey must cover a considerable terrain. For, as the inventory of Table XII.1 indicates, virtually every theoretically available combination and permutation of positions regarding the justification of induction has found its exponents. The aim of this survey is to consider the comparative strengths and advantages of the present methodological-

Table XII.1

AN INVENTORY OF MAJOR APPROACHES TO THE
JUSTIFICATION OF INDUCTION

(I)   Induction is *dispensable*; it is not needed, and should be replaced, with
      its mission accomplished by a fundamentally variant process of
      inquiry which proceeds simply by way of the elimination of untenable
      alternatives.
          – FALSIFICATIONISM (Popper)
(II) Induction (while needed) *cannot* be justified.
          – SCEPTICISM (Ancient Pyrrhonians)
(III) Induction *need not* be justified: it requires no justification, either (1)
      on the ground that induction is a perfectly natural process that does
      not rest on any discursive considerations at all, but on a purely
      instinctive or intuitive basis:
          – INTUITIONISM (Hume, Academic Sceptics)
      or else (2) because all justifications must stop somewhere and induc-
      tion is part of the rock bottom:
          – ANALYTICAL RATIONALISM (Strawson, Ayer)
(IV) Induction *can and should be justified*, and such justification is forth-
      coming through
          (A) grounds of *logico-conceptual necessity* by way of
              (1) considerations of strictly demonstrative necessity
                  – NECESSITARIAN APRIORISM (Peirce-early, D. C. Williams)
              (2) considerations of *hypothetically* demonstrative necessity
                  with regard to goal-attainment ("transcendental argu-
                  ments," "this-or-nothing argumentation")
                  – CONDITIONAL APRIORISM (one version of which is LONG
                  RUNISM [Peirce-late, Reichenbach])
              (3) purely theoretical considerations regarding the *modus
                  operandi* of probability as a quasi-demonstrative device.
                  – PROBABILISM (Laplace, Peirce-middle, Carnap)
          (B) empirical-inductive grounds
                  – INDUCTIVISM (Braithwaite, Black)
          (C) metaphysical grounds
                  – UNIFORMITARIAN DEDUCTIVISM (Mill, Russell)
                  – UNIFORMITARIAN PROBABILISM (Keynes)
          (D) methodological grounds
                  – PRAGMATISM

pragmatic approach to the justification of induction *vis-à-vis*
the competing alternatives.

It is, of course, possible to take the line that induction just
cannot be justified at all. But such an insistence on the impossibility of the venture reflects a despairing confession of defeat in
the face of the problem of justification. To be sure, the pro-

spect that a rational legitimation of induction is unachievable cannot be excluded out of hand. But this is surely a position of last resort. When a powerfully attractive goal lies before us, we would settle for its unattainability only after every prospect of its realization has been exhausted. As A. C. Ewing has sagely observed:

> [W]e cannot suppose it irrational to believe that if we jump from a height we shall fall; and even if we say that all induction is in some sense irrational, it will still be incumbent on us to explain the distinction between scientific inductions and those inductions which would be accepted by no sensible person. What is the difference between the two kinds if they are both irrational?[1]

There are also those who propose to abandon the project of a rationalization of our inductive reasonings not as impossible, but rather as unnecessary. They tell us that it is ultimately *pointless* to attempt a justification of induction, presumably because induction is an instinctive process, like respiration. Hume himself talks in this vein, and Hans Reichenbach follows his lead:

> To deem the inductive assumption unworthy of the assent of a philosopher, to keep a haughty reserve, and to meet with a condescending smile the attempts of other people to bridge the gap between experience and prediction, is cheap self-deceit. For at the very moment when the apostles of such a higher philosophy leave the field of

---

[1] A. C. Ewing, *The Fundamental Questions of Philosophy* (London: Routledge and Kegan Paul Ltd, 1951), p. 168. Compare the cogent objection that if induction is unjustifiable, then

empirical knowledge is at bottom a matter of convention. We choose, quite arbitrarily it would seem, some basic canons of induction; there is no possibility of justifying the choice. They are arbitrary in the sense that cognitive considerations do not force their acceptance. It is perfectly conceivable that someone else might select a different set of inductive canons, and if so, there would be no way of showing that one set was better than another for the purpose of gaining factual knowledge. Yet, such a person would regard certain inferences as justified which we would regard as unjustified. He would hold certain conclusions to be well established while we would hold the same conclusions to be disconfirmed. (Wesley C. Salmon, "Should We Attempt to Justify Induction," *Philosophical Studies*, vol. 8 [1957], p. 39.)

theoretical discussion and pass to the simplest actions of daily life, they follow the inductive principle as surely as does every earth-bound mind.[2]

Induction, on such a view, can dispense with any sort of further legitimation because it reflects an inherent commitment of the human mind, built into the programming of our thought, so to speak.

Such a position is all very well as far as it goes. But of course it does not *justify* induction – though, to be sure, it *explains* our recourse to it. And this alone is not very satisfying. Even if induction is "what comes natural," this does little towards its legitimation. Folly is not less natural to man than sagacity. Seemingly natural and common-sense procedures are not rationally justified by their mere possession of these features. It is in their suitability to common-sense *aims,* and not in their conformity to common sense *methods*, that we must seek the validation of our inductive practices. What we ask of a "justification of induction" is an account of what makes recourse to it appropriate and proper. The answer that induction is *natural* is an *ignoratio elenchi*: it manages only to *explain*, not to *justify* its use.

Any attempt at justifying induction – even by halfway adequate argumentation – has strikingly obvious advantages over an abandonment of the justificatory project, as unachievable or as unnecessary. For only thus can we obtain a usable legitimation of our cognitive techniques for the acquisition of information. We are not left at the tender mercy of instinct, custom, and other such noncognitive resources, but can secure a *rational* support for our inductive endeavors.

Yet the question remains: What advantage does the specifically *methodological-pragmatic* approach to the justification of induction have *vis-à-vis* the other available strategies? Since the demands of brevity preclude anything approaching an exhaustively detailed comparison of relative advantages and disadvantages, we must content ourselves here with indicating in each case the one or two key points that afford the most decisive advantage of the methodological justification over its main rivals.

[2] *Experience and Prediction* (Chicago, 1938), pp. 346–347.

2. NECESSITARIAN APRIORISM

The most radical and decisive mode of justification of induction would be one that proceeds on an entirely *a priori* basis. There are two prime possibilities here:

(1) *Necessitarian (or strict) apriorism.* The endeavor to provide a categorical demonstration that induction *must work* – that it must prove effective because every possible world must have *some* sort of internal order and that the utilization of inductive methods will (sooner or later) yield this.

(2) *Conditional apriorism.* The endeavor to provide a demonstration that induction *will work if anything does*. This envisages a "transcendental argument" to the effect that if any systematic method of inquiry can show how things actually go in the world, then induction can.

Let us begin with the former of these.

Necessitarian apriorism was in fact the position of the early Peirce – during the first of the many stages of his thought about this issue – and it has been revived more recently by Donald C. Williams.[3] Its leading conception is the idea that (1) every world must have *some* order (even a chaos is an order – a haphazard arrangement is a very definite sort of arrangement), and (2) that induction *must* eventually reveal this order as our sampling of nature grows more and more extensive. Thus Peirce, at an early stage, argued as follows for the inconceivability of a universe in which inductive procedures would not be reliable:

If men were not able to learn from induction, it might be because as a general rule, when they had made an induction, the order of things would then undergo a revolution. . . . But this general rule would be capable of being itself discovered by induction; and so it must be a law of such a universe that when the pursuit of the inductive venture by operate. But this second law would itself be

[3] See Donald C. Williams, *The Ground of Induction* (Cambridge, Mass., 1947).

capable of discovery. And so in such a universe there would be nothing which would not sooner or later be known; and it would have an order capable of discovery by a sufficiently long course of reasoning. But this is contrary to the hypothesis, and therefore that hypothesis is absurd.[4]

On this argument, it is inconceivable that inductive procedures should not succeed. After all, Peirce contended, the only sort of world in which induction could fail us, would be an absolutely chance world in which there were no regularities. But even such a disordered universe, seemingly without regularities, exhibits a definite and indeed very simple sort of order, since chaos too is a certain type of order. Thus any world must have some real uniformities,[5] and such uniformities will be discoverable by induction.

But this is a somewhat naive position, as Peirce himself eventually came to realize. For on this picture, a "chaotic" world is chaotic at the level of *events* only, and not that of *laws*. It admits a ready lawful characterization ("randomness" does just that) and is therefore insufficiently imaginative as to how bad a chaos – namely a *nomic* (i.e., law-correlative) chaos – can be. (Compare p. 95 above.)

To be sure, it is difficult to give a counterexample in other than approximate and suggestive terms. (After all, if one could characterize the hypothetical world in question by a neat verbal formula, then it wouldn't be all that chaotic.) But we can certainly envisage a powerful evil being – a combination of the demon of Descartes with that of Maxwell – who defeats all our inductive efforts. For the issue is not that of studying the world inductively *ab extra*, but that of the pursuit of the inductive venture by beings operating *within* the world. And a state of things can surely be imagined where their efforts are always frustrated. (Think here of the simple mathematical fact that any single specification of order in a finite series can be defeated as that series is extended.) Accordingly, a world not amenable to *our* inductive efforts – i.e. those of beings suitably emplaced within it – is certainly conceivable.

---

[4] C. S. Peirce, *Collected Papers*, vol. V, sect. 5.352.
[5] See also *ibid.*, 6.400–6.401.

Considerations along these lines create a well-nigh insuperable obstacle for a necessitarian and aprioristic approach to the justification of induction.

3. CONDITIONAL APRIORISM: LONG RUNISM

In view of the difficulties of the absolute, unconditionally necessitarian version of apriorism, it seems advisable to explore the promise of its less demanding conditional variant. The idea here is to show not that induction must inevitably succeed, but merely that induction will do the job effectively if any *method* whatever can do so. Hans Reichenbach's so-called *pragmatic* justification proceeds in just this way. He argues that induction is preferable to any other way of making predictions because it has the decisive merit of being certain ultimately to reveal regularities to us if they are regularities that we can find out at all – by *any* experience-exploiting process. Such a line of justification does not require showing that induction *must* work, but simply that we have nothing to lose by employing it.[6]

Peirce's self-correctionist approach also proceeds along these lines. It is based on the contention that, if any predictive *method* works, induction is bound ultimately to lead us to it – that if some other nonstandard predictive process is efficacious, induction itself is bound to reveal this in the end.

The guiding idea is that if we persist in the use of inductive methods regardless of our operational starting point, we are bound to be led, step by step, through inductively guided transformations, to a method that works (viz. the inductive method itself). Such an approach envisages the use of an inductive metamethodology for choosing among (possibly noninductive) basic, ground-level methods.

Unfortunately, however, this general strategy begs the question of the appropriateness of induction. After all, it is perfectly possible that a noninductive method might work (yield success) even though we are not in a position to learn this inductively, because there might be insufficient apparent stabilities in the situation for induction to take hold – our ortho-

---

[6] Hans Reichenbach, *Experience and Prediction* (Chicago, 1938), p. 354.

dox inductive vision being oriented in the wrong direction.

Peirce's specifically probabilistic long runism, on the other hand, affords an interesting and more promising variation of this theme, which was also operative in the thought of Hans Reichenbach. His leading idea is that induction emerges as inherently *self-authenticating* once we adopt a suitable construction of induction, namely, regard it as a *statistical* procedure aimed at yielding the real frequencies of traits in nature that establish the "true probabilities" of natural relationships. Construing probabilities as long-range relative frequencies, it is accordingly held that, as Reichenbach put it, "The aim of induction is to find series of events [in nature] whose frequency of occurrence converges towards a limit."[7]

On such an approach, the ratio:

$$\theta_t(\phi/X) = \frac{\text{\# of observed } X\text{'s with the trait } \phi \text{ (to time } t)}{\text{total \# of observed } X\text{'s (to time } t)}$$

is seen to represent the inductively appropriate answer to the question: "What is the probability that an X will have ϕ," because it offers our "best posit (at time t)" for the probability-value in question. As time moves on, we go along readjusting this ratio, with the result, so it is argued, that we are eventually *bound* to approximate the correct probability, because this is *by definition* given as the limit-ratio:

$$\text{pr}(\phi/X) = \lim_{t \to \infty} \theta_t(\phi/X)$$

Thus if the probability in question exists at all, that is if the limit exists, then our (the orthodox inductive) use of θ_t as its best approximation available at the time t is bound to reveal it to us in the long run.

Reichenbach formulated the point as follows:

[I]f there is any method which leads to the limit of the frequency, the inductive principle [= proportional induction] will do the same; if there is a limit of the frequency, the inductive principle is a sufficient condition to find it.[8]

---

[7] *Ibid.*, p. 350.
[8] *Ibid.*, pp. 346–347.

As Peirce liked to put it, statistical induction is a process of reasoning so designed that it is "destined" or "fated" to succeed in the long run if success is attainable at all. Max Black has formulated the underlying line of thought with characteristic cogency:

> A man who proceeds in this way can have no guarantee or assurance that his estimates, constantly revised as information about the series gradually accumulates, will bring him into the neighborhood of a limiting value of the relative frequency. These frequencies may, in fact, diverge. In that case no predictive policy at all will work, and successful induction is impossible. However, if this should not be the case and the series really does have a limiting value for the relative frequency in question, then we can know in advance, and with certainty, that the policy is bound eventually to lead the reasoner to estimates that will remain as close to the limit as desired.[9]

Thus if we are at all in a position to use our experience to arrive at true laws of nature (be they statistical or universal), then continued use of this (so-called) "straight rule" of proportional induction is *bound* to yield them up to us in the long run – and there is no comparable guarantee that any other, significantly different rule will do so.

However, this line of approach also encounters the most serious difficulties. They have already been examined in detail in Sect. 2 of Chapter VI (pp. 100–104) and it will suffice here to observe that the sorts of difficulties set out there cannot but decisively undermine the attractions of the conditionally aprioristic approach to the justification of induction.

4. UNIFORMITARIAN DEDUCTIVISM

The shortcomings of apriorism in *all* its forms suggests the need for a justification that is prepared to make room for *substantive* presuppositions regarding the nature of the world.

[9] Max Black, art. "Induction" in *The Encyclopedia of Philosophy*, ed. by P. Edwards, vol. 4 (New York, 1967), p. 176.

Let us consider some proposed justifications of induction that proceed along such lines.

The uniformitarian deductivist approach to the justification of induction goes back to J. S. Mill's contention that "there is a principle implicit in the very statement of what Induction is; an assumption with regard to the course of nature and the order of the universe."[10] On such a view, the validity of inductive argumentation is taken to follow from an auxiliary substantive principle and to derive its probative cogency on the basis of such an "ultimate major premiss of all inductions," as J. S. Mill calls it.[11] Consider the following argument by way of example:

- Within our experience, it has always happened that p [e.g., that 40% of all A's are B's]
- *Nature is uniform* – it is homogeneous in the specific sense that the same conditions pertain externally to human experience as apply within, so that (limited though it is in space and time) our experience samples nature representatively, and yields a result that is characteristic of the situation as a whole

∴ In nature at large, it always happens that p [that 40% of all A's are B's].

In such argumentation we supplement the specific factual data of the inductive situation with one, all-powerful "blockbuster" principle of randomness or uniformity, whose deployment

[10] John Stuart Mill, *A System of Logic* (8th ed., London, 1895), Bk. III, Chap. III, sect. 1.

[11] [E]very induction may be thrown into the form of a syllogism, by supplying a major premise. If this be actually done, the principle which we are now considering, that of the uniformity of the course of nature, will appear as the ultimate major premise of all inductions. . . . The real proof that what is true of John, Peter, etc., is true of all mankind, can only be, that a different supposition would be inconsistent with the uniformity which we know to exist in the course of nature. Whether there would be this inconsistency or not, may be a matter of long and delicate inquiry; but unless there would, we have no sufficient ground for the major premise of the inductive syllogism. It hence appears, that if we throw the whole course of any inductive argument into a series of syllogisms, we shall arrive by more or fewer steps at an ultimate syllogism, which will have for its major premise the principle, or axiom, of the uniformity of the course of nature. (J. S. Mill, *A System of Logic* [London, 1895; 6th ed.], Bk. III, Chap. III, sect. 1.)

then makes it possible to obtain the inductively warranted conclusion *deductively* from the information-in-hand.

As the issue is seen by Bertrand Russell, who elaborated this line of approach, the basic problem of justifying induction is set out by the question:

> What is the minimum form of the inductive postulate which will, if true, validate accepted scientific inferences? Is there any reason, and if so what, to suppose this minimum postulate true?[12]

Accordingly, Russell embarked on the quest for a suitable "minimal postulate" by recourse to which all our inductive inferences can be validated holus bolus. He envisaged recourse to a single, overarching superpremiss (akin to Mill's "principle of the uniformity of nature," or some analogous principle of ontological uniformity) as a means by which *all* sound inductive arguments can be justified in one fell swoop.

This approach to justifying induction, like that we have ourselves favored above, also views inductive argumentation as a mode of enthymematic deductivism – it too endeavors to justify inductive inferences by reconstruing them in deductive terms. But a difference – a vast difference! – resides in the character of the enthymematic premiss at issue. Our present approach views the question of this enthymematic premiss as a matter of plausibilistically guided selection among a diversified plurality of case-specific alternatives. By contrast, the enthymematic approach envisaged by Russell proceeds in *wholesale* terms, by invoking a single monolithic metaphysical superpremiss (like the principle of the regularity of nature) as capable of doing the job once and for all. Where our approach looks to a proliferation of case-specific enthymematic premisses by which particular inductive arguments can be validated, uniformitarian inductivism envisages an *omnium-gatherum* procedure, in which one single all-encompassing superpremiss is invoked for the justification of inductive reasoning in general.

Now the inherent difficulty of this monolithically enthyme-

---

[12] Bertrand Russell, *Human Knowledge: Its Scope and Limits* (London, 1948), p. 400.

matic approach is rather obvious. For how is one to *justify* the acceptance of this grand metaphysical assumption?[13] Just what is the cognitive standing of that monolithic enthymematic superpremiss which is being asked to bear singlehandedly and alone the whole weight of inductive justification? Is it an unreasoned postulate, an explanatory hypothesis, an inductive discovery, a deliverance of intellectual insight operating *a priori*, or what? No matter which way we turn, a host of difficulties bristles up. Does "intuition" justify it? But what justifies our *acceptance* of this intuition? (It is clearly not self-evident!) Are we to *postulate* it? What authorizes our making such a postulation? And is recourse to "intuition" or "postulation" not just a way of locating the problem rather than solving it? On the other hand, suppose that we say this substantive principle is validated as the result of empirical inquiry – i.e. is itself a product of induction – thus using the very process whose legitimation is *sub judice* as an instrument for establishing a premiss of the legitimative argument. This is obviously a highly problematic and questionable procedure.[14]

It is obviously a major advantage of our own *pluralistic* enthymematicism that this sort of difficulty does not arise. It is avoided because our enthymematic reliance is not placed upon any single substantive (metaphysical) superpremiss. Rather, the enthymematic labor is divided among a diversified mass of theses whose initial status is by no means secured, being (initially) no more than presumptions or plausible suppositions whose availability is underwritten by certain regulative (methodological) mechanisms of cognitive systematization. Its dispensing with any problematic ontological presupposition is clearly a major advantage of the methodological-regulative approach to the justification of induction.

[13] We certainly cannot validate it by a "transcendental argument" from the very possibility of induction, seeing that its role in the present probative context is to underwrite the justification of this very praxis.

[14] J. S. Mill himself characterized the uniformity-of-nature principle as on the one hand an *axiom* that is "the ultimate major premise in all cases of induction," and on the other hand "as itself a generalization from experience," i.e. as the product of an induction. (*Loc. cit.*) The untenability of such a proceeding needs little comment.

5. PROBABILISM

The attempt to justify induction on strictly *probabilistic* grounds has a long and distinguished history in which the names of Laplace, C. S. Peirce (in his middle phase), and Rudolf Carnap figure prominently.[15] The governing idea of such an approach is to treat induction as a type of probabilistic reasoning – relative to the mathematical theory of probabilities. On such an approach, a cogent inductive argument is one whose premisses are such as to render its conclusion highly probable.[16] Stanley Jevons articulated the matter with force and clarity:

> Nature is to us like an infinite ballot-box, the contents of which are being continually drawn, ball after ball, and exhibited to us. Science is but the careful observation of the succession in which balls of various character present themselves; we register the combinations, notice those which seem to be excluded from occurrence, and from the proportional frequency of those which appear we infer the probable character of future drawings.[17]

The version of probabilism which figures in the thought of C. S. Peirce ran roughly as follows. Just as an argument form is by definition *deductively* valid if it leads from true premisses to true conclusions in ALL cases, so it is by definition *inductively* valid if it leads from true premisses to true conclusions in MOST cases. A valid deductive argument form is *invariably* truth-preserving; a valid inductive argument form is *probabilistically*

---

[15] Much interesting historical information is given in Ian Hacking, *The Emergence of Probability* (Cambridge, 1975).

[16] Some writers suggest using the relative "more probable than alternatives" in place of the categorical "highly probable" here. Thus Richard Swinburne writes: "[A]n inductive argument is one for which . . . the premisses make the conclusion more probable than any equally detailed rival." (*Idem* [ed.], *The Justification of Induction* [Oxford, 1974], pp. 4–5.) This clearly will not do. If the evidence indicates that an otherwise fair die has a slight bias in favor of 6, this renders the conclusion "The die will come up 6 on the next toss" more probable than any of its comparable alternatives. But one would not want to say that we here have a cogent inductive argument for claiming the truth of this contention.

[17] Stanley Jevons, *The Principles of Science: A Treatise on Logic and Scientific Method* (2nd ed.; London, 1907), p. 150.

or majoritatively truth-preserving. There are certainly some argument forms that are inductively valid in this sense. For example:

(I)   Most A's are B's
       x is an A
       _____
       $\therefore$ x is a B

The inductive validity of form (I) arguments, in the specified sense of leading from true premisses to true conclusions in most cases, is – so one may plausibly argue – a *logical* fact, a circumstance that can be established by deductive reasoning alone (seeing that the first premiss to all appearances guarantees that most instances of this argument form will yield truths).

But this analysis does not quite do the job. For the question clearly still remains: Is it rational in the particular instances to *accept the conclusions* arrived at by reasoning from true premisses by argument forms that are inductively valid in the specified sense?

In responding to this question one clearly cannot argue that it is "rational" in the sense of *deductive* rationality. For it is clearly possible (i.e., *logically* possible) that such reasoning should have the deductively unsatisfactory feature of leading from true premisses to false conclusions. Is it, then, rational in the *inductive* sense? It surely appears so, because an argument that is *inductively* valid can be marshalled in behalf of the acceptability of the conclusion. This argument would run as follows:

Most [arguments that are of form (I) and have true premisses] are [arguments that yield true conclusions]
X is an argument of form (I) that has true premisses
_____
$\therefore$ X yields a true conclusion

Since this argument is itself of form (I), it is inductively valid. Hence whenever X is an argument that satisfies the second premiss here (i.e. takes form (I) and has true premisses), it is inductively appropriate to take the stance that X yields a true conclusion. *Quod erat demonstrandum.* The (inductive) validity of inductive argumentation can thus seemingly be demonstrated strictly *a priori*.

Though Peirce was at one stage persuaded by such reasoning that probabilistic operations can validate the rationality of inference by induction *a priori*, on the grounds of theoretical general principle alone, there are – as he himself came to see – grounds for serious dissatisfaction here.[18] Form (I) argumentation is not, strictly speaking, probatively cogent at all: what is actually needed if we are to arrive at its conclusion plausibly from true premises is not (I), but rather its cousin:

Most *A*'s are *B*'s
x is an (appropriately random instance of) *A*

∴ *x* is a *B*

For even if most *A*'s are *B*'s, it still remains a perfectly genuine prospect if *x* is an *A* arrived at by some inappropriate selection process, that most of the time *x* will fail to be a *B*. To make the argument go through, we must make some recourse to an additional, logically quite extraneous, and inherently problematic, condition of randomization.[19]

Attempts to reduce inductive to probabilistic reasonings undoubtedly have many attractions. But the implementation of such probabilistic approaches encounters one fundamental difficulty throughout, namely, that of somehow assuring that that sector of nature which we encounter in the course of our observational "sampling" is in fact sufficiently representative to yield the randomness requisite for probabilistic argumentation. To be sure, we know, *a priori* and with demonstrative certainty, that most of the samples drawn *randomly* from a population will have nearly the same descriptive composition

[18] See C. F. Delaney, "Peirce on Induction and the Uniformity of Nature," *The Philosophical Forum*, vol. 4 (1973), pp. 438–448; see especially p. 439.

[19] Another problem is no less serious here. How in the context of the inductive project could we ever establish the premises of the form "Most *A*'s are *B*'s" (or "*A*'s are probably *B*'s with such-and-such degree of probability"). Clearly only by inductive means. And so inductive reasoning based on argumentation in the style of form (I) could not ever get us off the ground. As long as our validation of inductive arguments is confined to this of the style of form (I), we will never be in a position to put our (*ex hypothesi*) validated modes of argumentation to work, because the sort of premiss they crucially require will not be available.

as the parent population as a whole, and that statistical inference based on such representative sampling is a "valid" process in the sense that it yields conclusions that are true most of the time. (This is something that follows *ex vi terminorum* from the definition of "random.") But all this hinges on presupposing the randomness or representativeness of our sampling – a point at which we stand on very shaky ground. (To realize that this worry is real, one need not impute malice to nature, believing that it somehow puts on a misleading show for us; the responsibility for the distortion could lie wholly on our side, in that we simply fail to look in the right places, say because our spatiotemporal setting in the scheme of things is somehow biased.) Moreover, no statistical or probabilistic inference from sample to population is possible in the absence of any information about the population as a whole. And any claims we might stake in this regard run into the roadblock of Hume's devastating critique of the argument from design. For to tell that the sectors of nature we have examined are representative of the whole we must determine just how great a part of the whole it is that we have actually examined. And this is difficult to do until we have actually taken full measure of the whole, what we cannot effectively do (and which, if we did *per impossibile* achieve it, would render our need for sampling processes otiose).

Security against the prospect of observational bias is only to be had from a metaphysical presupposition (e.g., a principle of uniformity or homogeneity assuring that when we look around in our own neighborhood we encounter a situation typical of nature-at-large). A metaphysical principle on the order of Mill's Principle of the Uniformity of Nature or some comparable metaphysical *deus ex machina* device is accordingly needed once more – this time to provide the key premiss of randomness on which the whole probabilistic argument hinges. There simply is *no way* to guarantee at the very outset of inquiry the appropriateness of probabilistic or statistical processes of inference without presupposing a metaphysical principle along some such lines.[20]

[20] Among the first to see this point clearly was C. D. Broad in *Scientific Thought* (London, 1923), where he maintained that our confidence in well-established inductions cannot be justified by any known principle of inference or of probability

A probabilistic approach to the scrutiny of nature always faces the big issue of *where the needed probabilities are to come from*. The calculus of probabilities merely enables us to move from some (preestablished) probabilities to others – to calculate derived probability numbers from those already given. It says nothing, and can say nothing, about how we are ever to extract probabilities in the first place from the nonprobabilistic facts that must provide our entry into the probabilistic arena. And it lies in the very nature of the case that induction is always required here. Authentic probability values are never *given*, but always inferred, and inferred by processes in whose operation induction must play a part. The *application* of probabilities in real-world situations only makes sense in a context where induction is *already* in hand, seeing that any invocation of definite and determinate probabilities with respect to actual phenomena and their laws presupposes the mechanisms of induction. We cannot use probabilities to justify induction, because we need induction (or else some randomness-assuring metaphysical assumptions) to obtain probabilities. Any assimilation of induction to probabilistic or statistical reasoning requires that we know something in advance concerning the constitution of the populations at issue – something that cannot be extracted from purely logical considerations and is itself of the factual sort that must be obtained by inductive means.[21]

To say all this is not to quarrel with the calculus of probabilities: the mathematics of probability is of unquestionable cogency. But its application to the statistical data garnered in the real world in effect begs all the big questions. Hume's basic point holds good: there is no decisive reason of purely theoretical general principle to suppose that what our data would have us class as "probable" conclusions will generally be true and

---

unless some further factual premiss about the physical world is assumed. (Pp. 403–404.) Broad thus generalized the train of thought implicit in Keynes' justification of induction in *A Treatise on Probability* (London, 1921). The point has become a commonplace of English philosophizing on the subject. Cf. P. F. Strawson, *Introduction to Logical Theory* (London, 1952), where however the point is turned (as at present) against the probabilistic justification of induction.

[21] Hans Reichenbach was quite right in holding that "a justification of induction must be given before the use of probability considerations." (*Theory of Probability* [Berkeley and Los Angeles, 1949], p. 446.)

"improbable" ones false. Probabilistic argumentation of itself is not a tool of sufficient power to underwrite the validation of induction, because we already need to have induction in hand to make any applicative use of it.[22]

A variant mode of probabilism takes the form of a deductivism that leads to a probabilistically formulated (rather than categorial) conclusion. Such an approach substitutes for the standard conclusion of an inductive argument, let it be C, its probabilized transform: "Probably C." Given an inductive inference from a family of premises $P_1, P_2, \ldots P_n$ to a conclusion C, probabilistic inductivism then maintains that the acceptability of this argument turns on the *deductive validity* of the corresponding argument to the probabilified conclusion "C is (highly) probable." On this approach – developed most fully by Rudolf Carnap[23] – the *inductive* cogency of the argument in view is made to hinge on the question of whether or not the argument

P_1
P_2
.
.
.
P_n
———
$\therefore$ Probably C (i.e., pr $(C) > 1 - \epsilon$ for some suitably small ϵ)

is *deductively* valid given the mechanisms of the calculus of probability. And this is tantamount to the question of whether the *conditional* probability of the conclusion relative to the premises is relatively high:

$$\text{pr}(C/P_1 \ \& \ P_2 \ \& \ \ldots \ \& \ P_n) > 1 - \epsilon$$

Accordingly, "inductive logic" is not an independent venture at all, it can be treated as a mere adjunct of the theory of probability.

*   *   *

[22] The lines of thought at issue here are developed elegantly in Dickinson S. Miller, "Professor Donald Williams *vs.* Hume," *The Journal of Philosophy*, vol. 44 (1947), pp. 673–684.

[23] See his *Logical Foundations of Probability* (Chicago, 1952, 2nd ed. 1962).

The difficulty, however, is that such a probabilizing of our inductive circumstances does not enable us to answer the questions we actually want to ask.[24] For when we ask "What is the color of the book?", then if all that we are told is that "The probability is high (relative to such-and-such data) that the color of the book is blue," this does not tell us what the color is. On such an approach we are constrained to abandon the traditional aim of describing the world. To take the turn of deductivistic probabilism in this present form is accordingly to become enmeshed in the fallacity of *ignoratio elenchi*, seeing that the mission of inquiry is to answer our questions about nature. And if we try to base judgments of fact on judgments of probability – i.e., by the move from "*C* is highly probable" to "*C* is true" – then we encounter the decisive difficulty that the nonoccurrence of each of initially exhaustive alternatives can be made as probable as we please, a fact that produces the anomaly which has been dramatized as the "Lottery Paradox."[25]

There are still other variants of probabilism. One especially interesting and influential approach along these lines envisages the use of Bayes' theorem to compute probabilities of generalizations relative to observational data that substantiate them. Such a strategy, attractive though it is, also encounters fatal difficulties. For, given the character of Bayes' theorem, it requires an assurance at the very outset that all the mooted generalizations have a non-zero *a priori* probability.[26] And how can such an assurance be obtained?[27]

[24] This issue is, of course, additional to the preceding worry about where probability numbers come from.

[25] The lottery paradox was originally formulated by Henry E. Kyburg, Jr., *Probability and the Logic of Rational Belief* (Middletown, Conn., 1961). For an analysis of its wider implications for inductive logic see R. Hilpinen, *Rules of Acceptance and Inductive Logic* (Amsterdam, 1968; *Acta Philosophica Fennica*, fasc. 22), pp. 39–49.

[26] This is so, because the definition of conditional probability

$$pr\ (h/e) = \frac{pr\ (h)}{pr\ (e\&h)}$$

plays a key role in the derivation. (Note: h = "the hypothesis"; e = "the evidence".) And here the fact that the denominator *pr* (e&h) must be nonzero, constrains the requirement that pr (h) must be nonzero.

[27] The strategy at issue goes back to W. Stanley Jevons, *The Principles of Science* (2nd ed., London, 1877; see Chap. XII). He solves this problem by assuming that every conceivable hypothesis possesses an equal *a priori* probability, which will certainly do the trick if one can somehow establish the finitude of the alternatives.

J. M. Keynes proposed recourse to a Principle of Limited Variety to meet this sort of requirement. The mission of such a principle – which stipulates that only finitely many logically independent properties are available to serve in the constant conjunctions represented by natural laws – is to assure that the *a priori* probability of any inductive generalization is non-zero. For if we know from the outset that only a finite number of types exists within nature, then there can only be a finite number of possible laws of combination. And in such a domain of finite alternatives, Bayes' theorem can be used to secure noncircular probabilistic support for our inductive generalizations.

But of course the problem at once arises: whence do we obtain this *a priori* stipulation of finite complexity? It surely cannot be through induction – only a vitiating circularity lies down that road. Keynes himself seems to have held that we have some manner of *direct intuitive apprehension* of this underlying grounding principle, an apprehension dependent on experience but not inductively derived from it. He suggested that the Principle of the Uniformity of Nature and the Law of Causality rest on the same sort of footing, obtaining "invincible certainty from some valid principle darkly present to our minds."[28] But this sort of contention is surely rather a formulation of the problem than a solution of it. The preferability of an approach that can dispense with such problematic metaphysical presuppositions is once again clear.

6. INTUITIONISM

A recourse to metaphysical principles along Keynes–Russell lines invites the invocation of intuition to validate this justificatory superpremiss. But some writers take the less circuitous route of invoking intuition to validate induction *directly*. They have it that we can simply "see with the mind's eye" that induction affords the proper mechanism for grounding claims regarding matters of fact and existence. On such an approach, the validity of induction is seen as a matter self-evident to

[28] J. M. Keynes, *A Treatise on Probability* (London, 1948), pp. 263–264.

intuition – a matter accessible to a suitably prepared and oriented mind. In the 14th century, John Buridan already taught "that the human intellect is compelled by its natural inclination (*inclinatio naturalis*) to truth to concede a universal proposition by having had [uncontradicted] experience of numerous singular instances of the universal."[29] Wesley Salmon has formulated the line of thought that underlies this approach in a way difficult to improve on:

> [I]t is sometimes said that we must utilize a kind of deductive intuition or logical common sense to 'see' that *modus ponens* is a correct and legitimate form of inference. . . . Similarly, the argument continues, if a person is so inductively blind that he cannot see the superiority of induction by enumeration . . . [over its alternatives] there is nothing to be done. We can no more logically compel a person lacking in inductive common sense to accept acceptable rules than we can in the case of deduction. . . . [T]he ultimate appeal for the justification of inductive rules is our intuitive sense for the concept of inductive evidence.[30]

But Salmon goes on to argue – quite rightly – that such a line of approach cannot achieve its justificatory aims:

> After a small dose of Hume's *Enquiry* we can, without difficulty, imagine all sorts of states of affairs in which practically all – if not absolutely all – of our future inductive inferences with true premises turn out to have false conclusions. We can, furthermore, construct perverse kinds of inductive rules (as judged in the light of our inductive intuitions) and describe possible worlds in which these rules would be very successful indeed. We cannot provide, without circularity, any reason for supposing that we do not, in fact, live in some such world. A Cartesian demon could addle our brains and throw us

[29] Julius R. Weinberg, *Abstraction, Relation, and Induction* (Madison and Milwaukee, 1965), p. 153.
[30] Wesley C. Salmon in Richard Swinburne (ed.), *The Justification of Induction* (Oxford, 1974), p. 54. (Note that Salmon does not here speak *in propria persona*.)

into linguistic confusion, but we cannot conceive of any-thing he could do to make *modus ponens* not literally truth-preserving. He would, however, have no trouble in completely subverting any inductive rule we can set forth. It is one thing to appeal to logical intuition con-cerning the acceptability of rules which, to the best of our most critical reflection, must be truth-preserving in all possible worlds. It is quite another to make such an appeal to our inductive-logical intuition for the accept-ability of inductive rules when critical reflection reveals that they may turn out to be entirely unsatisfactory in our actual world and distinctly less successful than others we can formulate.[31]

There is little choice but to reject intuitionism as evading, rather than solving, the problem of rational justification – seeking to obtain by theft what should be the product of hard work.

7. INDUCTIVISM

The failure of the various aprioristic and deductivistic ap-proaches enhances the attraction of any prospects of a some-how inductive approach to the justification of the inductive method of our science. On such an approach, induction is itself regarded as an empirically grounded principle of reasoning which is supported by the overwhelming weight of past experience.

The obvious difficulty of such a venture lies in its blatant circularity. Where the legitimacy of induction is itself at issue, we clearly cannot use this process as a means of validation. It is clearly problematic to let a particular probative technique sit in judgment on itself – it cannot give a rationally satisfactory ruling where its own jurisdiction is in question.

On the other hand, someone might argue as follows:

The entire search for a single, overall, synoptic and mono-lithic justification of induction is misguided. All we need

[31] *Op. cit.*, p. 55.

be able to do is to justify seriatim the various *particular* inductive arguments we use. We can thus proceed to justify induction on a retail rather than wholesale basis.

This approach is presumably to be implemented along something like the following lines. Let *a, a', a''*, etc., be (particular) inductive arguments; let *I* be the set of all (correct) inductive arguments; and let $a \rightarrow a'$ represent "*a* justifies (validates, warrants) *a'*." One can distinguish between the idea of a *collective* (wholesale, synoptic) justification of all inductive arguments on a once-and-for-all basis as per "There is one single argument *a* that validates all inductive arguments"

$$(J_1) \qquad (\exists a)(\forall a')[a' \in I \rightarrow a > a']$$

on the one hand, and on the other the idea of a *distributive* (retail, piecemeal) justification of all particular inductive arguments holding "For each inductive argument there is some validating argument or other":

$$(J_2) \qquad (\forall a')(\exists a)[a' \in I \rightarrow a > a']$$

Here (J_2) is to all appearances far weaker than (J_1), and yet it is nevertheless perfectly clear that if we manage to secure (J_2), we have achieved a perfectly adequate "justification" of induction that gives us all we need and can ask for. The justificatory distributionism of (J_2) is good enough for our purposes; we need not resort to the justificatory collectivism of (J_1).

All this is true as far as it goes, but it is not to the purpose. For the question remains: What effective route is there to the establishment of (J_2) save that of induction itself. To be sure, all's well as long as we can manage *in each particular case* to avoid – altogether, and "all the way back," so to speak – using the particular inductive rule of argument in question in its own defense. But the realization of this project leads to problems. For consider the sequence:

a_0 = some particular inductive argument

a_1 = the particular inductive argument ($\neq a_0$) used to
justify a_0

.

.

.

a_i = the particular inductive argument ($\neq a_0, a_1, \ldots, a_{i-1}$)
used to justify a_{i-1}

Now we are clearly not finished with the justificatory job until we have established not just that each argument of the finite (terminating) sequence $a_1, a_2, \ldots a_n$ is acceptable, but that the arguments of the whole series are – i.e. that $(\forall i)a_i$ is acceptable. We will be told – and quite rightly so – that an effective justification for a_0 hinges on the fact that the regress can be completed. And this is something that clearly cannot be done *deductively* but must proceed *inductively*. The generalization at issue is such that induction is the only means to its own establishment. And so it is clear that the regress can only be completed by an induction (presumably, induction by simple enumeration). Now let this inductive argument be a_0^1. How are we to justify it? Presumably by an inductive argument a_1^1. And this in turn must be justified by an inductive argument a_2^1. This process yields a sequence a_i^1 for which we must establish the acceptability of $(\forall i)a_i^2$. And this calls for a further inductive argument a_i^2. It is thus clear that the whole regress cannot be completed because the approach at issue (like that of Lewis Carroll's Achilles and Tortoise argument) sets the task up in such a manner that it cannot be discharged. The distributionism of a piecemeal justification of all particular inductive arguments is thus not an effective strategy. At some point one general argument must be deployed to do the whole job. And at this stage we are driven back from (J_2) to (J_1). The strategy of a seriatim approach thus proves unavailing.[32]

One ingenious recent attempt to justify induction by inductive means is due to Richard Braithwaite.[33] We can – so Braithwaite contends – move from a quite uncontroversial

[32] Then too there is the Peircean consideration that whatever argument does the job in schema (J_2) when the straight rule of statistical induction is at issue, will afford us a tool that can also justify the whole of induction in the manner of schema (J_1).

[33] R. B. Braithwaite, *Scientific Explanation* (Cambridge, 1953), pp. 264–292.

premiss via the mere *fact* that induction is justified to the desired conclusion that it is reasonable to believe in the effectiveness of induction. The argument he sets out runs essentially as follows:

> (i) *It is reasonable to believe that* induction has worked well in the past
> (ii) Induction affords an appropriate mode of reasoning (that is, an inference can properly be made from a character's being exhibited in the past to its obtaining in general)

> ∴ (iii) *It is reasonable to believe that* induction works well in general (and is thus an appropriate mode of reasoning)

Note that when the italicized qualifiers are suppressed, the conclusion follows from the premisses, given the mere fact of induction's being justified – as stipulated in the second premiss. Braithwaite maintains this to be an appropriate mode of reasoning because it conforms to the pattern

> (1) X's belief that p is reasonable
> (2) "*p* entails *q*" affords an appropriate principle of reasoning

> (3) X's belief that q is reasonable

Both cases exhibit an identical pattern: the move from a reasonable premiss and an (*ex hypothesi*) true implication to a reasonable conclusion. The mere fact that a (suitable) implication-relation obtains is seen as capable of transmitting reasonableness from premiss to conclusion.

But the difficulty in both cases is also the same. For (as Braithwaite himself clearly recognizes) if one insists upon inserting the reasonable belief operator also into premiss (ii) of his argument, then the argumentation is no longer able to do its appointed work, seeing that we now posit the very conclusion to be established as a premiss of the argument. Only as long as *the mere fact* of induction's validity is alone needed for the argument can it be seen as potentially serviceable towards the designated task of providing an inductive justification of induction.

But it is readily seen that the argumentation will not succeed unless its key implicational premiss too is reasonably believed. Consider the following case:

(1) X believes p and believes it reasonably
(2) While *in fact* "p entails q" holds and X indeed believes that p entails q, X believes this for a grossly inappropriate and incorrect reason, and his belief in q is predicated on his belief in the combination of p and p-entails-q.

In such circumstances one would not hesitate to *deny* that X believes q reasonably. For while his belief in q is indeed rationalizable it is – given the inappropriateness at issue – not in fact held by X himself on the basis that is reasonable. To be held reasonably, a discursive belief must be held on reasonable grounds reasonably exploited. Braithwaite's argumentation rests on the supposition that the reasonableness of a belief turns on whether the process of inference that *can* be used to desire it is effective, without reference to the question of whether the process of inferences by which the believer does *actually* derive it is reasonably believed by him. But this supposition is inappropriate. Cognitive rationality requires not just the correct alignment of beliefs but their correct alignment for the right sorts of reason – not some bizarre and idiosyncratic convictions that somehow "just happen" to yield correct results.

Reasonable belief is not subject to the inference pattern

$$\frac{\begin{array}{l} Bp \\ p \to q \end{array}}{\therefore \ Bq}$$

but rather to

$$\frac{\begin{array}{l} Bp \\ B(p \to q) \end{array}}{\therefore \ Bq}$$

As discussions of the "Gettier paradox" have served to indicate,[34] an argument cannot establish a conclusion in which a cognitive modality is present if the modal chain is broken by the presence of unmodalized premisses. In the epistemology of knowledge and rational belief, as in ethics of right conduct, what matters is clearly not just doing the correct thing, but doing it for the right sort of reasons. And in fact, the initial inference is clearly unacceptable – *inter alia* because it purports logical omniscience in yielding the consequence that someone who believes something reasonably thereby reasonably believes all of its consequences: that in reasonably believing the axioms we *eo ipso* so believe all of the theorems, *even those it has never occurred to us to recognize as such*. The first principle, accordingly, deals not with rational belief *per se*, but rather with its implicit commitments. The second inference principle, on the other hand, is relatively innocuous. Given that we are (*ex hypothesi*) dealing with *rational* believers, it is plausible enough to suppose that they are able "to put two and two together" in this way to extract the obvious consequences of their actual beliefs. But of course once we make the shift to the second mode of argumentation and insist that the implicational premiss too must be (not just true, but) rationally believed, then – as we have seen – the utility of Braithwaite's argument is destroyed because circularity now emerges in a vitiating form.

And how could it be otherwise? It is a fact of probative life that an argument can only establish its conclusion if its premisses are *available* – if they have *already* been rendered acceptable to us. For probative purposes we cannot simply fall back on the truth of the premisses as spontaneously generated *ex nihilo*: this is something that must be established. And due recognition of this fundamental fact engenders the collapse of Braithwaite's attempt to clear the inductive justification of induction of the charge of circularity.

It is a significant point of merit of the present erotetic-methodological approach that it affords the advantages of an inductive strategy for the justification of induction, but yet is

[34] See E. L. Gettier, "Is Justified True Belief Knowledge?," *Analysis*, vol. 23 (1963), pp. 121–123. A useful analysis of the Gettier problem is given in Roderick Chisholm, *Theory of Knowledge* (2nd ed., Englewood Cliffs, 1977), pp. 105–111.

able to do so without forcing us into a choice between vicious regress and vitiating circularity.

8. ANALYTICAL RATIONALISM: THE PROBLEM DISSOLVED

Analytical rationalism maintains, in effect, that induction does *not* stand in need of any justification designed to show that it somehow answers to the demands of rationality, because it itself forms part of the standard of rationality. Its position is as follows: Any attempt to "justify" induction is futile because the inductive style of argumentation serves to *define* what rational argumentation in inductive contexts is all about. To ask for a justification here is like asking for a measurement of the standard meter rod: the rationality of induction is implicit in the very conception of "rationality" as such. Thus P. F. Strawson writes that:

> [T]o ask whether it is reasonable to place reliance on inductive procedures is like asking whether it is reasonable to proportion the degree of one's convictions to the strength of the evidence. Doing this is what 'being reasonable' *means* in such a context. . . . In applying or withholding the epithets 'justified', 'well founded', &c., in the case of specific beliefs, we are appealing to, and applying, inductive standards. But to what standards are we appealing when we ask whether the application of inductive standards is justified or well grounded? If we cannot answer, then no sense has been given to the question. Compare it with the question: Is the law legal? It makes perfectly good sense to inquire of a particular action, of an administrative regulation, or even, in the case of some states, of a particular enactment of the legislature, whether or not it is legal. The question is answered by an appeal to a legal system, by the application of a set of legal (or constitutional) rules or standards. But it makes no sense to inquire in general whether the law of the land, the legal system as a whole, is or is not legal.[35]

[35] *Introduction to Logical Theory* (London, 1953), p. 257.

And A. J. Ayer writes in a similar vein that any justification of induction will have to postulate or

> assume that the future can . . . be relied on to resemble ˎthe past. No doubt this assumption is correct, but there can be no way of proving it without its being presupposed. So, if circular proofs are not to count, there can be no proof. . . . This does not mean that the scientific method is irrational. It could be irrational only if there were a standard of rationality which it failed to meet; whereas in fact it goes to set the standard: arguments are judged to be rational or irrational by reference to it.[36]

Such an approach in effect dissolves or dismisses the problem of justifying inductive argumentation, abolishing it *as a problem* by its stance that it is pointless or even senseless to ask for a justification for the standard that is itself determinative of the processes of rational justification. It insists that a proper understanding of induction automatically carries with it a rational commitment to accepting its authority. We have here a transcendental argument, reminiscent of Kant's, that embeds the rationality of induction within the very structure of human rationality.

The key shortcoming of such a view lies in its stand that, in

---

[36] *The Problem of Knowledge* (Harmondsworth, 1956), pp. 74–75. Again, Max Black describes the position at issue in the following terms:

> The challenge to the claim that inductive arguments cannot be said to be justified might be met in the following way: Suppose a man has learned, partly from his own experience and partly from the testimony of others, that in a vast variety of circumstances, when stones are released they fall toward the ground. Let him consider the proposition *K*, that any stone chosen at random and released will do likewise. This is, in the writer's opinion, a paradigm case for saying that the man in question (any of us) has a good reason for asserting *K* and is therefore justified in asserting *K* rather than not-*K*. Similarly, this is a paradigm case for saying that the man in question is reasonable in asserting *K* and would be unreasonable in asserting not-*K*, on the evidence at hand. Anybody who claimed otherwise would not be extraordinarily and admirably scrupulous but would be abusing language by violating some of the implicit criteria for the uses of "good reason," "justified," and "reasonable," to which he, like the interlocutor with whom he succeeds in communicating, is in fact committed. . . . (He would be behaving like a man who insisted that only stallions deserved to be called horses.) (Art. "Induction" in *The Encyclopedia of Philosophy*, ed. by P. Edwards, vol. 4 [New York, 1967], pp. 177–178.)

the course of exfoliating the *modus operandi* of rationality, we touch rock bottom with induction – that induction is of itself an ultimate component of rationality, a *ne plus ultra* of rational justification. To take this stance towards induction is surely to see the end of the line as being reached too soon.

There are certainly imaginable alternatives to the family of mechanisms that comprise scientific inductivism as we know it – other resources for arriving at explanations and predictions: guesswork, "intuition," custom, occultism, etc. Given the existence of such alternatives for filling the gaps in the structure of our information-in-hand, it seems altogether reasonable to ask for a justification of induction that manages not only to *say that* our reliance on induction is rational (which is true enough), but also to *explain why* it is so. No doubt induction is reasonable by the *established* canons of rationality, but we may still wonder whether in this instance these canons are themselves *appropriate*. To revert to Strawson's analogy: it is indeed senseless to ask why the legal system is *legal*, but it is perfectly natural and proper to wonder whether the legal system is *just* – that is, whether it is able to attain the ends for which legality is instituted in the first place. The key issue is whether the product of those standards and criteria actually *merits* acceptance. And even though it may well be senseless to ask whether induction is an *appropriate* mode of thinking – since this "goes without saying" relative to the accepted standards of appropriateness – it remains altogether sensible to ask why it is *rational* (i.e., actually serves the ends with reference to which our standards of appropriateness are instituted). To be sure, there is no doubt that by all the ordinary standards of "good reason" and "cogent grounding" our inductive arguments do furnish just such a basis for our inductive claims. Common sense, ordinary usage, and established custom are doubtless squarely on the side of induction. But the question remains: How is it that what the ordinary standards categorize in this way is actually so qualified – that we commonly *call* a "good reason" in this context really *is* a good reason.

A request for rational satisfaction along these lines seems altogether in order. Admitting that induction is an integral part of standard rationality, we want to know what there is about cognitive rationality as a whole that makes it reasonable and appropriate that induction should be a part of it.[37] The concept of rationality is inherently teleological; it is oriented towards the realization of the purposes of the intellectual enterprise. And we are perfectly entitled to ask whether – and how – an adherence to the standard ground-rules of induction can conduce to such a realization. There is just too little rational satisfaction to be derived from the "induction is the end of the line" stance that is at issue in analytical inductivism.

Accordingly, it emerges as a comparative advantage of our methodological-pragmatic approach that it takes the problem of justification seriously enough to endeavor to provide for our inductive methods a justificatory rationale of this sort. For it supports them through the purpose-oriented consideration that it is reasonable to expect induction to succeed in realizing the aims for which it is instituted as a process of inquiry and reasoning.

9. FALSIFICATIONISM

Falsificationism takes a very different sort of line. It does not represent an attempt to justify traditional induction, but rather a proposal to *replace* it – to put a very different sort of ampliative methodology in its place. Falsificationism sees the move from evidence to hypothesis – the process of answering an evidence-transcending question – as being at bottom a matter of *possibility-elimination*. Its basic strategy is that of excluding on the basis of suitably decisive tests or experiments all those hypotheses that are false. Laplace put the leading idea as follows:

> If we try all the hypotheses which can be formed in regard to the cause of phenomena we should arrive, by a process of exclusion, at the true one. This means has often been employed with success. Sometimes people arrived at several hypotheses which explain equally well all the facts

[37] The matter is one of overall coherence. And this applies to standards in general. If our standard meter rods were to shrink by one-half relative to everything else, we would no longer call them a meter long and would demote them from their position as standard as clearly unfit to continue to serve as such.

known, and among which scientists were divided, until decisive observations have made known the true one.[38]

The positive search for evidence supportive of a favored alternative is now replaced by the *via negativa* of an elimination-process to rule out rival alternatives. As falsificationism sees it, we answer our data-transcending questions about the world by a process of hypothesis and testing, of conjecture and refutation. The leading modern exponent of such a retreat from orthodox inductivism is Karl Popper, whose publications over many years have forcefully hammered at the point that no amount of confirmatory evidence can establish the truth or even the probability of a scientific theory.

Serious questions, however, confront the claims of such a falsificationist program to qualify as functional equivalent of inductivism – a genuine alternative to it. After all, the object of the enterprise of inquiry is the pursuit of truth – to find answers to our questions about nature that can reasonably and defensibly be held to be true answers. And how can the falsificationist program effectually help here? It is a prime weakness of the falsificationist approach that it proposes to pursue truth by the elimination of error. To falsify a conjectured truth-candidate is to do no more than to eliminate one possibility. And here lies a problem. Once one establishes, for example, that the value of the ratio of the circumference of a circle to its diameter, π, is not 3.12222. . . (with 2's *ad indefinitum*), is one really any closer to the true answer? If we know the fingerprint is not X's, that still leaves Y, Z, and a great many others. As any schoolmaster knows, the possibilities of "getting it wrong" are virtually endless. Error is hydra-headed – eliminate one possibility and a multitude of others spring up in its place. Only in those very special cases where it is given *a priori* that only a finite spectrum of possibilities exist, does the process of elimination yield a secure method for drawing near to the truth.

To be sure, when the totality of possible answers form a range of a suitably convenient structure – if we know (for example) that the correct answer must lie within one sector of a

[38] Pierre Simon de Laplace, *A Philosophical Essay on Probabilities*, tr. by F. W. Truscott and F. L. Emory (London and New York, 1902), Ch. XVII, *ad fin.*

certain grid – then an appropriate process of elimination will inevitably lead to the correct answer. If a problem is bound to have a solution within a certain delineated range, then a search-process of sequential elimination is bound to lead to it sooner or later. In all such cases, however, the circumstance that a process of elimination is a sure-fire method for drawing nearer to the truth hinges on its being fixed *a priori* that the range of possible answers has such a conveniently benign structure.[39] (If it is not to be fixed *a priori* but only *a posteriori*, other difficulties arise. For we then cannot avoid induction in delimiting the range of hypotheses that are *worth* trying to falsify.)

Again, if it were given that the mind of man possessed a Peirce-reminiscent natural tendency towards the truth – if it were assured that we will not ceaselessly stumble about from answers that are bad to those that are no better, but generally managed to replace incorrect answers by ones that "come closer to the truth" – then too we may be confident that a process of trial and error elimination will lead us nearer to the mark.[40] But of course this bit of epistemological metaphysics is highly problematic.

These observations indicate an important point. Falsificationism is an efficient instrument in the pursuit of the truth only if we are prepared to adopt a position akin to a doctrine of finite possibilities, or a doctrine of convenient range-structure, or a doctrine of truth-tropism. Only a metaphysical contention along some such lines could make falsificationism a promising tool in the search for truth.

Thus with falsificationism too we again confront the problematic issue of how the needed metaphysico-epistemological presupposition could ever be rendered available for use as a justificatory premiss. In this present context also, it once more proves to be a significant point of comparative advantage of the methodological justification of induction that it can dispense with any reliance on a problematic metaphysical presupposition.

[39] For a good discussion of eliminationism and its theoretical presuppositions see Chapter IV of G. H. von Wright, *The Logical Problem of Induction*, 2nd ed. (Oxford, 1957).

[40] This is in effect C. S. Peirce's position. See the author's *Peirce's Philosophy of Science* (Notre Dame, 1978).

10. CONCLUSION

One does not establish a philosophical doctrine by showing its rivals to have shortcomings – falsificationism fails us here in philosophical inquiry, even as it generally does in empirical inquiry itself. The fact that *other* philosophical positions have their problems and failings will never mean that the one in view does not. Nevertheless, the deficiencies of its rivals, as we have surveyed them, does lend credence to the idea that the methodological-pragmatic justification of induction that has been set out in these pages deserves careful and sympathetic scrutiny as a potentially promising strategy for the solution of this much-disputed problem.

Name Index

Subject Index

statistical reasoning 42–44
straight rule 98–115
systematicity of nature 162–165
systematicity, parameters of 31–32, 49
systematization, cognitive 30–47, 48–50, 179–182

teleology of induction 6–7
thesis-pragmatism 136
this-or-nothing argumentation 52–54, 72–73, 91, 112, 132–134, 149–152
this-or-nothing-better argumentation 64, 67–68
truth-conditions 143–149

truth-estimation 9–29, 19–26, 35–37, 59

Ultra posse Principle 53, 62, 94, 128
uniformitarian deductivism 187, 196–197
uniformitarian probabilism 187
uniformity 174–178
uniformity of nature 205
Uniformity Principle 41–44
uniformity requirement 24
use-conditions 143–149

validity 25

Wheel Argument 79–80